Paul Kegan

**The Reign of Terror**

A Collection of Authentic Narratives

Paul Kegan

**The Reign of Terror**
*A Collection of Authentic Narratives*

ISBN/EAN: 9783744662291

Printed in Europe, USA, Canada, Australia, Japan

Cover: Foto ©Thomas Meinert / pixelio.de

More available books at **www.hansebooks.com**

# THE REIGN OF TERROR

Mar. Ther. Louise de Savoye Carignan

PRINCESSE de LAMBALLE,

Née à Turin en 1749 et massacrée à Paris le 3 Sepre 1792

# THE
# REIGN OF TERROR

A

## COLLECTION

OF

## AUTHENTIC NARRATIVES

OF THE

### HORRORS COMMITTED BY THE REVOLUTIONARY GOVERNMENT OF FRANCE

UNDER

## MARAT AND ROBESPIERRE

WRITTEN BY EYE-WITNESSES OF THE SCENES

---

## TRANSLATED FROM THE FRENCH

INTERSPERSED WITH

### BIOGRAPHICAL NOTICES OF PROMINENT CHARACTERS

AND

## CURIOUS ANECDOTES

ILLUSTRATIVE OF A PERIOD WITHOUT ITS PARALLEL IN HISTORY

## VOL. I

WITH TWO FRONTISPIECES: BEING PHOTOGRAVURE PORTRAITS OF THE
PRINCESSE DE LAMBALLE AND M. DE BEAUMARCHAIS

## LONDON
## LEONARD SMITHERS
ROYAL ARCADE W
1898

PRINTED AT NIMEGUEN (HOLLAND)
AT B. C. A. THIEME OF NIMEGUEN (HOLLAND)
AND
36, ESSEX STREET, STRAND, LONDON, W.C.

# PREFACE

The period from the 31st of May, 1792, to the 9*th Thermidor,* 27th of July, 1794, when Robespierre and Marat usurped more than sovereign power, was very aptly designated The Reign of Terror. At that period, virtue and nobility were certain titles to proscription or the guillotine; debtors paid their debts by denouncing their creditors; criminals punished by the law denounced their prosecutors and judges; those who had not places denounced those who had; heirs denounced those whose fortunes would descend to them; husbands found it a commodious way of getting rid of their wives; and children denounced their parents. One crime and one crime only is wanting in this dark catalogue;—no parent denounced his child.

Partial details of the horrors committed have frequently been laid before the public; but this is the only work in which is completely embodied that mass of crime which stands without a parallel in the annals of the world.

Who has not heard of the massacres in the prisons of the 2nd and 3rd of September, where upwards of twelve thousand innocent victims, for the most part persons of the highest respectability, were inhumanly butchered by order of the committees which were then at the head of affairs? Yet these horrors were, if possible, surpassed in the provinces, where the natives rivalled in zeal the sans-culottes of Paris.

The relations here published are, with the exception of one or two, authenticated by the names of the authors who were themselves designated for the axe, and only escaped by miracles; they were themselves eye and ear witnesses of the scenes they describe. By turns terrific and affecting, they possess all the charms of romance with all the interest of history. Who can read without admiration the account of Mademoiselle Cazotte rushing to save her aged father's life when the assassin's pike was already at his breast? Who cannot but admire the vir-

tuous Loizerolles, * who, when his son, who had been condemned to the guillotine, was called to come and be bound
for the scaffold, answered in his name, and suffered in his
stead?—thus giving him a second time existence. Who can
read without horror the details of M. de Sombreuil, saved by
the heroic devotion of his virgin daughter from the massacres
of September?—and at what a price! The ruffians exacted
from her, as the price of her father's liberty, that she should
drink a cup of human blood, reeking hot from the wounds of
a newly murdered victim. The fate of the Princesse de Lamballe was accompanied with atrocities which the mind can
hardly conceive, and which the pen refuses to trace. †

During these horrors, the virtuous Abbé Sicard, who, as an
author has eloquently expressed it, gave "ears to the deaf and
a tongue to the dumb," did not escape denunciation. He was
a priest, and no merits could atone for such a crime in the
eyes of those who denied the existence of a God, and declared
themselves the personal enemies of Jesus Christ. A succession
of miracles saved this worthy man from the assassin's pike and
revolutionary axe; for had he gone to prison in the vehicle
destined for him, he would have been murdered. A series of
events, apparently fortuitous, but marking the special finger of
Providence, concurred to his being saved.

Such were the atrocities committed, that the moment the
period of horrors was passed, the public sought with avidity
details of the scene, even then scarcely credible. The interesting narrative of St. Meard, intituled his Agony of Thirty-Eight
Hours (which we have given), was published by him immediately after his escape, and two hundred thousand copies sold
in a few days.

The present edition is founded on the English edition of 1826;
some compressions of tedious or uninteresting matter have been
made; and an account of the Republican Marriages, "The
Wholesale Drownings at Nantes", has been added. The whole
has been prepared for the press by Mr. Percy Pinkerton and
Mr. J. H. Ashworth.

* Charles X., on his coronation, granted pensions to Messrs. Loizerolles and
St. Meard, as well as several other victims of the Reign of Terror.

† *Vide Appendix*, Note A.

# CONTENTS OF VOL. I

# MY AGONY

OF

# THIRTY-EIGHT HOURS

OR

## A RECITAL

Of what happened to me, and of what I saw and heard, during my
Imprisonment in the Prison of the Abbaye St. Germain, from
the 22nd of August, to the 4th of September, 1792

By M. DE JOURGNIAC ST. MEARD

CI-DEVANT CAPTAIN COMMANDANT OF THE CHASSEURS OF THE REGIMENT
OF INFANTRY OF THE KING

J'entends encore leurs cris, leurs lamentables cris.
VOLT. *Mérope.*

yet hear their cries, their lamentable cries.

.

# BIOGRAPHICAL NOTICE

ON

# M. DE JOURGNIAC ST. MEARD

The Chevalier François de Jourgniac St. Meard was born at
Bordeaux, in 1746, of an old and noble family, originally of
Le Limousin. He served in the regiment of infantry of the
king, from 1766 till the dissolution of that corps, at the commencement of the revolution. He was then captain commandant
of a company of chasseurs, and had passed through all the
regular grades. In 1786, the King named him chevalier or knight
of the royal and military order of Saint Louis.

At a time when France was at peace with Europe, M. de St.
Meard still found, in the midst of the leisure of his garrison,
opportunities of distinguishing his courage. He was at Nancy,
in 1784, when a dreadful conflagration threatened the richest
quarter of the city. The house of M. Hanner, printer, situated
in Rue Saint Didier, was on fire, and the timber-work of the
adjoining houses was about to be consumed. M. de Jourgniac
hastened to the spot, followed by forty of his soldiers, who,
like him, were excited by a generous sentiment of humanity.
He gave the first blow, with an axe, to cut off the communication, and saved the inmates and their property by this act of
courage. He was rewarded for it by a flattering letter, which
the Duke du Châtelet wrote him, at the desire of his Majesty
Louis XVI. It was also at Nancy that one of the most memorable events of his life happened. He was in that city at the
time of the military insurrection which broke out there in 1790.
The rebel regiments chose him as their commander, named him
their general, forced him to march at their head, and condemned
him to death three days afterwards, pretending that he had
betrayed them. He was the friend of that unfortunate young

3

man, whose soul was so lofty, and whose patriotism was so pure,
—Desilles, that affecting victim! who was sacrificed to the fury
of revolution and civil war.—The day before he ceased to
exist, Desilles said to him, "Accept, my dear St. Meard, the
sabre which I had on the 31st August; let it recall me to thy
recollection!" Simple words, which faithfully portrayed him who
uttered them.

In the midst of the troubles and of the divisions which were
appearing, the principles, the opinions, and the sentiments of
M. de St. Meard placed him in the ranks of the men who were
the most devoted to the monarchy. A writer in the *Journal de
la Cour et de la Ville*, his happy turn of wit and of sarcasm
rendered him formidable to the opposite party, and those whose
hatred he had excited by his cutting attacks basely devoted
him to the massacres of September. The reader will shortly
perceive, in the picture which he has himself traced of them,
and which he has imaged with so much interest, terror, and
pity, by what firmness of soul, by what sallies of an original
and courageous mind, he cheated the revenge of his enemies,
and disarmed the assassins.

Though he had miraculously escaped from these dreadful
scenes, yet neither the remembrance of the dangers which he
had run, nor the presence of those which still surrounded him,
could for a moment change his sentiments or character; even
in the midst of the most gloomy and threatening days of terror,
he preserved that sang-froid and that presence of mind to which
he owed his preservation under the sanguinary tribunals of the
Abbaye. A journal of that period relates the following anecdote.
M. de St. Meard, and M. L—— were on guard together. The
revolutionary principles of this citizen L—— had procured him
the surname of Marat of the Corn Market. In the evening
some members of the Committee of Inspection repaired to the
post, and asked if there was anything new. "Yes," exclaimed
the personage of whom we have spoken, "all is going on ill,
for we have amongst us a suspicious character; I require that
he be arrested immediately; it is St. Meard. I denounce him
as a moderate."—Scarcely had he pronounced these words,
before St. Meard, who was standing behind the speaker, aimed
a vigorous blow at him, thus replying to his accusation: "Well,

comrade, thou wilt not denounce that as moderate." Marat the Second preserved silence. How many individuals might, perhaps, have escaped death, if they had had the nerve to give such a severe reply to their accusers.

Who will credit it? M. de St. Meard, knight of Saint Louis, M. de St. Meard, one of the most ardent partisans of the royal cause,—he who could never consent to disavow, or even conceal, his opinions before the assassins of 1791, or the informers of 1793,—had, during all the continuance of the latter period, as his support and protector, Maillard, one of the most powerful agents of the 5th of October, and one of the sanguinary judges of September. Maillard had then discharged him, and ever afterwards protected him. Whether the wretch, astonished at having felt an emotion of humanity, had conceived a kindly sentiment towards him who had given him this new sensation, or whether he considered as thereafter sheltered from the revolutionary knife a life which had escaped himself, is doubtful; but M. de St. Meard owes to this strange good-will the security which he enjoyed during the reign of terror.

Always invariable in his opinions, yet tranquil in the bosom of the retreat which he had chosen for himself, M. de St. Meard afterwards passed through the Directory and the Empire without leaving any trace of his passage. Arrived at an advanced age, wholly removed from the discussions of politics, he lived in a repose which the storms of his former years rendered more delightful. When the King again set his foot upon the French soil, M. de St. Meard, who had fought twenty years for the cause of monarchy, found the most gratifying indemnity for his losses and his misfortunes in an event which he had long sighed for. His conduct, and his devotion to royalty, perhaps, deserved some recompense. He thought so at least, and in 1822 demanded the rank of colonel, and permission to retire on half-pay. We are fully disposed to think, that the administration is always just and always infallible: M. de St. Meard mentioned his services and his dangers; the administration opposed to him its rules and its instructions: "You have not emigrated," they replied to him, "and we can do nothing for you."

"But how!" returned M. de St. Meard, in a memoir which we have now before us, and in which we find the fire and vivacity of his other writings, "Is not the service of an old and good captain an active service,—a captain who, *during twenty years passed under the colours*, never ceased at Paris, at Nancy, at the Tuileries, to offer himself in February, June, August, and September, to bayonets, pikes, and poniards? and who, in every catastrophe, until the decisive crisis, thought it his duty, without observations and without fear, to wait at the post *which his sovereign had appointed him*, the hour for devoting his life?——

"Is it necessary to ask him, who formed a part of the crew *swallowed up in the revolutionary storm*,—is it necessary to ask him what place he occupied in the vessel which perished? Is it not enough that death was present everywhere? Does it import whether he happened to be at the prow or at the stern?"

These reasons appeared, at all events, good. The terrible affair of September was assuredly more bloody and more murderous than many battles would have been. At every age, and under every circumstance, M. de St. Meard had moreover given proofs of zeal.

In the month of March, 1815, he repaired to the house of Lieutenant-General Count de Viomenil, to sign an engagement as a royalist volunteer. M. de Jourgniac consulted more at that time his ardour than his strength; for, aged fully seventy, it was not very probable that he could support the fatigues of war. When he saw himself forced to lay down his arms, he returned to continue his peaceful existence, in an asylum where the remembrance of the dangers which he had run, the approbation of a pure conscience, a few friends, and his taste for literature, consoled him for a neglect which was not merited.

Besides *My Agony of Thirty-Eight Hours*, which has gone through fifty-seven editions, as well in the departments as abroad, M. de St. Meard was the author of several works. He published at Nancy various writings; and, amongst others, a tragi-comedy, in three acts, on the insurrection of which that city was the theatre, in 1790. The public are indebted to him for another pamphlet, entitled *The Order of the Day*. In 1785, he composed, in concert with Messrs. Fortia de Piles and Louis de Boisgelin, a volume in 12mo., *Correspondance de Mesmer*, on the three discoveries of the *baquet octagone* (octagon bucket), of *l'homme baquet* (man-bucket), and of the *baquet morale* (moral bucket), a work in which he has given full scope to all the gaiety of his imagination. Literature had always been a relaxation to him. He never demanded either places or emoluments, and we are not aware of any other employment he had than that of president of the *Société des Gobe-mouches* (Society of the Fly-catchers).

Spirited productions and honourable actions throughout marked the career of M. de St. Meard. We cannot terminate this notice without reminding our readers, that while he was menaced himself, he succeeded in rescuing from death, during the reign of terror, the Count and the Chevalier de Murat, Marsollier de Vivetierres, a literary character, Bertrand, Fortia de Piles, and other unfortunate men, whose heads were just on the point of being submitted to the fatal axe. Happy is he who can at once interest his fellow-citizens by his writings, and preserve them by his courage!

# MY AGONY

## OF

# THIRTY-EIGHT HOURS

## BY M. DE ST. MEARD

### CHAPTER I

#### FOURTEEN HOURS OF THE COMMITTEE OF INSPECTION OF THE COMMUNE

On the 22nd of August I was arrested by the orders of this committee, and carried to the office of the mayoralty at nine o'clock in the morning, where I remained until eleven at night.* Two gentlemen, *no doubt members of the committee*, ordered me to enter into a hall; one of them, worn out by fatigue, fell asleep; the other interrogated me if my name was M. Jourgniac de St. Meard? I replied in the affirmative.

"Sit down—we are all equal. Do you know why you have been arrested?"

"One of those who conducted me hither has informed me that I am suspected to be the editor of an anti-constitutional newspaper."

"Suspected is not the word; for I believe that Le Gautier, who is the reputed editor of the *Journal de la Cour et de la Ville*, is a man of straw."

---

\* I was arrested by M. Niquette and by M. Pommier. They were accompanied by ten or twelve soldiers, whom they dismissed when I assured them that it was my intention to submit myself to the law. They informed me that they had brought this considerable force with them, in consequence of the assurance they had received, that it was my intention to make a vigorous resistance. The latter of these gentlemen was afterwards shot by the orders of Moreau. He had formerly served in the king's regiment, in which he had been appointed president of the revolutionary club of the soldiers.—*Note of the Author.*

" Your credence has been imposed upon, Sir; for his editorship is as easily to be proved as his physical existence."

" I must believe——"

" Nothing but the truth; for you will be *just*, as you are a *judge*, and I give you my word of honour——"

"Oh! Sir, it is no time now to speak of words of honour."

" So much the worse, Sir, for mine is yet unblemished."

" You are accused of having been upon the frontiers ten or eleven months since; of having raised recruits, whom you led to the emigrants; and that, on your return, you were arrested, and escaped from prison."

" If I could suppose that this was a serious denunciation, I would only demand one hour to prove that I have not been out of Paris for three-and-twenty months. And if——"

"Oh, I know, Sir, that you have ability, and that, by your cunning, you would find——"

" Allow me to say, that the word cunning is rather too much; that it is dealing in absurdity, for we are only speaking of denunciations which have been made against me."

" Do you know M. Durosoi, editor of the *Gazette de Paris?*"

" I know him well from reputation, but not otherwise; I have never even seen him."

" That surprises me, for there have been found, amongst his papers, letters which you have written to him."

" Only one has been found; for I only addressed one to him, by which I apprised him that I had sent him a speech which I made to the chasseurs of my company, at the time of the insurrection of the garrison of Nancy, and which he printed in the *Gazette de Paris*. This is the only correspondence I have had with him."

" That is true enough, and I may tell you that this letter hazards your safety."

" None of my letters, none of my writings, none of my actions, can hazard me."

" I have seen you at the house of Madame Vaufleury; I have also seen you with M. Peltier, editor of the Acts of the Apostles."

" That may be, as I go frequently to the house of that lady, and I sometimes walk with M. Peltier."

"Are you not a knight of Saint Louis?"

"I am, Sir."

"Why do you not wear the cross of the order?"

"Here it is: I have always worn it during the last six years."

"This is enough for to-day. I shall go and report to the committee that you are here."

"Do me the favour also to tell them, that if they do me justice, they will send me away free; for I am neither editor, recruiter, conspirator, nor denunciator."

A moment afterwards three soldiers beckoned to me to follow them; when we reached the court, they invited me to mount with them into a hackney coach, which drove off, after having received orders to take us to the *Hôtel du Faubourg St. Germain.* *

---

\* The history of the revolution of the 10th of August, by Peltier, furnishes a curious paragraph on the arrest of St. Meard. The facts contained in it are not mentioned anywhere else, yet they appear authentic.

"The chevalier Jourgniac de St. Meard, captain in the regiment of the king, was known for an individual who had furnished many puns for the *Journal de la Cour et de la Ville.* He was arrested, but it was less for this offence that he was imprisoned, than for a quarrel which he had had, some time before the 10th of August, with the magistrate Manuel, at the shop of the bookseller Desenne. It made so much noise at the moment, that St. Meard thought it necessary to have his apology printed in the form of a dialogue, in order that he might not be torn to pieces by the volunteers of Manuel."—*Note of the Editors.*

# CHAPTER II

ON my arrival at the hotel pointed out by my fellow-travellers, which turned out to be the prison of the Abbaye, they presented me, *with my lodging billet*, to the keeper, who, after having addressed the usual observation to me, *It is to be hoped that it will not last long*, ordered me to be placed in a large hall, which served as a chapel for the prisoners of the *ancien régime*. I counted nineteen persons who were there sleeping upon folding beds. I was supplied with that of M. Dangremont, whom they had beheaded two days before.

On the same day, when we were just about to sit down to table, M. de Chantereine, colonel of the constitutional household of the King, and inspector of the wardrobe of the crown, inflicted three wounds upon himself with a knife, after having exclaimed, "We are all destined to be massacred!——Oh, God! I am about to meet Thee!" He died a few minutes afterwards.

*23rd.*—I composed a memoir, in which I unmasked the turpitude of my denunciators, and sent copies of it to the minister of justice, to my own section, to the Committee of Inspection, and to all whom I knew took an interest in the injustice which was done me.

*Five o'clock, p.m.*—We received, as a companion in misfortune, M. Durusoi, editor of the *Gazette de Paris*. Immediately on hearing me named, he said to me, after the usual compliments, "Ah, Sir! how happy I am to meet with you! I have long esteemed you, and yet I only know you by the affair of Nancy; allow an unfortunate man, whose last hour is approaching, to pour out his heart to yours." I cordially saluted him. He afterwards made me read a letter which he had just received, which one of his female friends had written to him.

"My friend, prepare yourself for death; you are condemned, and to-morrow . . . . . . I rack my soul, but you know what I have promised. Adieu."

During the reading of this letter, I saw the tears trickle down his cheeks; he kissed it several times, and I heard him say, in broken accents, "Alas! she will suffer from it much more than I." We lay upon my bed, and, thinking of the means that had been employed to accuse and arrest us, our wearied spirits became exhausted, and we fell asleep. Immediately as daylight dawned upon us, he employed himself in writing a memoir in his justification, which, although written with great energy and full of powerful argument, produced no favourable effect, for the following day the guillotine severed his head from his body.

25th.—The commissaries of the prison at length permitted us to procure ourselves the evening paper.*

In the sacristy of the chapel which served us as a prison, there had been placed a captain of the regiment of the Swiss guards, named Reding, who, in the affair of the 10th of August,

---

* A fresh prisoner brought us several papers: in one, entitled the *Courrier Français*, I read *what my readers may very well dispense with perusing:*—

"M.M. St. Meard and Beaumarchais have been arrested; the former was the author of the scandalous journal which appeared under the title of *Journal de la Cour et de la Ville.* He was captain in the regiment of the king; and, what is somewhat remarkable, he is the owner of the estate which the celebrated Montaigne possessed near Bordeaux. M. St. Meard has an annual income of upwards of 40,000 francs."

I pardon this manufacturer of news for having given me that estate, though it belongs to M. de Segur, and more than 40,000 francs per annum, though I never had half that income, even before the revolution. I do more: I will not suppose that he had any bad intention, so far; but I cannot believe that he had good ones, when he has chosen the moment in which I was under the restraint of the law, in order to publish that I was an anti-constitutional journalist; for, *although he was formerly a journalist feuillant (that is, most constitutional),* he knew that M. Gautier was editor of the journal in question. In fine, how will he be able to agree, on the subject of the considerable fortune which he has given me, with the author of the Revolutions of Paris, who affirms that I *worked* at that paper to gain a livelihood? If he had added to this piece of stupidity, that I had never *worked* to procure it from any one, he would have spoken one truth, and I would have pardoned him the falsehood.—*Note of the Author.*

received a shot from a musket, which broke his arm; he had also been wounded in four different places in the head, from sabre blows. Some citizens saved him, and carried him into a lodging-house, from which he was dragged as a prisoner to the Abbaye, where his arm was a second time set. I have frequently, in the course of my life, met with objects which have surprised me, but never was I more astonished than in recognising here, in the person who acted as sick-nurse, one with whom I had been intimately connected for twelve years.

The particular circumstances of this singular anecdote having nothing in common with my narration, I pass on to the order of my narrative.

*26th, midnight.*—A municipal officer entered into our apartment, to register our names and the days that we had been arrested. He gave us reason to hope that the municipality would send commissaries the next day to order the discharge of those against whom there were only vague denunciations. This information enabled me to pass a tranquil night, but my expectations were not realised; on the contrary, the number of prisoners continued to increase.

*27th.*—We heard the noise of a pistol fired in the interior of the prison, and, immediately afterwards, hurried steps on the staircases and in the corridors; locks and bolts were opened and closed with great rapidity; our room, amongst the rest, was entered by one of the turnkeys, who, after he had counted us, desired us to remain tranquil, as the danger was past. This was all that we could learn of the cause of this disturbance, from this blunt and taciturn personage.

*28th and 29th.*—Our attention was withdrawn from our own miserable situation only by the arrival of conveyances, which were constantly bringing in fresh prisoners. We could see them from a small tower which communicated with our room, the windows of which looked into Rue St. Marguerite. We paid most dearly in the end for the pleasure we had in hearing and perceiving what passed in the street, and more particularly opposite the gate of our prison.

*30th, eleven o'clock, p.m.*—A man of nearly eighty years of age was brought to sleep in our room: we learnt, the next day, that he was M. Cazotte, author of the poem of Olivier, of

the Diable Amoureux, * etc.   The gaiety of this old man, which
had something silly in it, and his oriental style of speaking,
caused a diversion to our *ennui:* he endeavoured very seriously
to persuade us, by the history of Cain and Abel, that we were
much more happy than those who enjoyed liberty.   He appeared
mortified that we appeared to think very differently, and absolutely wished to make us admit that our situation was only an
*emanation of the Apocalypse, etc., etc.*   I piqued him to the very
quick by telling him that, in our position, we were much happier
in believing in *predestination* than in all which he said.   Two
*gendarmes*, who came to take him before the revolutionary tribunal,
terminated our discussion.

I did not lose a moment in procuring the attestations which
could serve to prove the truths that I advanced in my Memoir.
I was assisted by a friend--by such a friend as is rarely met
with, who, while my companions in misfortune were abandoned
by theirs, laboured night and day to render me service.   He
forgot that, in a moment of fermentation and mistrust, he might
run the same risks as I had done, and that he rendered himself *suspected* by interesting himself for a suspected prisoner:
nothing intimidated or impeded him; and he has well proved
to me the truth of the proverb, *adversity is the touchstone of
friends.*   It is chiefly to his exertions and to his zeal that I am

---

* "Jacques Cazotte was seventy-three years of age, and was born at Dijon:
his father, an upright man, was registrar of the states of Burgundy.   Jacques
Cazotte had rendered himself useful to his country in the administration of the
navy, and had, besides other situations, filled with great distinction that of intend-
ant-commissary of the Windward Islands, in the wars prior to those of 1778.
He was a valuable friend, a good father, and an excellent husband; no one had
a more lively character, a more sprightly wit, or a more feeling heart: *Olivier,
Le Diable Amoureux,* and *The Impromptu Lord,* are evidences of this, and are
works of great merit.   The bald forehead and grey hair of this amiable man
gave him the appearance of a venerable patriarch: he retired at Pierry, in
Champagne, in the midst of a family whose happiness he constituted, with two
sons, one of whom was in the King's Body Guard, and the other had served
abroad in the army of the Bourbons,—and a daughter of twenty, a model of
loveliness and filial piety, Elisabeth Cazotte.   This lady acted as her father's
secretary in his retirement, and had written a part of the fatal letters which
sufficed as a pretext for his death.   On the 18th of August, a detachment of
national *gendarmes* surrounded his house, and he and his daughter were conducted
to Epernay, then to Paris, into the prison of the Abbaye."  - *Extract from the
History of the Revolution of* 10th *August, by Peltier.*

indebted for my life. I owe it to the public, to myself, and to truth, to name this excellent man,—M. Teyssier, merchant, Rue Croix des Petits Champs.

*The last days of the month of August* reminded me of the cruel situation in which I had been placed at the affair of Nancy. I employed my imagination in comparing the risks I was running with those I had incurred the same days, when the army, composed of the regiments of the King, of *Mestre de Camp*, of Chateauvieux, and of some battalions of *national guards*, named me its general, and forced me to lead it to Lunéville, in order to carry off Malseigne from the *Carabineers*.

*1st September.*—Orders were received to liberate three of our companions, who were much less astonished at their discharge than they had been at their imprisonment, as they were the most zealous patriots of their sections. Their names were, St. Felix, Laurent, and Chignard. The two latter only left us on Sunday the 2nd September: they were claimed by their sections. Some others were liberated from the adjoining rooms, in particular M. de Jaucourt, member of the Legislative Assembly, who, some time before, had given in his resignation as deputy.

# CHAPTER III

## COMMENCEMENT OF MY AGONY OF THIRTY-EIGHT HOURS

SUNDAY, the 2nd of September, our turnkey served us our dinner sooner than usual; his wild manner and his haggard eyes gave us a presage of something sinister.* At *two o'clock* he entered again; we eagerly surrounded him, but he was deaf to all our questions, and after, contrary to his custom, he had collected all the knives which we had placed upon our napkins, he abruptly drove out the nurse of the Swiss officer, Reding.

*Half-past two o'clock.*—The dreadful noise which the people made, was terribly increased by that of the drums, which were beating the general alarm, by the three guns of alarm, and by the tocsin, which was ringing on all sides.† In these moments of terror, we saw three carriages pass, escorted by an innumerable crowd of furious women and men, who were crying aloud, *A la Force! A la Force!* § They were going to the cloister of the

---

* His name was Bertrand. He had been *barker* at the Opera, for calling the carriages and hackney-coaches.

† It will be recollected that the report of the taking of Verdun having been circulated in the capital, proclamations were addressed to the people. Arms were given to them, and it seemed to be the design to direct them towards the places which were occupied by the enemies. The tocsin was sounded. The apparent object was to assemble the citizens preparatory to their departure. One cannot but shudder to reflect that sanguinary men found, in the defence of the territory, a pretext for the atrocious projects which they meditated. This tocsin which the prisoners heard, these drums which were beating, were, in the opinion of all, except the assassins, the signal of the dangers of the country, and not the command for carnage. The French doubtlessly thought they were marching against a foreign enemy, and little imagined that they were moving to the murder and massacre of their fellow citizens.—*Note of the Editors.*

§ We knew not yet that these words, *à la Force!* were an intimation which was given when the tyrants were sending victims to death.—*Note of the Author.*

16

Abbaye, which had been converted into a prison for the priests. A moment after, we heard it said, that all the bishops and other ecclesiastics, who, it was observed, had been *penned up* in that place, had just been massacred.

*Four o'clock.*—The piercing cries of a man whom they were hacking to pieces with a sabre, drew us to the window of the small tower, and we perceived, opposite the gate of our prison, the body of a man extended dead upon the pavement; an instant after, another was butchered, and so they went on with others.\* It is utterly impossible to express the horror of the profound and gloomy silence which reigned during these executions; interrupted only by the cries of those whom the barbarians were immolating, and by the blows which were inflicted on their heads with swords.† At the moment the wretched victim fell, a dreadful murmur would arise, which was immediately drowned by shouts of *Vive la Nation!* a thousand times more horrifying to us than the awful silence that preceded them. In the interval between one murder and another, we heard several voices beneath our windows, saying, "We must not suffer one to escape; we must kill all, and more especially those who are in the chapel, where there is none but conspirators." It was of us that they were speaking: it is scarcely necessary to say, that we thought the situation of those who were immured in the most obnoxious dungeons far preferable to our own. The most agonizing suspense and anxiety tormented us, and occupied our painfully gloomy reflections. To add to our misery, the moments of silence that prevailed without the walls of our prison were constantly interrupted by the most discordant and terrifying noises in the interior.

---

\* After all the priests shut up in the cloister had been massacred, the wretches began the massacre of the other prisoners by killing a hundred and fifty-six Swiss soldiers, shut up likewise in the Abbaye, not one of whom was saved. The turn of others then arrived, at the head of whom were M. de Montmorin, and M. Thierry, valet-de-chambre of the king. To certain prisoners a burning torch was applied to the face, when they issued from the gate to be massacred. This precaution was taken in order that the people might not recognise them.— *Note of the Author.*

† We have extracted from an extremely curious pamphlet, entitled *The Truth on the Massacres of September,* some details which the reader may consult; they form a part of the Appendix, Note B.—*Note of the Editors.*

*Five o'clock.*—Many voices called loudly for M. Cazotte; a moment afterwards, we heard loud exclamations, the clashing of arms, and the shrieks of a crowd of persons traversing the passages, men and women. It was that unfortunate old man and his daughter, the former of whom they were leading away to murder. Upon his issuing from the prison-gate, this courageous girl rushed forward, and threw her arms around the neck of her parent. The people, who were deeply affected by the scene, implored his pardon, and obtained it.*

*Seven o'clock.*—We saw two men enter, whose bloody hands were armed with swords; they were conducted by a turnkey bearing a torch, who pointed out to them the bed of the unfortunate Reding. In this frightful moment I pressed his hand and endeavoured to cheer him. One of the men made a motion,† as if he were going to carry the Swiss away; but the ill-fated man stopped, and exclaimed, with a dying voice, "Ah! Sir, I have suffered enough: I do not fear death; but, as a favour, I entreat you to give me the last blow here." These words rendered the wretch motionless; but his comrade, by looking at him, and saying to him, "Come along," decided him. The officer was taken up, placed upon the shoulders of one of the

---

* "Some days before the 2nd of September, Mademoiselle Cazotte, imprisoned with her father in the Abbaye, was acknowledged to be innocent; but she would not leave her parent there, alone and without assistance, but obtained permission to remain in prison with him. Those dreadful days, which were the last of so many Frenchmen, arrived; the evening before the massacres commenced, Mademoiselle Cazotte, by the charms of her countenance, the purity of her soul, and the eloquence of her language, had succeeded in interesting the feelings of some Marseillois who had entered the prison, and afterwards assisted her to save Cazotte. This old man, condemned after thirty hours of carnage, was about to perish under the blows of a group of assassins. His daughter, pale and dishevelled, and more beautiful from her disorder and her tears, threw herself between him and them. ' *You shall not,*' the heroic creature exclaimed, '*reach my father till you have pierced my heart.*' A cry of pardon was heard in the crowd. It was repeated by two other voices: and the Marseillois opened a passage for Mademoiselle Cazotte, who led her father away, and restored him to the bosom of his family."

This piece is extracted from the notes of the Women of Merit, by Legouvé.— *Note of the Editors.*

† I have become acquainted with this man since. He appears to have possessed some virtue, for I know that he saved the life of a young man of Besançon, a prisoner confined in the same chamber as myself.—*Note of the Author.*

assassins, and carried into the street, where he received his death-blow.* .... My eyes are dim with tears; I can no longer see what I am writing.

We gazed upon each other without uttering a word—we pressed each other's hands, and mutually embraced. Immovable,—in deep and solemn silence,—with our eyes fixed in inexpressible grief, we contemplated the pavement of our prison, lighted by the moon, through the spaces formed by the triple-bars of our windows. .... But shortly the cries of fresh victims produced again our former agitation, and recalled to our recollection the last words which were uttered by M. de Chantereine, when he plunged the knife into his heart: "We are all destined to be massacred." ....

*Midnight.*—Ten men, with swords in their hands, preceded by two turnkeys who carried torches, entered our prison, and ordered us to place ourselves each at the foot of our beds. After they had counted us, they told us that we were answerable for one another, and swore that, if a single one escaped, we should all be massacred *without being heard by the president.†* These last words afforded us a gleam of hope; for we knew not whether we should be *heard or not* before we should be murdered.

*Monday the 3rd, two o'clock a.m.*—One of the doors of the

---

* In the History of the Revolution of the 10th of August, by M. Peltier, we find the following details of the unfortunate Reding:—

"St. Meard has not dared to relate a horrible circumstance that took place under his own eyes. The following is the manner in which he described it to me. The executioners who came to fetch this unhappy man to lead him to the place of his destruction, perceiving that his wounds prevented him from supporting himself, placed him upon their shoulders. Pain forced the most piteous cries from him. A third executioner, who followed, determined, in order to put an end to the noise, to cut the poor victim's throat with his sword, and he commenced the cruelty under the very eyes of the prisoner's companions.—Reding had scarcely reached the first steps of the staircase, before those who remained behind discovered, by the cessation of his cries, that he had ceased to breathe."—*Note of the Editors.*

† This president, or popular judge, who had established himself at the post to see the sentences executed, was the constable Maillard, one of the men of the 5th of October and of the 10th of August, residing in the Faubourg St. Antoine. He exercised, during the whole of the revolution, a great influence over this terrible faubourg.—*Note of the Editors.*

prison was burst open, after repeated blows: at first we thought it was that from the street, which had been broken through for the purpose of admitting the assassins to massacre us in our chambers; but we were somewhat comforted when we overheard it said, on the staircase, that it was the door of a dungeon in which some prisoners had barricaded themselves. Shortly afterwards, we learnt that all who had been found in it had been slaughtered.

*Ten o'clock.*—The Abbé l'Enfant, confessor of the King,* and the Abbé de Chapt-Rastignac † appeared in the pulpit of the chapel which served as our prison, and into which they had entered by a door leading from the staircase. They informed us that our last hour was approaching, and invited us to prepare our minds, in order to receive their benediction. By a kind of electrical motion, we all fell on our knees, and with clasped hands received the promised blessing. That moment, although consolatory, was one of the most awful that we ever experienced. On the eve of appearing before the Supreme Being, kneeling before two of his ministers, we presented a spectacle that defies description. The age of these two old men, their position above us, death hovering over our heads and surrounding us on all sides,—everything shed over the ceremony an august but gloomy colouring: it drew us near to the Divinity;

* Abbé l'Enfant, member of a celebrated society, preacher of the late Emperor Joseph II., by whom he was greatly esteemed, and afterwards of Louis XVI. It has also been said, that, at a later period, he was confessor of this monarch. To him has been attributed the discourse read to the council, on the project of granting civil rights to the Protestants, which appeared in 1787. He was upwards of seventy at the time of his execution. His tender piety, the affability of his character, and the sincerity of his friendship, caused him to be deeply regretted by his friends.—*Note of the Editors.*

† Abbé de Chapt-Rastignac was aged upwards of seventy when he lost his life. He was of the ancient and illustrious house of Périgord, Doctor of the Society of the Sorbonne, Vicar-General of the Diocese of Arles, and Deputy to the Constituent Assembly. He had cultivated literature with great advantage, and was author of a work entitled "On the Agreement of Revelation and Reason against Divorce;" of another production "On Divorce in Poland;" and also of the translation from Greek into French, of the Synodal Letter of Nicolas, Patriarch of Constantinople, to the Emperor Alexis Commenes, on the power of the Emperors, relative to the election of the Metropolitan Ecclesiastics. *Vide*, further, on, the relation written by Madame Fausse-Lendry, niece of the Abbé de Rastignac.—*Note of the Editors.*

it restored our courage and our fortitude; our senses appeared in a manner invigorated; and the coldest and most unbelieving received as much impression from it as the most ardent and the most susceptible. Half an hour afterwards, these two priests were massacred, and we heard their shrieks! *

Who is there that will be able to read the following details, without feeling the tears rush to his eyes, without experiencing the contractions and the shudderings of death! Who is there that will not involuntarily start with horror!

Our most important occupation was to reflect and determine upon the best position for us to assume, that we might receive our death with the least pain, upon entering the place where the massacres were perpetrated. From time to time we sent some of our companions to the window of the small turret, to inform us of the positions taken by the unhappy beings who were sacrificed, in order that we might decide, from their report, how we should act upon the occasion, to endure the least suffering. They reported to us that those who stretched out their hands suffered much longer, as the blows of the sabres were deadened before they reached their heads; that there even were some whose hands and arms fell before their bodies, and that those who placed them behind their backs appeared to suffer much less than the others. . . . . . Alas! it was upon such horrible details as these that we were driven to deliberate. We calculated actually the advantages of the last-mentioned position, and reciprocally recommended each other to take it, when our turn to be massacred should arrive!!

*About midnight.*—Overwhelmed and completely cast down by a more than supernatural agitation, and absorbed by reflections of inexpressible horror, I threw myself upon a bed, and slept profoundly. Everything induces me to believe, that I owe my existence to these moments of sleep. It appeared to me, that

* They were included in the general massacre of the priests. The History of the Revolution of the 10th August, which we have already had occasion to quote, relates the following fact:—

"The fate of these unfortunates had been so certainly determined for several days, that the gravediggers of the parish of St. Sulpice had received in advance an assignat of a hundred crowns, in order to prepare, at Montrouge, the grave that was to receive their bodies. The next morning, in fact, they were buried there. Ten carts carried them thither."—*Note of the Editors.*

I made my appearance before the formidable tribunal that was
to judge me; I was listened to with attention, notwithstanding
the dreadful noise of the tocsin, and of the cries which I
fancied I heard all around. As soon as my defence was
finished, I was dismissed free. This dream produced such a
cheering effect upon my spirits, that it totally discarded all my
anxieties, and I awoke with a presentiment that it would be
realized. I related the particulars of it to my companions in
misfortune, who were astonished at the confidence I felt from
that moment until the period when I was summoned before
my terrible judges.

*Two o'clock.*—A proclamation was made that the people
appeared to have a discontented air; a moment after, some
meddling people, or rather, perhaps, some individuals who
wished to point out to us the means of saving ourselves, placed
a ladder against the window of our apartment; but others
prevented them from ascending it, by crying out, "*Down!
down! it is to carry them arms.*"

All the torments of thirst were united to the agonies which
we every moment experienced. At length our turnkey, Bertrand,*
appeared alone, and we prevailed upon him to bring us a
pitcher of water,† which we drank with so much the more
eagerness, as we had not been able to obtain a single drop for
*six-and-twenty hours.* We spoke of this negligence to one of
the federated body, who came with others to visit our prison;
he was so indignant at it, that he requested us to tell him the
name of this turnkey, and he assured us he would exterminate
him. He would have done as he had said, and it was only
by many supplications that we obtained the man's pardon. This
little alleviation was very soon disturbed by some plaintive cries
which we heard over us. We perceived that they proceeded

* It was the fault of circumstances and not his, nor was it the fault of the
gaoler, Citizen Lavaquerie, who, while he remained at the Abbaye, fulfilled the
duties that humanity imposes upon an honest man.—*Note of the Author.*

† It was at this period that he informed us he had prevented *evil-disposed*
persons from bringing us twenty-eight sabres; that they had been seized, and
had been deposited at the guard-house. He told us, also, that M. Manuel was
in the room of M. Lavaquerie, the gaoler; that he was looking at the commitments of the prisoners, and that he had made many crosses beside their names.
—*Note of the Author.*

from the tribune, and we informed all those who passed along the staircases of it. At length some one entered the tribune, and told us that it was a young officer, who had inflicted upon himself several wounds, not one of which was mortal, as the blade of the knife he had used, being round at the end, could not penetrate deep enough.* This only served to hasten the moment of his execution.

*Eight o'clock.*—The agitation of the people abated, and we heard several voices cry out "Pardon, pardon for those who remain!" These words were applauded, but only very feebly. Yet a ray of hope began to beam upon our hearts: some even believed their deliverance so near at hand, that they had already taken their bundles under their arms; but soon afterwards new cries of death plunged us into our former agonies.

I had formed a particular intimacy with M. Maussabré, who had only been arrested because he had been aide-de-camp of M. de Brissac. He had often given proofs of courage; but the fear of being assassinated had completely sunk his heart. I had, however, partly succeeded in calming his anxieties, when he came and threw himself into my arms, exclaiming, "Oh, my friend, I am undone; I have just heard my name pronounced in the street." In vain did I urge, that it was, perhaps, by some individuals who took an interest in his situation; that, moreover, fear could cure nothing; but that, on the contrary, it might ruin him: all was useless. He was so entirely subdued by terror, that, finding no place in the chapel where he could conceal himself, he mounted into the chimney of the sacristy, where he was stopped by some gratings, which he had the madness to endeavour to break with his head. We requested him to come down, and, after many difficulties, he returned amongst us; but he had wholly lost his reason. This was what caused his death, of which I shall shortly speak.

M. Emard, who, the evening before, had given me some hints

---

* The name of this young officer was Boisragon. Some other prisoners killed themselves in their rooms; amongst others, one who broke his skull against the lock of the door of his prison. M. Loureur, who had been our companion in misfortune, in the chapel, and who had been removed into another apartment before the fatal days of the 2nd, 3rd, and 4th of September, related to me this fact, which occurred in his presence.—*Note of the Author.*

for making a holograph will, communicated to me the motives for which he had been arrested. I considered them so unjust, that, in order to give him a proof of the certainty I felt that he would not perish, I made him a present of a silver medal, entreating him to preserve it, and to show it to me ten years afterwards, if we met. . . . If he should read this article, it will recall to his mind his promise. If we have not since seen each other, it is not my fault; for I know not where to find him, and he knows where I am.

*Eleven o'clock.*—Ten persons, armed with swords and pistols, ordered us to arrange ourselves in a line with each other, and conducted us into the second turnkey's room, placed by the side of that where sat the tribunal that was going to try us. I cautiously approached one of the sentinels who guarded us, and I gradually succeeded in getting into conversation with him. He told me, in a dialect which enabled me to comprehend that he was either from Provence or Languedoc, that he had served eight years in the regiment of Lyonnais.* I spoke *patois* (provincial dialect) to him: this appeared to give him pleasure; and the interest I had in pleasing him gave me such a persuasive Gascon eloquence, that I succeeded in interesting him so far as to obtain from him the following favourable remark, which it is impossible for any one to appreciate who has not been at the portentous wicket, as I then was. "*I do not know thee, but yet I do not think that thou art a traitor; on the contrary, I think thou art a good fellow.*" I racked my imagination for everything which it could furnish me, in order to confirm him in this good opinion. I succeeded in it; for I obtained permission from him to enter into the formidable room, in order to see a prisoner sentenced. I saw two tried, one of whom was purveyor of the King, who, being accused of forming one in the plot of the 10th, was condemned and executed; the other, who was weeping, and who could only utter broken sentences, was already undressed, and was going to depart for La Force, when he was recognised by a workman of Paris, who proved that they took him for another. He was sent before a judge who had more ample means of information

---

* Maillard has informed me that he was a federate native of Ville-Neuve-les-Avignon, and that he set out for the frontiers a few days after the massacres of September.—*Note of the Author.*

respecting him; and I have since learnt that he was declared innocent.

What I had just seen was a ray of light to guide me on the turn which I ought to give to my means of defence. I went back into the second turnkey's room, where I met some prisoners who had just been brought from without. I entreated my Provençal friend to procure me a glass of wine. He went for it, when he received orders to take me back again into the chapel, which I entered again, without having been able to discover the motive for which we had been made to go down. I found there ten fresh prisoners, who replaced five that had previously been tried. I had no time to lose in composing a fresh memoir; and I was working at it, well convinced that it was only firmness and frankness that could save me, when I saw my Provençal friend enter the room. After he had said to the keeper, "Close the door merely with the key, and wait for me on the outside," he approached me, touched my hand, and thus addressed me:

"I come for thee.—Here is the wine which thou requested; drink." I had drunk more than half of it, when he placed his hand upon the bottle and said to me, "Zounds, my friend, how thou guzzlest it; I wish some for myself: to thy good health." He drank the rest. "I cannot remain long with thee, but recollect what I tell thee.—If thou art a priest or a conspirator of the castle of M. Veto" (a name given to the King of France by the revolutionists), "thou art undone; but if thou art not a traitor, don't be afraid: I'll answer for thy life."

"Well, my friend, I am very sure of not being accused of all that; but I am considered a little aristocratic."

"That is nothing; the judges know very well that there are honest men everywhere. The president is a good fellow, and is no fool."

"Do me the favour to entreat the judges to hear me; I only ask them for that."

"Thou shalt be heard, I answer for it; and now, adieu, my friend; cheer up—I am going to my post again—I will endeavour to make thy turn come as soon as possible. Embrace me; I am at thy service with all my heart."

We embraced, and he went out.

A man must have been a prisoner at the Abbaye on the 3rd Sept. 1792, to form a just idea of the influence which this short conversation had upon my hopes, and how it re-inspired me.

*About midnight.*—The unnatural noise, which had never for a moment ceased for six-and-thirty hours, began to diminish. We thought that our judges and their executive power (thus we called the murderers), worn out with fatigue, would not try us till they had taken some rest. We were occupied in arranging our beds, when a fresh proclamation was made, which was generally hooted. A little while afterwards, a man demanded the attention of the people, and we very distinctly heard him say to them, "The priests and the conspirators who remain, and who are there, have bribed the judges; this is the reason why they do not sentence them." He had scarcely finished speaking, before we fancied we heard them strike him down. The agitation of the crowd became dreadfully vehement, the noise increased every moment, and the ferment was at its height, when some one came for M. Défontaine, formerly one of the King's body-guard, and very soon afterwards we heard his cries of death.* In a little while two others of our companions were torn from us, which made me presage that my fatal hour was approaching.†

At length, on Tuesday, at one o'clock in the morning, after having suffered an agony of thirty-seven hours, which one cannot

* They likewise came to fetch a superior officer of the new household of the King, on the part of one of the Commissaries of the Commune. He was accommodated with a chamber above ours. We demanded the same favour, but without effect.—*Note of the Author.*

† The first was M. Vaugiraud, formerly an officer in the French guards, who had been put in prison because the tyrants had not found his son in the country-house in which he resided, whom the Committee of Inspection had given orders to arrest. Three or four hours before his death, he had gone to the window of the turret to see what was passing opposite the prison-gate. He came back again, weeping bitterly and tearing his hair. He told us that he had just seen his son massacred; and he died with this dreadful idea upon his mind, which it afterwards appeared was false. I have since learnt that, as he was accustomed to stammer, the means of defence which he availed himself of appeared suspicious. He passed, in the eyes of the judges, for one of the *conspirators of the Palace of the Tuileries,* who were irrevocably proscribed.—*Note of the Author.*

even compare to death; after having drunk a thousand and a thousand times of the cup of bitterness, the door of my prison was opened. I was called, and made my appearance. Three men seized upon me, and dragged me into the dreadful room of judgment.

# CHAPTER IV

## LAST CRISIS OF MY AGONY

BY the light of two torches, I perceived the dreadful tribunal which was going to give me either life or death. The president, in a grey coat, with a sword by his side, was supported standing against a table, upon which were seen papers, an inkstand, some pipes, and some bottles. This table was surrounded by ten persons, sitting or standing; two of them had jackets and aprons on; others were stretched out upon benches sleeping. Two men, in their shirt-sleeves, stained with blood, sword in hand, guarded the entrance of the room; an old turnkey had his hand upon the bolts. In the presence of the president, three men were holding a prisoner, who appeared to be about sixty years of age.

I was placed in a corner of the room; my keepers crossed their sabres upon my breast, and warned me, that if I made the least movement to escape, they would run me through. I was gazing around for my Provençal friend, when I saw two national guards present to the president a petition from the section of the Croix-Rouge, in favour of the prisoner who was opposite to him.* He said to them, "that these demands were useless for traitors." The prisoner then exclaimed, "This is dreadful; your sentence is an assassination." The president answered him, "I wash my hands of it; conduct M. Maillé †..."

---

* One of them was drunk, and the language which he used probably caused the death of M. de Maillé, who had been wounded at the Palace of the Tuileries on the 10th August. He was denounced by an old surgeon of his house, in whom he had placed all his confidence.—*Note of the Author.*

† I fancied that I perceived that the president pronounced this sentence against his will. Many assassins had entered into the room, and caused a great ferment in it.—*Note of the Author.*

These words having been pronounced, he was pushed into the street, where I saw him massacred through the opening of the door of the turnkey's room.

I have frequently found myself in dangerous situations, and I have always had the good fortune to know how to keep my mind in tone; but in this, the alarm inseparable from what was passing around me would infallibly have made me sink under my sufferings, had it not been for the conversation of the Provençal and more especially for my dream, which was continually recurring to my imagination.

The president sat down to write, and, when he had apparently registered the name of the unhappy being who had been despatched, I heard him say, "*Another.*"

Immediately I was dragged before the expeditious and sanguinary tribunal, in the presence of which the best protection was not to have any, and where all the resources of the mind were of none effect, if they were not founded on truth. Two of my keepers held, each of them, one of my hands, and the third took me by the collar of my coat.

*The president addressing me.* — "Your name?—your profession?"

*One of the judges.* —"The least falsehood undoes you."

"My name is Jourgniac St. Meard; I have served twenty-five years as an officer; and I appear before your tribunal with the confidence of a man who has nothing to reproach himself with, and who, consequently, will utter nothing false."

*The president.* —"That is what we are going to see; a moment. . . . (He here looked at the commitments and the denunciations, which he afterwards passed to the judges). Do you know what are the motives of your arrest?"

"Yes, Mr. President,* and I must believe, from the falsehood of the denunciations against me, that the Committee of Inspection of the Commune would not have had me put in prison, had it not been for the precautions which the safety of the people require it to take.

---

* To my great mortification, the attention of the president and of the judges was often drawn aside. Individuals were whispering to them and bringing them letters; one amongst others was given to the president, which had been found in the pocket of M. Valcroissant, major-general, addressed to M. Servant, minister of war.—*Note of the Author.*

"I am accused of being editor of an anti-constitutional paper, entitled *Journal de la Cour et de la Ville.* The truth is, that such is not the case. It is an individual named Gautier, the description of whom is so unlike mine, that it can only have been through pure wickedness that they can have taken me for him; and if I were able to search in my pocket . . . ."

I made a motion ineffectually to take out my pocket-book: one of the judges perceived it, and said, to those who held me, "Let the gentleman loose." I then placed upon the table the affidavits of several clerks, dealers, shopkeepers, and owners of houses where he had lodged, which proved that he was editor of that paper, and sole proprietor.

*One of the judges.*—"But in fact there is never fire without smoke; you must tell us why you are accused of that."

"That is what I was going to do. You know, gentlemen, that this journal was a sort of box, in which people deposited the puns, jokes, epigrams, and witticisms, good or bad, which were made at Paris, and in the forty-three departments. I might say that I have never made any for this paper, as there does not exist any manuscript in my handwriting; but my frankness, which has always been serviceable to me, shall be of service to me again upon this occasion, and I will confess that the liveliness of my character frequently inspired me with witty ideas, which I sent to M. Gautier. Here, gentlemen, is the simple cause of this great denunciation, which is as absurd as that of which I am about to speak is monstrous. I am accused of having been upon the frontiers,—of having raised recruits there,— of having led them to the emigrants. . . ."

A general murmur arose, which did not disconcert me; and I said, raising my voice,—

"Well, gentlemen, gentlemen! I have the word, and I entreat Mr. President to be good enough to maintain my right to speak; never was it more necessary for me."

*Almost all the judges laughed, and said,* "It is just,—it is just; silence!"

"My denunciator is a monster; and I am about to prove this truth to judges whom the people would not have chosen, if they had not believed them capable of discerning between the innocent and the guilty. Here, gentlemen, are affidavits, which prove that I have not been out of Paris for twenty-three months. Here are the declarations of the masters of three houses, where I have lodged during that time, which prove the same thing."

They were occupied in examining them, when we were interrupted by the arrival of a prisoner, who took my place before the president. Those who held him said that it was another priest whom they had rooted out from a corner of the chapel. After a very short examination, he was sent to La Force. He threw his breviary upon the table, and was dragged to the outside of the gates, where he was massacred. That affair finished, I appeared again before the judges.

*One of the judges.*—" I do not say that these affidavits are forged, but who will prove to us that they are genuine?"

"Your remark is just, Sir; and, to put it in your power to judge me with a full knowledge of the circumstances, order me to be conducted into a dungeon, till messengers, whom I entreat Mr. President to be good enough to appoint, have ascertained their validity. If they are forged, I merit death."

*One of the judges,* who, during my examination, appeared to *interest himself about me, said in a low voice,* "A guilty man would not speak with that confidence."

*Another judge.*—"Of what section are you?"

"Of that of the Corn-Market."

*A national guard, who was not amongst the number of the judges.*—"Oh, oh! I am likewise of that section. With whom do you live?"

" With M. Teyssier, Rue Croix des Petits Champs."

*The national guard.*—"I know him: we have even had transactions together, and I can pronounce whether this affidavit is by him." He looked at it, and said, "Gentlemen, I certify that this is the signature of Citizen Teyssier."

With what pleasure could I have thrown myself around the neck of this tutelary angel! But I had things more important to treat upon, which prevented; and scarcely had he finished

* The features of his face are engraven in my heart; and if I ever have the happiness of meeting him, I will embrace him, and endeavour to express my gratitude.—*Note of the Author.*

speaking before I made an exclamation, which recalled the attention of all, in saying,—

"Well, gentlemen, after the testimony of that worthy man, which proves the falsehood of this denunciation, which might have caused my death, what idea can you have of the denunciator?"

*The judge who appeared to feel an interest in me said*, "He is a scoundrel; and, if he were here, we would punish him. Do you know who he is?"

"No, Sir; but he must be known to the Committee of Inspection of the Commune; and I declare that, if I did know him, I should think I rendered a service to the public in warning them, by hand-bills, to mistrust and avoid him as they would a venomous reptile."

*One of the judges.*—"We see that you are not an editor of newspapers, and that you have never raised recruits. But you do not speak of the aristocratical language which you used at the Palais Royal, at the shops of some booksellers."

"Why not? I have not been afraid to acknowledge what I have written: I will still less fear what I have said, and even thought.—I have always advised obedience to the laws, and preached up the necessity of example. I confess, at the same time, that I have profited by the permission which the constitution gave me, and I have said that I did not think it perfect, because I thought I perceived that it placed us all in a false position. If it is a crime thus to have spoken, then the constitution itself laid the snare for me; and the permission which it gave me to make known its defects, was nothing more than an ambuscade. I have likewise said, that almost all the nobles of the Constituent Assembly who have shown themselves such zealous patriots, have laboured much more to promote their own interests and ambition, than the good of their country; and when all Paris appeared so smitten with their patriotism, I said, they deceive us. I appeal to you, gentlemen, whether the event has not justified my idea of them? I have often blamed the cowardly and unskilful manœuvres of certain personages, who only wished for the constitution, the constitution itself, and nothing but the constitution. For a long time I had been predicting a great catastrophe, the necessary result of that constitution, revised by egotists who, like those of whom I have already spoken, laboured only for themselves; and more especially of the character of the intriguers who defended it. Dissimulation, cupidity, and pusillanimity, were the attributes of these political quacks.* Fanaticism, intrepidity, and frankness, formed the character of their enemies. It was not necessary to have telescopes of any great power to discover who would derive the advantage."

The attention which had been paid to my observations, and which I confess I did not expect, encouraged me, and I was going to urge a thousand reasons which made me prefer the republican régime to that of the constitution—I was going to repeat what I said daily in the shop of M. Desenne, when the gaoler entered, wild with alarm, to inform the judges that a prisoner was escaping by the chimney. The president gave orders that he should instantly be fired at: but that, if he escaped, the turnkey should answer for him with his head. It was the unfortunate Maussabré. They fired several musket-shots at him; but the keeper, seeing that this method was unsuccessful, set fire to some straw beneath. Half stifled by the smoke, he fell; and was massacred before the gate of the prison.

I resumed my speech, continuing,—" No one, gentlemen, has wished for the reform of abuses more than I have. Here are pamphlets which I composed before and during the sitting of the States-General; they prove what I say! I have always thought that we went too far for a constitution, and not far enough for a republic. I am neither a jacobin nor a constitutionalist. I did not like the principles of the former, although

---

* It is with pain that we see M. St. Meard accuse the Constituent Assembly. The *attributes* which he gives to the members who composed it do not belong to them. If the nation had followed strictly, to the letter, that constitution which Mirabeau, Barnave, Lameth, and Lanjuinais voted for, France would not have been covered with the veil of mourning which so long shrouded her: anarchy would not have raised her sanguinary head; the unfortunate Louis XVI. would not have ascended the steps of a scaffold; and, finally, those horrible days which stained our generous country would not have furnished history with a few dark pages, which should be torn out from her book, if they ought not to remain in it in order to bear witness against crime. The Constituent Assembly committed many errors; but those errors were effaced, and the fruits of the good which it did have been reaped.—*Note of the Editors.*

much more consistent and frank than those of the latter, which
I shall detest, until it has been proved that they are not the
cause of all the evils which we have experienced. At length
we are rid of them" . . . .

*A judge, in an impatient tone.*—" You continually tell us that
you are neither this nor that; what are you, then?"

" I was a downright royalist."*

There arose a general murmur, which was miraculously checked
by the judge who appeared to feel an interest for me, and who
said, word for word,

" It is not to judge opinions that we are here; it is to judge
and decide upon their results."†

Scarcely had these precious words issued from his lips, when
I exclaimed, " Yes, gentlemen, I have been a *downright royalist*,
but I have never been paid for being so. I was a *royalist*, because I believed that a monarchical government was suitable for
my country; because I loved the King cordially, and for himself.
I preserved this sentiment in my heart until the 10th of August."

The murmur which now arose had something in it rather
flattering than otherwise; and, in order to maintain the good
opinion which appeared to be entertained of me, I added,—

" I have never heard plots spoken of but with the greatest
indignation. Whenever I have found an opportunity of assisting
a man, I have done it, without inquiring from him his principles. Behold some journals,§ even patriotic journals, which prove

---

* We know not whether we ought on this occasion most to admire the
frankness or the presence of mind of M. de St. Meard. Although the event
decided in his favour, it is not the less true on that account that his imprudent
confession exposed his life; but a man is doubly happy when, like him, he can
save it with honour.—*Note of the Editors.*

† If the geniuses of Rousseau and of Voltaire had been united in pleading
my cause, they could hardly have expressed themselves more happily.—*Note of
the Author.*

§ I showed them some newspapers, in which favourable mention was made
of me.

M. Gorsas, who had, more than any one else, reason to complain of the
*Journal de la Cour et de la Ville*, would not have said, *the day after my
liberation*, if he had thought me the editor of it, that which he has said in the
sixth number of his journal (*Le Courrier des 83 Départements*):

"The Chevalier de St. Meard had furnished some articles for the *Journal
de la Cour et de la Ville*, but these articles bore no character of malignity.

what I have the honour to assert. I have always been loved by the peasantry of the estate of which I am the proprietor; for at the very moment when they were burning the *châteaux* of my neighbours, I was in mine at St. Meard. The peasants came in crowds to express to me the pleasure they had in seeing me again, and planted a may-pole in my court. I know that these details must appear to you trivial; but, gentlemen, put yourselves in my place, and judge whether this is not the moment to take advantage of every truth that may be beneficial to me. I can affirm, that not a soldier of the regiment of infantry of the King,* in which I served twenty-five years, has had occasion to complain of me: I may even pride myself on being one of the officers whom they most loved. The last proof which they gave me of this is by no means equivocal, since, two days before the affair of Nancy, the very period at which their mistrust of the officers was at its height, they appointed me their general, and obliged me to command the army which went to Lunéville to liberate thirty dragoons of the regiment of Mestre-de-Camp, which the carabineers had made prisoners, and to carry off from them General Malseigne."

*One of the judges.*—"I will soon see whether you have served in the regiment of the King. Did you know in it M. Moreau?"

"Yes, Sir; I knew even two of that name: one, very tall, very fat, and very clever; the other, very little, very lean, and very "——

I made a motion with my hand, to express a light and shallow head.

*The same judge.*—"That is the same; I perceive that you have known him."

The Chevalier de St. Meard candidly confesses that he had been a royalist because he had believed Louis XVI. sincere. He did not deny his articles; and the Chevalier de St. Meard was borne off in the arms of the people, and carried in triumph to his own house: he even received a title to protection on his discharge. The Chevalier de St. Meard was not the author of those revolting articles which were often met with in that journal; and he has proved, in some circumstances which *we have mentioned*, that he was capable of good actions, and that he had an excellent heart."—*Note of the Author.*

* One of the judges trod upon my toe, apparently to warn me that I was going to expose myself to danger. I was sure of the contrary.—*Note of the Author.*

We were in this part of the trial, when one of the doors of the apartment which communicated upon the staircase opened, and I saw an escort of three men, who were conducting M. Marque ——, late major, formerly my comrade in the regiment of the King, and recently my fellow prisoner at the Abbaye. They placed him, until my trial should be finished, in the place where I had been put when I was first led into the room.

I resumed my speech.

"After the unfortunate affair of Nancy, I came to Paris, where I have remained since that time. I was arrested at my apartments twelve days ago. So little had I expected it, that I had not ceased to show myself abroad as usual. The seals were not placed at my lodgings, as nothing suspicious was found there. I was never inscribed upon the civil list: I never signed a petition: I have had no reprehensible correspondence: I have not been out of France since the revolution. During my abode in the capital, I have lived there peaceably; I have given myself up to the natural gaiety of my character: which, being in consonance in this respect with my principles, has never permitted me to mix seriously in public affairs, and still less to do harm to any soul living. This, gentlemen, is all I can say of my conduct and my principles. The sincerity of the confessions which I have made ought to convince you that I am not a dangerous man. This is what induces me to hope that you will have the goodness to grant me the liberty which I demand, and to which I am attached both from necessity and from principle."

*The president, after taking off his hat, said,* "I see nothing which ought to make us suspect this gentleman; I grant him his liberty. Has this decision your approbation?"

*All the judges.*—"Yes, yes; *it is just.*"

These *divine* words were scarcely uttered before all those who were in the room embraced me. I heard above me shouts of applause, and cries of *bravo!* I raised my eyes, and perceived several heads grouped against the bars of the vent-hole of the room where I was; and as they had their eyes eagerly open and in motion, I imagined that the murmuring and uneasy buzz, which I had heard during my examination, proceeded from that place.

The president named three persons to go as a deputation to

proclaim to the people the sentence which had just been pronounced. During this proclamation, I requested from the judges
an extract of what they had just pronounced in my favour, which
they promised me. The president asked me why I did not wear
the cross of St. Louis, which he knew I had. I answered him
that my fellow prisoners had advised me to take it off. He told
me, that as the National Assembly had not yet forbidden it to
be worn, individuals excited suspicion in doing the contrary.
The three deputies entered again, and made me put my hat
on: they then led me out of the door of the turnkey's room.
As soon as I appeared in the street, one of them cried out,
*Hats off, citizens, behold him for whom your judges request aid and
protection.* After these words were uttered, the *executive power*
took hold of me; and, placed in the centre of four torches, I
was embraced by all those who surrounded me. All the spectators loudly exclaimed, *Vive la Nation!* These honours, to which
I was deeply sensible, placed me under the safeguard of the
people, who, heartily applauding, suffered me to pass, followed
by the three deputies, whom the president had charged to escort me to my own house. * One of them told me that he was
a mason, and established in the Faubourg St. Germain; another
was a native of Bourges, and was apprenticed to a hair-dresser;
the third, dressed in the uniform of the National Guard, told
me that he was one of the federated body. As we were pro-
ceeding along, the mason asked me if I was afraid. "Not more
than yourself," I replied; "you must have perceived that I was
not intimidated in the turnkey's room, and I shall not tremble
in the street."

"You would be wrong to be afraid," said he, in return, "for
at present you are sacred to the people; and if any one struck
you, he would perish on the instant. I clearly perceived that
you were not one of those caterpillars of the civil list; but I
trembled for you, when you said that you had been an officer

* Pétion thus reports one of the days of September :—"I perceived a dozen
executioners, with their arms bare, covered with blood, some with clubs, and
others with swords and cutlasses, which were dripping with gore! Citizens were
impatiently waiting outside for the decisions of the judges, preserving the most
melancholy silence at the sentences of death, and crying out for joy at the
orders for liberation."—*Note of the Editors.*

of the King. Do you recollect that I trod upon your foot?"
—"Yes, but I thought it was one of the judges." "In good
faith it was I; I thought you were going to thrust yourself into
the fire, and I should have been mortified to see you sacrifice
your own life; but you have got well out of the scrape: I am
very glad of it, for I like people who do not shrink." On our
arrival at Rue St. Benoît, we got into a hackney coach, which
carried us to my residence. The first action of my landlord, of
my friend, on beholding me, was to offer his pocket-book to my
conductors, who refused it, and who said to him, in honest
terms,—"We do not follow this trade for money. Here is your
friend; he has promised us a glass of brandy; we will drink it,
and will then return to our post."

They requested from me a certificate, declaring that they had
conducted me to my lodgings without accident. I gave it to
them, and entreated them to send me the document which the
judges had promised me, as well as my effects,* which I had
left at the Abbaye. I accompanied them to the street, where
I embraced them most heartily. The next day one of the
commissaries brought me the certificate, of which the following
is a copy:—

"We, commissaries appointed by the people to try the traitors
detained in the prison of the Abbaye, have made appear before
us, this 4th September, citizen Jourgniac St. Meard, late officer,
decorated with an order, who has proved that the accusations
made against him were false, and that he never entered into
any plot against the patriots. We have had him proclaimed
innocent in the presence of the people, who applauded the
liberation which he had received from us. In proof of which
we have delivered to him, at his own request, this certificate:
we invite all the citizens to grant him aid and protection.

"Signed, POIR . . . . BER . . . .

"<i>At the Abbaye, year 4th of Liberty,<br>
and 1st of Equality.</i>"</div>

---

* In consequence of a claim which I have since made for them, M.M. Jour-
deuil and Leclere, administrators in the department of inspection, have had the
politeness to promise me, by letter, an order for the delivery of the said effects:
I have not yet received either it or the things, but I am bound to believe that
I shall lose nothing by the delay.—*Note composed several days after the manuscript.*

After some hours' repose, I eagerly hastened to fulfil the duties which friendship and gratitude imposed upon me. I got a letter printed, in which I communicated my happy liberation to all those who I knew had felt any interest in my misfortunes. I went the same day to walk in a public garden: I saw several individuals rubbing their eyes, in order to assure themselves if it was myself whom they beheld; while others started back with alarm, as if they had seen a spectre. I was embraced even by those who did not know me; in fact, it was completely a day of congratulation and rejoicing for me. But what has since been said to me, what has been written to me, and what I have seen printed, has made me reflect how very prejudicial my imprisonment may have been to me in its effect upon the minds of those who are not acquainted with me, and particularly at a period when people believe, condemn, and execute so precipitately. I have, therefore, thought that it behoved me to produce a counter effect, and I have made known the truth.*

* In order that the reader may embrace, at one glance, all the various scenes of this fatal drama, we have comprised, in the Appendix, Note C, a recital of the massacres which took place in each prison.—*Note of the Editors.*

# CHAPTER V

## TO MY ENEMIES

IN the sketch of the dreadful events which I have just traced, I promised to observe exactness and truth.* I have scrupulously fulfilled my promise. The details into which I have entered unquestionably prove that my intention has been not to omit any, because there is none which occurred, at that fearful epoch, that is not interesting, and which will not be written in characters of blood in the pages of history; they will doubtlessly furnish to others reflections on the causes which produced them. I have merely indulged in those which grief and terror inspired in my mind.

A stranger to every kind of intrigue, and an enemy to those dark conspiracies which degrade the dignity of man and dishonour the French character, which, till now, was always distinguished for loyalty, I entered pure into that terrible prison, and it was my ingenuousness alone which saved me.

I know, however, that the justice which was done me, at a moment when it might possibly have been pronounced by chance, has excited mortification in the minds of my enemies,

---

* I do not affirm that what was addressed to me at the Committee, and at the time of my trial in the Abbaye, as well as my answers, are reported word for word; but I do aver, that the sense of the expressions is given with the greatest exactness. It will without doubt be a matter of surprise, that, at such a critical moment, I spoke on my examination with so much connection; but the astonishment will cease when I state, that I had learnt by heart what I intended to say, and that I had even requested four of my companions in misfortune to hear me repeat the defence which I had composed, and which I had determined to make. My resolution was taken; I was, as it were, identified with the idea of death: I neither feared it nor sought it.—*Note of the Author*.

whose hatred, which I have never merited, has not been extinguished by my dreadful agony. I know that at the very time when I was pronouncing, in the tribune of my section, the oath prescribed for all the citizens, they were proclaiming, in one of the coffee-houses of the Place de la Révolution, that I had solemnly sworn never to take it.

Well, gentlemen, recollect that never did any one live with the certainty of death so completely before his eyes; recollect, that during thirty-eight hours the knives and the axes were raised over me. Could the moment that separates us from life be more dreadful than this? You have done me great wrong, but I forgive you for it with all my heart; but I implore you, by your patriotism, to leave me to terminate in peace the remainder of my life.

I will confess, if you desire it, that a decree of the Legislative Assembly, by taking away more than half of my patrimony, which myself and my family had long enjoyed, may have made me a little fretful and discontented; but put yourselves in my place for a moment, and tell me honestly if you could have experienced this reduction in your property with satisfaction?

However, at the moment I am writing these lines, I feel really consoled for my loss, with the reflection that the suppression of the seignorial rents is favourable to those of my former tenants, who were somewhat poor, whom I have always esteemed as well as the others, and who, I am persuaded, will not be ungrateful to me. Amuse yourselves with my narration; I abandon to your criticism both the work and the *author,* as an *author;* but no more malignity I entreat you: it produces effects of too melancholy a nature.

Think not, however, that I demand your favour or indulgence. Having all my life been a faithful observer of the laws, I will not disobey those which the national sovereignty has dictated. I have always loved my country, and will not injure her, but will willingly join with those who would put an end to her misfortunes. If you see me swerve from these principles, denounce me. But speak the truth, and, above all, remember that, if I had been guilty, I should not have been arrested in my apartments *twelve days after the* 10*th of August,* 1792; that, if I had entertained the design of injuring my country, I should not have remained at Paris; and that, if I did her injury, I should not have appeared as an evidence against myself, but should have remained silent.

LAZARE, *ci-devant* JOURGNIAC ST. MEARD,
*Ne Varietur.**

*Paris, 1st year of the Republic,*
15*th Sept.* 1792.

* The courageous publication of this pamphlet exposed the author to constantly increasing dangers; assassins tracked his footsteps. He only escaped by opposing to them that calmness and that resolution which he had preserved during the fearful scenes of the Abbaye. *Vide* Appendix, Note D.—*Note of the Editors.*

SOME OF

# THE BITTER FRUITS

OF THE

## REVOLUTION

AND A

FEEBLE SKETCH OF THE DAYS OF THE SECOND
AND THIRD OF SEPTEMBER, 1792

Ils s'abreuvent de sang, et le sang les altère.

They bathe in blood, and blood renders them athirst.

# BIOGRAPHICAL NOTICE

ON

# MADEMOISELLE DE PAYSAC

THE narration which we are about to present to the reader was furnished by M. de St. Meard, who received it himself from the courageous woman by whom it was written. Its author, Mademoiselle de Paysac, born in Le Périgord, about the year 1750, had married M. de Fars, Marquis of Fausse-Lendry. She was unfortunately living in Paris, with Madame de Rastignac, her mother, and Abbé Chapt de Rastignac, her uncle, during the fatal days of September. When this worthy and estimable ecclesiastic, whose virtues and religious sentiments the tyrants wished to punish, was torn from his family, Madame de Fausse-Lendry solicited and obtained permission to go and visit him in prison.

As heroic as, but less fortunate than, Mademoiselle Cazotte and Mademoiselle de Sombreuil, she had not the happiness to rescue from the murderers their destined victim. The devoted tenderness of Madame de Fausse-Lendry could not save her uncle. The revolution gave her a further and more agonizing cause for grief. Madame la Marquise de Rastignac, her mother, soon afterwards was brought to the scaffold. Overwhelmed by these cruel events, Madame de Fausse-Lendry would, doubtlessly, have been condemned in her turn, had it not been for the revolution of the 9 Thermidor. That day, which saved her life, could not, however, alleviate her misery. The dreadful deprivations she had experienced in the execution of her mother and

her uncle, strengthened her attachment to the cause for which
they had perished. She shared the transports of joy which the
restoration excited in the friends of royalty. During the hundred
days, she offered a flag to the pupils of the School of Law
(Ecole de Droit), who repaired to Ghent.

# SOME OF

# THE BITTER FRUITS OF THE REVOLUTION

It is not with the vain desire of fixing upon me the eyes of the public, that I have undertaken to write the recital which is about to be presented to the reader. I would taste the melancholy but sweet consolation which remains for the unfortunate, —the consolation of communicating their sorrows. I have wished, moreover, to fulfil a sacred duty, the only one of which I have it in my power to acquit myself, to the memory of a man whose death will appear dreadful to those who look for nothing beyond this visible world; but which eyes enlightened by faith will regard as the reward due to an estimable priest, whom Heaven, by an astonishing revolution, destined at the close of an honourable and peaceful career, to receive the bloody palm of a martyrdom.

With a moderate fortune, which satisfied my wishes, I enjoyed every comfort which can alleviate the sufferings of a susceptible heart. The affection and the tender attentions of two much-loved uncles shed a degree of serenity through my soul, and made me every moment feel the delights of pure friendship. One was in the church, and the other in the army: the former united with the virtues of his profession all the learning which it requires, and his erudition was ornamented by the flowers of a brilliant and varied literature; the latter was full of honour and generally esteemed. In the month of July, 1791, he was appointed, by the National Assembly, colonel of the 15th regiment. It was at this period that my misfortunes commenced. I hoped that my uncle would refuse a post which he could only hold from the King; but an ardent desire to serve his master misled him in the choice of means, and he accepted the appointment, thinking that he should thereby be able to be useful to the unfortunate monarch whose faithful subject he ever remained.

I had written to this brave and worthy officer a letter, in which I explained to him the reasons which ought to determine him to decline a command conferred upon him by unfaithful governors. My indignation had induced me to indulge in strong and energetic expressions; this letter miscarried, and fell into the hands of the Committee of Examination. M. Voidel, who performed the functions of grand national inquisitor, preserved it with great care. Through a piece of good fortune it is signed, and my *amour-propre* is flattered at the idea that my name is at the foot of a document which does honour to my principles, and in which I had the courage to brave the dangers to which the declaration of such sentiments exposed me.

My uncle set out to join his regiment, and I had at once to support the grief which his departure caused me, and the mortification of beholding him deviate in appearance from the path of honour; I say in appearance, for I was well convinced of the purity of his intentions. He departed at the end of August, and, on the 10th of November, I had the misfortune to lose him.* I will not attempt to describe the state to which I was reduced by this melancholy event; alas! my heart was destined to receive a wound still more severe and desolating.

His brother, the ecclesiastic, as deeply affected as myself, but supported by religion, was occupied solely in administering to me all the consolation of which I was susceptible. After he had lavished upon me all the attentions of the most tender affection, when my heart gave this dear uncle, with his own natural share of my respectful attachment, that of which his brother had been the object, I had the grief to see him fall sick, and for nearly three months he lay in a dying state. It was now my turn to bestow all my attention upon him. His affection for me rendered my little cares gratifying to him, and I was ultimately rewarded

---

* He was in garrison at Revel. An epidemic disease had seized a great part of his men; he wrote several times, without success, to M. Duportail, then minister of war, entreating him that the regiment might change garrison. He did more: in order to attend himself to his sick soldiers, he passed several days and nights successively in the hospital. He was fortunate enough to contribute to the recovery of some of them; but, attacked in his turn by the same disease, his life was the price of his attentions to others.—*Note of the Author.*

by his restoration to life again. But, alas! how short was this enjoyment permitted me.

On the 25th of August, at eleven o'clock at night, a band of four hundred armed ruffians came to carry off this worthy old man, who, having been confined to his bed for so long a period, could hardly make use of his limbs. In seizing their victim, there was no sort of outrage or insolence which crime could lavish on virtue, which was not committed. The unfortunate bore it all with that serenity which springs from the peace of a good conscience and the deep resignation of a Christian. He was conducted to the office of the Mayoralty, where all present feigned that they did not know the pretexts of the arrest, for which, in fact, no order appeared upon the registers, not even his name. Pétion, then mayor, refused to listen to him; and, without any formalities being observed, he was taken to the prison of the Abbaye.

Let the reader judge of my situation during these wretched moments. Yet the Supreme Being did not suffer me to be overwhelmed with my grief, but filled my soul with new strength. At seven o'clock in the morning I repaired to the Hôtel de Ville, where I saw Manuel, and all the assassins who then formed the Commune. I addressed them all. None of them knew that the Abbé de Rastignac was arrested. I solicited, as an especial favour, permission to become a prisoner with my uncle; but they harshly refused my application. How imperious are the necessities of the soul, and what courage do they not inspire! From Sunday till the following Wednesday I did not quit the Hôtel de Ville, except to take a few hours' sleep. On Tuesday they came and arbitrarily forced me away, and took me to the section of the Luxembourg, where I remained in a state of arrest from two o'clock in the afternoon till eight in the evening. At length, on Wednesday, by dint of urgent importunities, I obtained the much-desired permission. M. Sergent, and others, told me that I was committing an imprudence, and that the prisons were not safe. Ah! how could such motives stop one impelled by affection! I was only the more eager to share all the dangers of him whose days I would willingly have preserved at the expense of my own.

I at length saw him who had always been a second father

to me, and pressed him in my arms. He expressed to me the
pleasure which my presence gave him; but his joy was mingled
with the fear that he might see me suffer with him. Alas! I
could only suffer from his sufferings. He was one of seven in
a room where it was scarcely possible to turn around. The air
of the place was infected,—sufficient of itself to have destroyed
an unfortunate old man, enfeebled by age and by sickness.
His eyes had not closed once in the horrible abode. What
would I not have given to have seen him take one hour's
repose! The frightful aspect of the prison, the corrupted air
which I breathed, the continual sight of the prisoners who shared
the misfortune of my uncle,—nothing affected me—I was beside
him.

Thursday, Friday, and Saturday, passed with tolerable tranquillity. Every night, at ten o'clock, the gaoler fetched me to
sleep in his chamber, occupied by the Princesse de Tarente* and
Mademoiselle de Sombreuil.

On Sunday, at an early hour in the morning, the gaoler
removed his wife and children from the prison. This precaution
alarmed me, inasmuch as I saw consternation depicted upon his
countenance. On other days it was sometimes four o'clock before the prisoners were served with their dinners; but on this

* The following fact proves the courage a woman can evince when required
by circumstances:—

"Madame la Princesse de Tarente is placed between life and death by her
judges: they promise her life, if she will accuse the Queen; instead of accusing
her, she pleads her cause. She is acquitted.—They seize her again, and she
demands either death or perfect liberty. These traits of virtuous courage astonish
her very assassins, and they suffer her to go."

Madame la Princesse de Lamballe was less fortunate. She likewise refused
to swear hatred to the Queen and to the King. It will be recollected that
her head was exhibited under the windows of Louis XVI. at the temple, and
that the unfortunate monarch was constrained to see it. On this subject a
most touching anecdote is related, which our readers will be gratified in having
related here.

"When this lady's head was exhibited to the King, a soldier, with an atrocious appearance of pleasure, directed his attention to it; another soldier did
what he could to conceal the horrid sight from him. The King was asked if
he should recognise the soldier who had conducted himself so savagely. *No*,
he replied: *but I should perfectly well remember him who evinced so much
feeling.*"—(Extract from the Spy of the French Revolution.)—*Note of the
Editors.*

day, a day for ever execrable! they dined before two o'clock.
Another frightful presage! The turnkeys took care to carry away
all the knives and forks.

At length the fatal hour arrived. We heard the most horrible
cries and howlings. We were told that the populace wished to
force their way into the prison. Nearly three hours elapsed before the assassins had penetrated the gates. If the public officers
had not consented to the massacre, they could undoubtedly have
prevented it.*

At the beginning of the night, some national guards and the
gaoler came and tore me from my uncle. . . . I saw him no
more. . . . I was led into a chamber whither all the women
had been conducted. We heard the cries of joy of the ferocious
murderers, and the groans of the victims whom they were
sacrificing. The gaoler came to inform us that he was forced
to permit some of the prisoners to be destroyed for the safety
of the others. I told him that the lives of all had been confided to
him, and that it was his duty to save them or perish. I saw
with indignation that I was not heeded. Alas! in what place,
and to whom, was I speaking of duty and heroism? All the
night passed in agonies worse than death.

At seven o'clock in the morning (Monday), the turnkey announced Manuel. He appeared to condemn the cruelties which
had been perpetrated, but prevented nothing. He passed the greater
part of the day in the prison; but his presence was either use-

---

* On the subject of the horrors of September, two speeches, one by Robespierre, and the other by Louvet, contain the following passages:

"They hurried to the prisons.... Could the magistrates stay the people?
It was a popular movement, and not the partial insurrection of a few wretches,
paid for assassinating their fellow citizens." (Robespierre.)

"We are then arrived at the fatal period. The former friends of the people
have wished to fix upon them the horrors by which this week is marked: they
have hereby inflicted the most grievous outrage on the inhabitants of the capital,
whom I well know, and amongst whom I have lived. They are, I am aware,
powerful; but, like all brave men, they are good and generous. I do not mean
here to speak of that portion of the people which is misled, but of the immense
majority of the citizens of Paris. It is false that the people were seen before
and in the interior of the prisons, on the horrible day of the 2nd of September.
How many were there of them? Not two hundred persons. And on the
outside, how many spectators were there led by a curiosity truly inconceivable?
Not twice that number." (Louvet.)—*Note of the Editors.*

less or fatal.  As I had before seen him, when entreating permission to share the captivity of my uncle, I now addressed
him, and expressed my fears of the dangers which surrounded
the object of my tender veneration.  "Be satisfied, Madam,"
said he to me; "nothing will happen to him: I answer for it
with my life."  As if his life, and the lives of all his fellows,
could pay for that which I am weeping for!  He added, "Do
not speak of your uncle; you would make them think of him,
and he will be forgotten."  The keeper then promised me, that
if they came to ask for my uncle, he would immediately inform
me of it.  Oh! if he had kept his word, I might have saved
the good old man, or I should have died with him.*  While I
was in this dreadful situation, the minutes appearing hours to
me, a turnkey brought me a note from my uncle, who com-

* In a pamphlet, written at the period of the revolution, against Brissot,
Pétion, Manuel, etc., menacing each, we find the following details, which we
give verbatim to our readers:—

"At the time of the massacre of the prisoners, of which people were apprised
some days previous, Madame de la Trémoille, apprised of the approaching horrid
event, hurried to the house of Manuel, with the intention of preventing the
murder of Madame St. Brice, her friend, then confined in the prison of La
Force, and addressed him thus:—'If I thought it possible, Sir, that you would
refuse to accompany me, and secure the immediate liberation of my dearest
friend, I declare to you that I would blow my brains out this instant.'  With
this the lady took a pistol from her pocket, and appeared prepared to execute
her design.  Manuel, alarmed, vainly attempted to disarm and calm her; but
she added, that her resolution was taken; that she was resolved to destroy
herself, if he did not yield to her entreaties, and accompany her in her carriage
to the prison.  Manuel, urged by this energetic and sensitive lady, yielded to
her urgent solicitations; and, in his character of Syndic Procurer of the Commune, caused Madame St. Brice to be released.  This lady, after tenderly
embracing her friend, declared, in her turn, to Manuel, that she would not
leave the prison until he had put the finishing stroke to his generosity, by
restoring Mademoiselle de Tourzel, to liberty.  Manuel, again embarrassed,
sought for excuses, and alleged a thousand reasons to avoid the performance of
this noble action.  In the end, he was constrained to yield, and to procure,
against his will, the liberation of Mademoiselle de Tourzel."  Who or what
forced Manuel to act thus?  He either had a secret motive, or he was really
moved by a sentiment of humanity.  Who can explain the heart of man, capable
as it is of such conflicting emotions?  It will be seen that Manuel saved, in the
same manner, the celebrated Madame de Staël from the dangers she incurred
at the Hôtel de Ville; but it will also be seen what insensibility he evinced
amidst the bloodiest scenes of massacre.—Note of the Editors.

plained of not having seen me. (Alas! the tyrants kept me chained as well as him). This beloved uncle told me, that they were going to take him home, and entreated me to repair thither as soon as possible, in order to relieve his anxiety. He charged me to take care of a very voluminous portfolio, which would be troublesome to him, on account of the difficulty he had in walking. This portfolio was never delivered to me, and was doubtlessly stolen.

At nine o'clock in the morning, they came to inform us that all those who remained had their pardon. We were nearly to the number of twenty. The two first who went out were butchered. A national guard, who doubtlessly was not one of the assassins, exclaimed, "It is a snare which they have laid for you; go up again, and do not show yourselves." It was thus that he saved our lives. Two hours afterwards some one announced to us that Mademoiselle de Sombreuil, the model of every virtue, had saved her father's life. What an affecting spectacle of truly heroic filial tenderness! Could we behold without emotion, and without the liveliest admiration, a daughter surrounded by assassins, forcibly clasping in her arms the body of her father, whom the wretches wished to assassinate, and demanding from the tyrants that their first blows should be aimed at her! Oh, admirable trait of tenderness, the memory of which will endure as long as that of the ever-detested day !*

This event restored us to some degree of tranquillity ; but, a few minutes afterwards, the assassins began again to slaughter their victims. Their arms were wearied, but their rage for blood was insatiable. They soon came to conduct the females to be examined. We were led into a turnkey's room, where a great number of prisoners had already met their death. The judges of the sanguinary tribunal would not hear us, and we were taken back to our chamber. From that moment we were haunted by men covered with blood, and armed with swords and pistols. The

---

* Legouvé, in *Le Mérite des Femmes* (Merits of Women), has commemorated this heroic instance of filial piety. He has, however, omitted one terrible circumstance, which, perhaps, he despaired of giving with full poetic force. The murderers presented a glass of blood to Mademoiselle de Sombreuil; she was obliged to drink it. This was the price of her father's life, and the devoted angel swallowed the horrid potion.—*Note of the Editors.*

intoxication occasioned by the united power of wine and carnage
was depicted in their frightful countenances, and shone in their fiery
looks.   They related to us, with savage delight, the manner in
which they got rid of the aristocrats, and the terror with which their
descriptions inspired us was highly gratifying to these cannibals.

In this horrible situation, Mademoiselle Cazotte eagerly entreated to see her father; she evinced so much sensibility, and such
sublime virtue, that her petition was complied with.   They led
her into the room where he was, and almost immediately she
was conducted back to ours.   Some moments afterwards, this
interesting young creature, hearing her father, who was going
down to meet his fate, darted through the guards, and grasped
the unfortunate old man, and it was impossible to separate her
from him.   She displayed the same heroism of which Mademoiselle de Sombreuil had given so rare an example.   In imitation
of that generous girl, Mademoiselle Cazotte succeeded in softening the hearts of the murderers, whose fury her father was on
the point of experiencing; but, alas! she saved the head which
was already whitened by age, only to see it a few days afterwards
delivered up to the steel of the executioner.   Horrible assassination, the more revolting from being invested with judicial forms.*

* It was on the 12th September that he was imprisoned again.  His daughter
passed both day and night at his side.  She had already succeeded in securing
the same Marseillois to whom she was so indebted in her former danger.  She
was beginning, in fact, to hope, when she was ordered into close confinement.
Her zeal had been so formidable to the adversaries of Cazotte, that they took
these means of assuring themselves that he should not escape a second time.
In the absence of his daughter they did, in reality, assassinate him.—*Extract
from the Notes of "The Merits of Women," by Legouvé.*

The decree pronounced against him by the tribunal installed after the 10th
of August, was executed on the 25th December, 1792.  His condemnation was
founded upon the pretext of several letters which he had written to his friend,
M. Ponteau, secretary of the civil list, in which he pointed out certain means
which he thought would check the progress of the revolution.  Cazotte exclaimed,
upon the scaffold:—"I die as I have lived, faithful to God and to my King."

It appears that his religious ideas gave to his sentiments all the ardour of
supernatural enthusiasm.  He went to his death as the first Christians ran to
martyrdom.  He said, with an affecting exaltation of soul, to the prisoners
whom he left behind him:—"My friends, I die content, if you assure me that
my fate does not excite your envy."  He believed that he left amongst them
men who were ready to dispute with him the merit of his devoted attachment
to God and to his sovereign.—*Note of the Editors.*

At six o'clock in the evening, collecting all my strength of mind, and urged alone by the desire of seeing my uncle again, I earnestly entreated to be led before the tribunal of blood, in order to endeavour to quit at last a place so fatal, or to terminate an existence so insupportable. I was conducted by men stained with the blood of the murders they had just perpetrated. I advanced through sabres and pikes until I reached the president. This man, who had no appearance of humanity but the conformation of his features, was seated beside a table, surrounded by funeral torches; his clothes were covered with blood, his wild and haggard eyes appeared greedy for the murder of the unfortunate beings of whom the influence of crime had rendered him the sovereign judge; hatred for every virtue appeared seated on his brow. This monster, placed upon a throne erected by infamy, said to me:—

"For what reason are you here?"

"It is not by a warrant that I am detained: I voluntarily became a prisoner in order to fulfil the duties of gratitude and humanity."

"Towards whom?"

"It was to bestow my attentions on a worthy old man, who is my uncle and my benefactor, the friend and the support of the unfortunate."

"All this does not tell his name."

"It is the Abbé de Chapt de Rastignac."

"You have committed a great piece of imprudence."

"No, Sir, I request to share his fate."

"You are free, and you may depart."

One of the judges, who had listened to me with great attention, said to me:—

"No, Madam, do not depart; the moment is not favourable. Go up again into your room, and, as soon as you can go without danger, I will send and inform you."

A man with a short jacket then said to me:—

"Do not attend to that: if you wish to go, I will push you through, and you will very soon be out."

When individuals were pushed out, it was to be slaughtered. I was ignorant, as it may well be imagined, of these dreadful formalities. Carried away by a desire of seeing my uncle again,

I believed this man to be my preserver. I accompanied him
to the fatal passage, where so many honest individuals had died
with glory. Suddenly I felt myself seized by the arm that was
disengaged, and heard a voice exclaim, "You shall not go out."
Strange effect of my blindness! I repulsed the humane man who
wished to save me, and seconded with all my strength the executioner who was dragging me to punishment. This struggle lasted
for ten minutes: at least, it appeared to me as long. We had
reached the door, and I was about to enter the fatal passage
which led to destruction; the man who still held me back cried
out to the other, "Let go, or I will shoot you." The assassin
did not require the order to be repeated. The person to whom
I owe the preservation of my days (if it can be considered an
advantage in the melancholy position in which I find myself) is
called M. Pochet. Let this man here receive the tribute which
is due to his humanity, and to the perseverance with which he
snatched me from the fate that threatened me

I ascended to my room, accompanied by my liberator, who
then described to me the danger which I had just avoided.
"Remain quiet," said he to me, "I will go and get one of my
comrades to accompany us, and will furnish myself with an order
of the president, and will save you. I will return for you at
nine o'clock." I waited for him with patience, being still supported by the hope of seeing my uncle again.

My preserver returned at the hour which he had mentioned
to me, accompanied by one of his comrades, a man as humane
as himself. These two worthy individuals gave me their arms.
The formidable door opened. I saw myself covered with swords,
without being able to make a motion,—I saw the blood flowing
under my footsteps. Alas! without doubt, my feet were covered
with thy blood . . . . . . I walked over arms . . . . hands . . . ·
over those which had been the support of the unfortunate, which
had so often succoured me! . . . Oh, God! oh, God! give me
strength to support the grief which lacerates my bosom! . . . .
My preservers demanded protection for me, which was granted
to them; I was not worthy to receive a death so glorious.

My conductors, thinking I was going to sink at the frightful
sight which I had just witnessed, made me enter into a coffee-
house. I entreated M. Pochet to continue his good work, and

to conduct me to the house of my uncle. This excellent man requested me, as the only reward which he wished for the service he had rendered me, to permit him to pass his house with me, in order that his wife might share the happiness which he experienced in having preserved me. Ah! let my relations and my friends assist me to repay the sacred debt which I have contracted towards this worthy man. I followed him to his house, and it was there that I learnt the dreadful misfortune which will be an eternal source of sorrow to me. M. Pochet and his wife lavished their attentions upon me; they offered me their house for an asylum, telling me that I should no longer find in mine what I sought there . . . . My unfortunate uncle had been massacred! The pen falls from my hand; I leave it to feeling souls to conceive all the horrors of my situation.

PAYSAC DE FAUSSE-LENDRY.

# RELATION

ADDRESSED

# BY THE ABBÉ SICARD

INSTRUCTOR OF THE DEAF AND DUMB

## TO ONE OF HIS FRIENDS

ON THE

DANGERS WHICH HE RAN ON THE SECOND AND
THIRD OF SEPTEMBER 1792

# RELATION OF THE ABBÉ SICARD

*etc., etc.*

THE unfortunate events of the 2nd and 3rd September, of which I was one of the appointed victims, occupy too important a place in my remembrance to deprive me of the power of always being able to give an exact recital of them. But you are not contented, my too sympathetic friend, with what I have related to you in the intimacy of full confidence, but would have a history of them in writing. I owe too much to your excellent heart, to refuse you anything. I will therefore pen this history, so disgraceful to our age, all the horrors of which it will be difficult for posterity to conceive.*

The oath of the civil constitution of the clergy, required from all the public functionaries who were ecclesiastics, had sown in the sanctuary the germs of a fatal division. The Constituent Assembly, in decreeing the obligation of this oath, left the functionaries free to take it or to refuse it. A refusal, in the terms of the law, amounted to a dismissal from employment. Some took it; but the greater number refused it, and were deprived of their functions. The law gave them free choice; but to the former they applied the title of *good citizens*, while the latter were called *the refractory*.

---

* It would have been superfluous to have prefaced this relation by any biographical details. The name of the Abbé Sicard is *known to France* and to all Europe. The loss which, by his decease, was experienced by the deaf and dumb, by literature, and by religion, is irreparable. The recollection of the services which he rendered to humanity, of the dangers which he incurred on the memorable days of September, can never be effaced. The recital which he himself penned of them was published, for the first time, in a periodical collection that appeared under the name of Religious Annals; it is from this collection that we have extracted the interesting relation about to be presented to the reader.—*Note of the Editors.*

61

In the month of August, 1792, the same assembly thought
proper to command a second oath, which was denominated the
oath of *liberty* and of *equality*. The first was not according to
my religious principles, and it was not required of me; but
when I learnt that another oath had been decreed, purely civil,
I thought it my duty to take it, and I accompanied the formality
with a civic gift of two hundred livres.

This was at the time when the municipality of Paris was
filling the prisons with the unfortunate victims whose massacres
had been determined upon. Several sections, by its orders,
arrested all the priests called *refractory*, and those who were
known to have any connection with them. Every bad passion was
then awakened, and no good man was sheltered from suspicion.

I had only one enemy, whose name and intrigues I shall
conceal, and who was indebted to me for more than one benefit.
He only waited for a favourable moment to effect my ruin. He
associated himself with some factious individuals, whose numerous
crimes were punished by the 9th Thermidor, and thereby obtained a warrant against me, and it was put in force on the 26th
of August, 1792.

It was at the moment that I was about to give a lesson to
the deaf and dumb, and was occupying the few leisure moments
previous, in writing to a friend, that I observed a carpenter of
the neighbourhood, of the name of *Mercier*, enter my study; he
was accompanied by a municipal officer, followed by about sixty
men, armed with muskets, swords, and pikes. Mercier told me
that he came, by orders of the commune, to put me under
arrest. I listened to him with great coolness, and asked him if
I might be allowed to finish the letter which I was then writing,
in order to send it to the post. Mercier replied that he should
seize my letters, and that I must even empty my pockets, in
order to give him all which they contained; and that he was
about to place seals upon all my effects. I asked him if I
should be permitted to take with me my breviary, and I furnished
myself at the same time with a volume in addition, entitled *The
Christian Religion contemplated in the True Spirit of its Maxims*.
Mercier tore this book out of my hands, and while he was
endeavouring to read the title of it, he said at each word:—
"This is counter-revolutionary; it will be necessary to mention

it in the *procès-verbal* that Sicard wished to take this book and to carry it away, instead of his breviary." The carpenter searched in all the cupboards, like a true man of the trade, and went so far as to take out the bottoms, suspecting that there might be some writing in them deserving of his censure.

At length, four hours having passed in the search for, and in the sealing up of my effects, I was led away with all this military parade to the committee of my section: it was that of the Arsenal. The committee was full. Several members, upon observing my arrival, could not help evincing secret satisfaction. I was ordered to take a seat on one side; they looked at each other, and the person who was to draw out the *procès-verbal* said to the president, in a low tone of voice, *What motive shall we assign for his arrest?—It is only necessary to state*, replied the president, *that there were meetings of priests at his house.* No one addressed a word to me. Mercier alone was called upon to know who should conduct me to the office of the mayor. He answered that he had some persons to dine with him, and that he could not return till very late. They laughed at his scruple, and invited him to return only at his convenience. *Sicard*, added they, *was made for waiting.*

They then retired, and left me under charge of some *sans-culottes.*

At five o'clock Mercier and his satellites came back to conduct me to the Committee of Execution. It was proposed to me to take a coach, in order to avoid the unpleasantness of being conducted by soldiers. I replied to Mercier, that if the shame belonged to me, I wished to suffer it wholly; but as it was justly theirs, I should not screen them from it. We walked therefore on foot towards the mayor's office, preceded and followed by bayonets.

One of the two officers, having some business in a house near the Place de Grève, left us there; the other followed him, and I found myself alone with my guards. One of these volunteers, astonished to see them thus lead to prison a man whose serene manner betokened nothing criminal, asked me my name. He had no sooner heard it, than he raised his eyes and hands towards heaven, and exclaimed, "What! is it you whom they lead to prison,—you, the friend of humanity, the father, as

well as the instructor, of the poor deaf and dumb! And of
what are you accused? What is your crime? Ah! permit me
to go and admire your labours when you shall be restored to
your family, whom your imprisonment will fill with grief." I
suppress the more flattering eulogies which this worthy volunteer
lavished upon me, calling me, in the heat of his enthusiastic
feelings, the worthy successor of the Abbé de l'Epée, the rival
of Locke, of Condillac, and honouring me with various other
illustrious titles, which were less flattering to my heart than the
interest which this unknown took in my fate, adding, at last:
"And it is you, rare and valuable man, whom they imprison!"
When my two satellites in command returned, they took me to
the mayor's office. I was introduced into a low hall, where the
Committee of Execution was held. There, around a large table,
several men, with their hair dressed in the jacobite fashion,
received the prisoners, who followed each other into this den,
in order to be registered and stripped of the keys of their sealed
secretaries. A motion was made to me to seat myself in a corner. Mercier said to one of them :—"This is the Abbé Sicard
whom we bring you; we should have many others to introduce,
if we had greater powers." "Greater powers," replied the man,
"you cannot want! To give you greater would be to limit those
you have already. Do you then forget that you are the sov-
ereigns, since the sovereignty of the people is confided to you,
which you exercise at this moment? Bring us, then, all those
whom you may be able to discover."

It was now six o'clock in the evening, and I had fasted during
the whole day, when a piquet of men received orders to lead
me to the hall for deposits. I passed into the hall of registry,
where my name caused the same surprise as it had done to
the soldiers of my escort. At length I ascended into the large
hall, which, at the time the hotel of the mayoralty was occupied by the first president of the Parliament, served as a gran-
ary. Before I entered, the small pieces of paper which were
employed as references to my breviary, were examined with
extraordinary attention. They were compared together, and
endeavours were made to discover some counter-revolutionary
words upon them. Finding nothing upon them, however, they
thrust me into this large room, filled with a crowd of men of

all classes, shut up there without knowing for what fault. I advanced a few paces into the midst of them, and immediately a respectable old man, the curé of St. Jean-en-Grève, rushed into my arms, and, forgetting his own arrest, seemed alone occupied with mine. Several prisoners surrounded me, and I received from them the same evidences of interest. I found amongst them many acquaintances, and some friends; and their society afforded me every consolation I could experience in this wretched situation. Night arrived, and I shared the straw bed of the worthy old man to whom I have just alluded. I had scarcely lain down, to endeavour to find some repose, when there were brought in, as prisoners, two friends, peculiarly dear to me, who were employed in the institution. One was a priest, named *Laurent*, my deputy instructor, the most gentle, virtuous, and constant of men; the other was a lay inspector, named *Labrouche*, whose friendship for me had rendered him *suspected*. "Here I am, my dear Sir, the associate of your persecution, as I was of your principles," said the Abbé Laurent to me; "how happy do I esteem myself, in having been considered worthy of persecution in such a noble cause!"

Yet the deaf and dumb, my pupils, from whom I had been torn away, could not console themselves for my removal. They came the next morning to my prison, to ask my permission to claim me at the bar of the Assembly. Massieu,* on beholding me closed up and guarded like a criminal, made, in the presence of the guards of the prison, signs of such affecting interest, that he touched all their feelings. He gave me a copy of the petition which he was going to address to the Assembly. The following is an abstract of it :

"Mr. President,—they have borne away from the deaf and dumb their instructor, their nurse, and their father. They have imprisoned him as a malefactor; yet he has neither murdered nor robbed; neither is he a bad citizen. All his life is passed in instructing us to love our God and our country He is virtuous, just, and pure. We demand from you his liberty: restore

---

* All those who have frequented my lectures are acquainted with the distinguished talents of this deaf and dumb youth, who is as interesting from the various conceptions of his mind, as from the affections of his heart.—*Note of the Author.*

him to us, his children, for we reverence him as sons, and he loves us as a father. It is he who has taught us what we know. But for him we should be as the beasts of the field. Since he has been torn from us, we are melancholy and unhappy. Restore him to us, and you will make us happy."

This letter carried to the bar by Massieu, was read by a secretary, and greeted with applause. A decree was passed, which ordered the Minister of the Interior to render an account, as soon as possible, to the Assembly, of the motives for the arrest of the teacher of the deaf and dumb.

A young man, called *Duhamel*, since appointed one of my assistants, went and joined the deaf and dumb at the bar, offered himself as hostage, and requested that he might be imprisoned in my place. This act of courage was greatly admired and applauded.

Yet the days rolled along, and this decree was not executed. The 2nd of September was now approaching. It was just forty-eight hours before the terrible destruction which took place in the prison of the mayoralty, that Manuel, then attorney of the commune, was announced. Upon his entrance, he was immediately surrounded by most of the prisoners, who hoped to learn from him something positive respecting their destiny. The following is the perfidious language which this wretch held to us:—
" I come, gentlemen, to bring you tidings of peace and consolation: in thirty-six hours you will receive from the municipality an account of their intended measures for the execution of the law of transportation, to which all those are condemned who have not taken the civic oath; twelve hours afterwards you will be free, and you will have fifteen days allowed you for your departure. But it will be necessary that each should prove himself a priest; for the advantage of leaving France at this moment is a favour which many would envy."

Some of the prisoners showing themselves sensible of the kindness which this speech apparently contained, were checked by the greater number, who dared not trust to the words of Manuel.

Our moments passed in peace and tranquillity. Our conversation, free from the least sentiment of illiberality or dislike to each other, having our own improvement for its sole object, turned upon morality and our relative duties, all joining in the anxious hope and expectation that our principles, as well as our intentions, would one day be better known, and that justice would then be rendered to us. Each afterwards formed schemes for the future. I resolved, if I were transported, to retire into a capital city, whither I was advised to go and found an establishment for the deaf and dumb. I wrote to this effect to one of my friends. It became a question whether this letter should pass, and it was stopped at the door. The officer on guard said to me, on perusing it, that this letter could not pass; that no Frenchman would be permitted to go and carry any discovery whatever to foreigners.

"Ah! if you did but know what this discovery is: it is the art of teaching the poor deaf and dumb."

"Oh, if that be all," he replied, "your letter may pass, and you will be able to depart."

The intelligence of Manuel was partially realised. We received the publication of the law of transportation, with the measures for its execution, decreed by the municipality. Twelve hours more passed away. Nothing more was now spoken of but preparations for departure, and the means of rendering exile more tolerable. Three commissaries presented themselves on the Saturday, the day before the second of September, to take the names of those who, it was said, were to be set at liberty. They were eagerly surrounded and pressed upon. Each was anxious to give his name, in order to have it inscribed upon the fatal list. One of my assistants, Laurent, was the first. I was talking with a new friend, whom I had made in the prison, when some one came to reproach me with my tardiness in getting my name inscribed. I advanced, and gave my name. It was written down; and it suddenly occurred to me to request them to add, that I was teacher of the deaf and dumb. I was told that I could not go out that day with the others, and my name was erased. The superintendent, Labrouche, wished to give his; but, on being asked if he was employed in my institution, and on replying in the affirmative, they refused to add him to the list.

What was I to think of this singular exception? I fancied that the motives for my arrest had not been communicated to the Assembly, and that I was detained till that should be effected. All my companions became my friends, and embraced me when they left me. All expressed their grief on leaving me behind. One of them, in particular, gave me the greatest marks of tenderness. Nothing draws people so much together as the idea of misfortune. "Our two souls," said he to me, "had become linked to each other; they had touched on every point. I will come and see you again," he added. "My heart remains with you—we can no longer live separately."

The whole prison became in a moment a real desert. I remained there alone with the inspector, Labrouche, and a former counsellor to the Parliament of Paris, named *Martin de Marivaux*. The spacious hall appeared to me as if covered with a funeral veil; and nothing could appear more sad than this frightful solitude.

But it was soon to be filled with fresh victims. In the night, between the first and second of September, twenty-four prisoners arrived, and took the place of my former companions, who, I imagined, had obtained their liberty, and retired home.

But what was my surprise when, the next day, those who had regularly visited their friends in prison again came to see them. "You will find them at their own residences," said I to all those who presented themselves; "persons came yesterday evening and set them at liberty."—"They are not at their own houses," replied they; "for we have come from thence.—Perhaps they have been transferred to another prison." They were, in fact, at the Abbaye: news to this effect was brought to me, and I was perfectly thunderstruck by it.

In the meanwhile, the Minister of the Interior had caused inquiry to be made of Pétion, then Mayor of Paris, of the causes of my arrest. He had replied, that it was a matter that did not concern him, and that it was necessary to apply to the *Committee of Execution*. The committee replied, in its turn, that the seals having been placed upon my papers, it could not render an account of these causes. It was known at the mayor's office, that the Legislative Assembly wished to preserve me, if my accusers could not prove anything against me; and it was clearly seen, that the motives for my arrest would not be found sufficient. The General Assembly of the Section of the Arsenal had issued a decree, the day before, inviting all the constituted authorities *to make me suffer the law in its full extent,* " as it had been proved that I was a favourer of tyranny; that I kept up a correspondence with the coalesced tyrants; and that it was necessary to hasten and deprive me of my functions, and replace me by the learned and modest Salvan." It was further said, that this order would be immediately carried to all the turnkeys of the prisons, to the commune, etc.

The reader may recollect that, at the time the agents came to remove the prisoners from the Mayoralty Prison to the Abbaye, I was excepted from the number of those transferred. It was evident that they then wished to save me; but the decree, determined on by three reptiles of the Section of the Arsenal, in the night which preceded the second of September, had changed all these good dispositions. My ruin had just been plotted a second time. Already were they preparing for the horrid massacre, and we were on the brink of the fatal hour. Dinner was brought to us at two o'clock; guns of alarm were heard firing; the prisoners were astonished at the uproar, and a sudden dread agitated the souls of all; everything inspired affright and horror. One of us, uneasy and terrified, clambered to the window of the prison, whence he distinguished several soldiers in the court before the prison. He asked them the cause of these guns of alarm. "It is," was the answer to him, "the taking of Verdun by the Prussians." This was a falsehood: Verdun was not taken till some days afterwards. Every one now knows that the cannon of alarm on that day of blood was to be the signal for the massacre. All the assassins had orders to commence the murders at the third shot.

At that instant, some soldiers of Avignon and Marseilles rushed in a crowd into our prison. They upset the tables, seized upon us, and dragged us out, without giving us time to take our luggage. Assembling us together in the court, they informed us that we were about to be taken to the Abbaye, whither our companions had been transferred the day before. They left it optional with us, whether we would go thither in coaches or on foot. *Martin de Marivaux* requested to go in a coach. I should have been undone, before I had arrived there, if I had preferred any other means. Six coaches were ordered:

we were twenty-four prisoners. Here every particular becomes
truly interesting, for it is to a union of a few of the minor events that
I am indebted for my preservation. I was about to suffer my
companions to occupy the first coach; and it was essential to my
safety to choose the first. *Martin de Marivaux* made me get in;
he took the second place, and another the third. We occupied the
back part: *Labrouche*, inspector of my institution, took the fourth;
and one other prisoner got up after him. Here we were then
five in the first coach. The rest of the prisoners filled the five
others. A signal for departure was given, with a recommendation
to the coachmen to drive very slowly, under pain of being massacred
upon their boxes, and with a thousand abusive epithets lavished
upon us. The soldiers who accompanied us informed us, that
we should not arrive at the Abbaye; that the people, to whom
they were going to deliver us, would at length do justice on
their enemies, and would massacre us on the way. These dreadful words were accompanied by every expression of rage, and
by blows of their sabres and their pikes, which these wretches
levelled at each of us. The coaches started; and immediately
the mob collected and followed us with insults. "Yes," said
the soldiers, "these are your enemies, the accomplices of them
who delivered up Verdun; those who only waited for your departure to slaughter your wives and your children. Here are our
swords and our pikes,—inflict death on these monsters."

Let the reader imagine how the cannon of alarm, the news
of the taking of Verdun, and these stimulating observations,
must have excited the naturally irascible character of a misled
populace, to whom we were announced as their most cruel
enemies. As we advanced towards the Abbaye, by the Pont
Neuf, the Rue Dauphine, and the Place de Bussy, the multitude
increased in the most alarming manner. We attempted to close
the windows of the coach several times; but the mob forced us
to leave them open, that they might be able with greater ease
to commit their horrid outrages. One of my companions received
a cut with a sabre on the shoulder; another was wounded in
the cheek; and a third over the nose. I occupied one of the
places at the back, and the blows which were aimed at me fell
upon my companions. Imagine, if you can, my wretched situation during this painful ride;—the blood of my companions

flowing before my eyes; unprotected in the midst of an enraged populace, actually excited to violence by those who were placed over us as our guard, expecting every moment to be massacred. Our guards could not have protected us, had they been inclined, nor could we ourselves have opposed it.

At length we arrived at the Abbaye: the butchers were waiting there. They had orders to begin with us. The court was filled by an immense crowd.—Our coaches were surrounded. One of our companions, who thought he might escape, opened the coach door, and leaped into the middle of the crowd. He was immediately butchered. Another made a like attempt: he pushed through the crowd, and was just escaping, but the assassins fell upon him, and blood again flowed; a third suffered in the same way. In the meanwhile, the coach advanced towards the hall of the Committee. A fourth attempted likewise to spring out, but he received a stroke with a sabre, while in the act, which did not prevent him from pushing forward, and seeking an asylum in the Committee.* The assassins fancied there was nothing more to do in this first coach: they had killed three prisoners, and had wounded the fourth and last, as they thought, not knowing that there was one more left; they therefore left it, and proceeded, with the like fury, upon the second coach.

Recovered from the stupor into which I had been thrown by the massacre of my companions, and no longer seeing near me the monsters who were glutting their fury and their cruelty upon other unfortunates, I seized the favourable moment, darted out of the coach, and rushed into the presence of the Committee. "*Oh! gentlemen*," I emphatically exclaimed, "*preserve an unfortunate man.*" The commissaries repulsed me. "*Go along,*" said they to me; "*do you wish us to get ourselves massacred?*" I should have been undone, if one of them had not recognised me. "*Ah!*" he cried out, "*it is the Abbé Sicard. How do you happen to be here, Sir? Enter; we will preserve you as long as we can.*" I entered into the hall of the Committee, where I

---

* The Committee here alluded to was neither the frightful tribunal which sat in the turnkey's rooms, nor the Committee of Execution, of which the abbé spoke three or four pages back, but a committee charged with the civil affairs of the section of the Quatre Nations, which at that time held its sittings in this formidable spot.—*Note of the Editors.*

should have been in safety with my remaining companion who had escaped, but a woman had seen me enter. She hurried to inform the assassins of the circumstance. They continued their bloody work for several minutes, and I thought myself forgotten; but suddenly some one knocked rudely at the door, and demanded the two prisoners. I deemed myself lost. I pulled out my watch, and presented it to one of the commissaries. "*You will deliver it,*" I said to him, "*to the first deaf and dumb youth who shall come and inquire for me.*" I was certain that this watch would reach its destination. I knew the attachment of Massieu; and that to give this recommendation was to name him.

The Commissary refused the watch. "*It is not time,*" said he, "*to take your resolution; the danger is not yet sufficiently pressing; I will inform you when it is.*"

In the meantime the blows were becoming louder at the door, and the assassins were about to burst it open. I presented my watch a second time, with the same entreaty. "*Now,*" said the same commissary, "*it is well; I will deliver it to him whom you mention.*"

The delivery of my watch was like my last will. There no longer remained any thing for me to leave to my friends. I fell on my knees, and offered the sacrifice of my life to God. I had scarcely finished my prayer, when I arose and embraced my companion, saying, "*Let us clasp each other; let us die together; the door is going to open; the executioners are there; we have not five minutes to live.*" At length the door opened. What horrible men rushed towards us! What brutality! Their fury deceived them for some moments. I was in the midst of the commissaries, clothed like them, perhaps less agitated, and with a more tranquil soul. At first they mistook; but a prisoner who had escaped, and whom the press of this dreadful horde had hurried into the hall, was recognised. We were at length discovered, and two men, with pikes, cried out, "Behold those two b—— whom we are seeking." Immediately one of them seized my fellow prisoner by the hair of the head; the other struck his pike into his bosom, and stretched him dead at my feet. His blood flowed in a stream through the hall, and mine was about to mingle with it. The pike was already raised; when a man, whose name will ever be dear to me, informed by his children that massacres were going on at the Abbaye, and that mention had been made of the Abbé Sicard, hurried thither, broke through the throng, and, throwing himself between the pike and me, displayed his breast, and exclaimed to the monster who was going to stab me, "Behold the bosom through which you must pass before you reach him; it is the Abbé Sicard, one of the most benevolent of men, the most useful to his country, the father of the deaf and dumb: you must pass through my body to reach him."

At these words, uttered with an accent of courage and of patriotism, the pike fell from the hands of the murderer. But that was only one danger avoided. Fury was yet upon every countenance; and my ruin would only have been retarded, had I not determined upon an act which might have accelerated it, if Providence had inspired me with less *sang-froid* and courage.

Almost all the assassins were in the interior court, upon which the windows of the committee looked. It was necessary to gain them, as they were the arbiters of life and death. I mounted up at a window, and there, demanding of the unruly troop a moment's silence, I thus harangued them:—"My friends, behold an innocent man; am I to die without being heard?" "You were," exclaimed they, "with the others whom we have just killed: therefore you are guilty, like them." "Listen to me for a moment," I replied, "and if, after having heard me, you decide upon my death, I will not complain: my life is yours. Learn first who I am, and what I do, and then you may pronounce my fate. I am the Abbé Sicard." (Here several spectators exclaimed, "It is the Abbé Sicard, father of the deaf and dumb: we must hear him!") I continued, "I am instructor of the deaf and dumb from their birth; and, as the number of these unfortunate beings is far greater amongst the poor than amongst the rich, I belong more properly to you than to the rich." I was interrupted by a voice, which exclaimed, "We must save the Abbé Sicard; he is a man too useful for us to suffer him to perish. His whole life is employed in doing good works; he has not time to be a conspirator." They all repeated these last words, and all added, at the same time, "He must be saved, he must be saved."

Immediately the assassins, who were waiting behind me for

the effect of my speech, took me up in their arms, and bore me into the midst of their troop of murderers, who all embraced me, and proposed to conduct me back in triumph to my own residence. You will ask how could I refuse this proposal which would have restored me at once to life and liberty? But a scrupulous respect for justice induced me to prefer a new imprisonment. I said to those around me, who wished to be my preservers, that a constituted authority had imprisoned me, and that I must remain until the decision of a constituted authority pronounced me innocent. They urged me, but I persisted, and I was taken back to the committee; I there again found that energetic patriot, that courageous watchmaker, who had protected me at his own peril. I asked him his name and address, and immediately, without informing him of it (his modesty would not have allowed it), I wrote to the president of the assembly the following letter:—

"Mr. President,

"The National Assembly will not, without grief, learn the massacre of several citizens, who, after being detained some days in the lock-up-house of the Mayoralty Office, were transferred to the prison of the Abbaye St. Germain-des-Près. I hasten to raise my feeble voice of gratitude in favour of the courageous citizen to whom I owe my life; his name is *Monnot*, a watchmaker, Rue des Petits-Augustins.

"Seventeen unfortunate beings had been butchered under my eyes. The public force had not been able to save them, and I was about to be massacred in the like manner, when the worthy Monnot threw himself between me and my assassins, and baring his bosom, exclaimed:—

"'*Behold, citizens, the bosom that you must strike before you reach that of this good citizen. You do not know him, my friends, and, when you hear his name, you will respect him, love him, and fall at his feet: he is the most benevolent, the most worthy of men; he is the successor of the Abbé l'Epée; he is the Abbé Sicard.*' The people were not at first satisfied, but thought that there was a design of preserving a traitor under my name. I firmly advanced, and, mounting the balcony of a window, spoke to the multitude, having no other defence than the courage of innocence, and my firm confidence in this misled people.

"I told my name and my functions. I dwelt upon the special protection of the National Assembly in favour of the Institution of the Deaf and Dumb, and of the head of that institution. Reiterated applauses succeeded shouts of fury. I was placed by the people themselves under the safeguard of the laws, and was received as the benefactor of mankind, by all the commissaries of the section of the Quatre Nations, which ought to feel proud in having such a man as Monnot among them.

"Permit me, Mr. President, to confide to the Assembly the testimony of my gratitude, in order to give to such a generous action the greatest possible publicity. A nation in which such citizens as he to whom I owe my life are not rare must be invincible. To recite such acts of heroism is to fulfil a duty. To attempt to express the admiration which they excite is out of my power, but I can never forget them; I am more gratified to live with such citizens, than to have escaped from death.

"I am, etc."

"*Abbaye St. Germain,*
     *2nd September,* 1792."

This letter was taken to the president of the Legislative Assembly by one of the keepers of the Abbaye. It was publicly read, and followed by a decree which declared that Monnot, for having saved the teacher of the deaf and dumb, had merited well of his country. Three copies of this decree were sent to me; one for my liberator, one for the committee of the section, and one for myself. *

---

* *Decree of the National Assembly of the 2nd September,* 1792, *the fourth year of Liberty:*—

A secretary has read a letter from M. Sicard, teacher of the deaf and dumb, confined at the Abbaye St. Germain-des-Prés; he has transmitted to the chamber a statement of the danger which has threatened his life, the heroic devotedness of M. Monnot, watchmaker, who exposed his life to save him, and the profound gratitude which he feels towards his generous liberator and preserver.

The National Assembly solemnly acknowledges that citizen Monnot has merited well of his country, and decrees that an extract of the *procès-verbal* shall be sent to him.

Collated with the original, by us, the President and Secretaries of the National Assembly; Paris, 2nd September, 1792, 4th year of Liberty.

HÉRAULT, President,<br>GOSSELIN, ROMME, Secretaries.<br>—Note of the Editors.

The committee was then assembled. The assassins were murdering, under the windows in the courts of the Abbaye, all the prisoners on their way from the great prison; and the members of the committee were calmly deliberating, without troubling themselves upon public affairs, and without paying any attention to the cries of the victims whose blood was streaming in the court. Individuals brought to the table of the committee the ornaments, the pocket-books, and the blood-stained pocket-handkerchiefs found in the pockets of these unfortunate beings. I was seated close to the same table; they saw me shudder at the sight. The president (citizen Jourdah) manifested the same sentiment. One of the commissaries, addressing his discourse to us:—" *The blood of enemies*," said he, " *is, in the eyes of patriots, the object which pleases them most.*" President Jourdan himself could not restrain an emotion of horror.\*

One of the executioners, with his sleeves tucked up, armed with a sword reeking with blood, entered into the place where the committee was deliberating: "I come to ask you, in behalf of our brave brethren in arms who are slaughtering these aristocrats," he exclaimed, "for the shoes which the latter have upon their feet. Our brave brethren are barefooted, and they set out to-morrow for the frontiers." Those who were in deliberation looked at each other, and they all replied at once, "Nothing is more just; granted."

To this request another succeeded:—"Our brave brethren have been long labouring in the court," exclaimed another assassin, who entered the committee-room quite out of breath; "they are fatigued, their lips are dry; I come to ask you for some wine for them." The committee decided that there should be delivered to them an order for twenty-four pots of wine.

Some minutes afterwards, the same man came to renew the same demand. He obtained again another order. Immediately there entered a wine-dealer, who came to complain that they gave the *custom* to strange dealers when there was *a good feast.* He was appeased by being allowed to send also some of his wine to the brave brethren who were *working* in the court.

\* Vide, at the end of the Memoir of the Abbé Sicard, the unedited relation which has been left by the same president to whom he alludes.—*Note of the Editors.*

The door-keeper announced a commissary of the commune, who was making a course through the different sections, by order of the commune. He entered, and addressed these words to the committee:—"The commune desires me to say to you, that if you have need of *assistance*, it will send you some." "No," replied the commissaries to him, "all is passing well here." "I come," rejoined he, "from the Carmes, and from the other prisons; *all is passing equally well there.*"

This observation will explain to those who may yet be ignorant of it, what part the *commune of Paris* took in the events of that dreadful day.

The night being already far advanced, I requested from the committee permission to retire. They did not very well know whither to send me. The gaoler of the Abbaye offered to conduct me to his house, where I might find an asylum. I preferred being put in a small prison, named the *Violon* (violin), which was close to the hall of the committee. This, also, was a signal mark of divine protection; for if I had retired to the house of the keeper, I should have perished, as was the case with two other unfortunate beings who went thither upon my refusal, and were there massacred.

What a night was that which I passed in this prison! The assassinations committed under my very windows,—the cries of the victims,—the blows of the sabres aimed at their innocent heads,—the howlings of the murderers,—the applause of the witnesses of these scenes of horror,—all thrilled to my very heart. I even distinguished the cries of many of my companions who had arrived the day before from the prison of the mayoralty. I heard the questions proposed to them and their answers. They were asked if they had taken the civic oath. None of them had taken it; all might have escaped death by a falsehood; all said in dying:—"We are obedient to your laws, we all die faithful to your constitution; we only except in it what relates to religion, and concerns our consciences."

They were immediately pierced with a thousand wounds, in the midst of the most horrible vociferations. The spectators applauded, and cried out,—*Vive la Nation!* and these cannibals indulged in the most horrible dances around each corpse.

About three o'clock in the morning, when there was no

longer any one to destroy, the murderers recollected that there
were some prisoners in the *Violon;* they came and knocked at
the small door which looked into the court. Every knock was
a signal of death to us. We thought ourselves lost. I knocked
gently at the door which communicated with the hall of the committee, and in knocking I trembled lest I should be heard by
the assassins, who were threatening to break open the other
door. The committee brutally answered us, that they had no
key. It was therefore necessary to await our destiny patiently.

We were three in this prison. My two companions fancied
they perceived, over our heads, a floor which offered us means
of safety. But this floor was very lofty. One alone could reach
it by mounting upon the shoulders of the other two. One of
them addressed these words to me;—" One alone of us can be
preserved above there; you are more useful upon earth than
we, and it must therefore be you. We will form a ladder for
you with our two bodies." They stood up one upon the other.—
" No," said I, to these generous victims, " I will not profit by
an advantage which you will not share. If you cannot preserve
yourselves by the way you offer to me, I can die with you.
We must be saved together, or we will all die together." This
struggle of generosity and self-devotion lasted for some minutes;
they reminded me of the deaf and dumb, whom my death
would render orphans; they even exaggerated the little good
which I could yet do, and forced me to profit by the innocent
stratagem which their generous friendship had contrived. It was
necessary to yield to their earnest solicitations, and to consent to
owe to them my life, without being able to contribute to save theirs.
I threw myself on the necks of these two preservers, and never was
there a more affecting scene. They were going invariably to die;
they forced me to survive them. I mounted then upon the shoulders
of the first, then upon those of the second, and at length upon the
floor, addressing to my two companions the expression of thanks
of a soul oppressed with grief, with affection, and with gratitude.

But Heaven did not will that I should preserve my life at
the price of that of my two preservers; I should have been too
unfortunate. Just at the moment when the door was about to
yield to the efforts of the assassins, just when I was going to
see my friends perish in my presence, we heard in the court

the accustomed cries of *Vive la Nation!* and the song of the *Carmagnole*. It was occasioned by their having torn from their beds two priests, whom they were dragging into the court, already strewed with dead bodies. The murderers all rallied at this signal for slaughter and carnage; they all wished to have a share in the massacre of the victims. Our prison was then forgotten.

I descended from the height of my floor, to mingle anew my fears and my hopes with those of my generous companions. Oh, how long was that frightful night, which saw so much innocent blood flow!

The furious troop of the murderers questioned the two victims who had just been led to the scene of carnage. They replied with the same gentleness, the same calmness, and the same courage, as we have already remarked in others. "Behold," said they to each, "this mountain of the dead bodies of those who would not submit to our laws; take the oath, or thou shalt instantly go and increase the number." "Give us time to prepare ourselves for death; permit us to confess ourselves to each other: this is the only favour which we demand of you. We are as obedient as you to all your civil laws: we should be bad Christians if we were not good citizens; but the oath which you require of us is not merely a civil oath,—it is a renunciation of essential articles of our religious faith. We prefer death to the crime which we should commit by taking it."

"Well, let the rascals confess themselves," replied the assassins, with one voice; "for we have no others of them to-day to amuse the neighbours with. Let them confess themselves; they will give time to the curious part of the neighbourhood to get up, and see us do justice on these *rogues*. In the meantime we will clean the court. Go and fetch some carters; let us send these aristocrats to the dogs; they would infect this court."

The order was immediately given: carters arrived; their conveyances were loaded with the dead bodies, and they were carried beyond the Porte St. Jacques, a long way into the country, to the foot of the first iron cross, where a large grave was dug to bury them all.

But the court of the Abbaye streamed with blood, and was like the reeking ground on which several cattle have just been butchered.

It was necessary to wash it: the labour was extreme. In order that they might not have the trouble a second time, some one proposed to have some straw fetched, and to make with it a sort of bed, upon which should be put the clothes of all the unfortunate victims who should be taken to that place to be slaughtered. The advice was approved of. Another complained that the aristocrats died too quickly; and that the first only had the pleasure of striking them. It was therefore determined that, for the future, they should only be struck with the back of the sword, and that they should afterwards be made to run between two rows of assassins, as was formerly practised towards the soldiers who were condemned to run the gauntlet. It was likewise decided, that there should be erected around the place benches for the *ladies*, and benches for the *gentlemen* (for there were then ladies and gentlemen). A sentinel was placed at this post, in order that all might take place in a regular manner. I saw with my own eyes, and heard all that I have just been stating. I saw the ladies in the neighbourhood of the Abbaye assemble around the bed which was prepared for the victims, to take their places there, as they would have done at a theatre or any public entertainment.

At last, about ten o'clock, the two priests said they were ready to die, and they were led forth. I saw nothing further after that moment. Ah! how could I have had the courage to turn my eyes upon a scene so heartrending? All that day passed in going into the city to seek for the priests, whom wretches came to denounce, and in murdering them. Around these victims there were still the same shouts, the same songs, the same dancing. The night was not more tranquil. I passed it in the same fears which had agitated me during the preceding days. "How is it," said I to my companions, "that the city of Paris, which must be aware of these horrors, does not rise in a mass, and come to prevent them?" The unfortunate beings only replied to me during that day by words without coherency, and with wild and wandering manners and looks. They had lost their reason. One of them gave me his knife, and requested me, as the greatest favour, to kill him; the other entered into a room adjoining that where we were, undressed himself, and, with his pocket-handkerchief and his garters, he endeavoured to hang himself. His madness preserved him, for he could not succeed in his object.

While all this was passing, the door of our prison was opened with a loud noise, and a new victim was pushed in. Good God! it was one of my companions of the prison of the mayoralty, whom I thought dead, the Abbé S**. He had been removed on the first of September, with sixty others; and, by an inconceivable miracle, after being dragged with those unhappy beings into the middle of the court, to be massacred with them, he had found himself, without knowing how, in the ranks of the murderers, around the murdered; and, taking advantage of the disorder which pervaded the execrable scene, he had slipped away into the committee, where he had implored his life with that earnestness of despair which will touch even the hardest hearts. The only reply he received was shutting him up with us. What an interview! and what a moment for both! I had learnt, by means of the gaoler, the massacre of all the prisoners with whom I knew he was. I had heard the sixty, of which he was one, struck, as I believed, by the fatal blow. Each of us had wept for the death of the other. In beholding him, I fancied I saw again all my other friends. It was he who informed me of the heroic and glorious death of the worthy Curé of St. Jean-en-Grève; of that venerable old man, who replied with so much courage to the executioners who interrogated him upon his faith, and who preferred death to the oath which was proposed to him; who demanded, as the sole favour he should solicit, in consideration of the weakness of his age, the speediest kind of death, which he obtained. They were preparing to cut off his head, when he addressed these affecting words to his executioners:—"For what are you going to punish me, my children? What have I done to you?—what have I done to the country of which you consider yourselves the avengers? The oath which I have not been able to take would not have been against my conscience, and I would even take it at this moment if, as you believe, it was purely civil: I am as obedient as you to the laws of which you consider yourselves the ministers. Let me be allowed to except from this oath which you propose to me all which relates to religion, and I will do it most heartily, and no man shall be more faithful to it."

The most ferocious of the horrid crew seized the old man by the hair of the head, threw him down upon the threshold, and struck him on the head with his sabre; another smote off his head. Thus commenced the destruction of that multitude of victims, to whom Manuel, ten days before, had come to announce liberty. Such was the recital which was made to me by my old companion, who had escaped, as if by miracle, from this sanguinary tragedy.

The court of the Abbaye was again covered with dead bodies. Orders were given to remove them elsewhere. While this removal was going on, another priest was led forth and massacred, to the reiterated cries of *Vive la Nation!* This was on Tuesday morning. My enemies of the section of the Arsenal had sent their famous decree to the commune; and the latter had doubtlessly given orders that I should be destroyed. They were already preparing in the court for the execution of this order, but they were fatigued, and wished to dine. It was decided that they should come at four o'clock to cut off my head. My companions, of whom more than one had been given me in the course of the morning, heard this conversation, and repeated it to me. They heard the question asked of the carter, why he did not remove a body which he had at first placed upon his cart. "You are to give me that of the Abbé Sicard to carry at four o'clock; I will take them all at once."

When I was told of this conversation, I saw myself at last undone. I procured a sheet of paper, and I wrote to a deputy, my intimate friend, the following letter. The original has been returned to me.

I have marked the passages which were scratched out and suppressed, when it was read to the Legislative Assembly.

" *Tuesday, 4th Sept.* 1792; 4*th of Liberty.*

"Ah, my dear Sir, what will become of me, after having escaped from death, if you do not come and save my life, by removing me from prison, *around which furious cannibals commit a thousand massacres every moment.* I have been a prisoner seven days, and for three days I have continually heard my head demanded, with loud cries, under my window, and indignant threats to break open the feeble shutters which separate me rom them, if the commissaries of the Abbaye do not give me up to their fury. They no longer know how to preserve me; and all advise me to seek a refuge in the bosom of the National Assembly, but not to go thither except in the company of two deputies; otherwise I shall be butchered on my departure hence.

"Good God! what have I done to be treated thus? *At the very moment while I write, they are cutting off the head of a priest; and they are leading out two others, who are going to endure the same fate. What have we done, that we should perish thus cruelly? for, too surely, I shall no longer be spared.* In what am I a bad citizen? Am I even a useless citizen? It is for all France to answer. My pupils are, perhaps, dying of grief at this very hour. I sink myself under the weight of so many anxieties. What is my crime? I have not been questioned during the seven days that I have been here. I shall not exist to-morrow, if you do not come to my assistance. I do not ask for liberty; I ask life for my poor children. Let the National Assembly constitute me a prisoner in one of its halls. Let it urge a report upon my affair. Have I time to be a bad citizen?

" *What cruelty to remove me in broad day, at three o'clock, on a holiday, at the instant when the cannon of alarm fired, in the company of soldiers of Avignon and Marseilles, who denounced me to the populace, when they ought to have defended me from their rage, across the Pont Neuf, and through all the streets which lead to the Abbaye!*

"Come, my dear Sir, come and do a good action; come and preserve an unfortunate man; protect him with the inviolability of yourself and of another of your colleagues, who will perhaps with pleasure share the troubles with you. But how do I know whether you will be here in time? *My executioners are here, reeking with blood; they gnash their teeth, and demand my head.*

"Adieu, my dear countryman: I know not whether you will find me alive at the Abbaye.

"The unfortunate teacher

"Of the deaf and dumb,

"SICARD."

The parts of this letter particularly marked were not read to the Assembly; the letter even was not read by him to whom I had addressed it. He entreated one of his colleagues to communicate it, as having more favour and consideration than himself. It interested both the deputies and the Commune; and they immediately passed a decree, which ordered the Commune to set me at liberty. This decree was not attended to. In the meantime the hours rapidly glided on, and I saw that fast arriving which had been fixed for my death. Three o'clock struck, and I was to perish at four. I was ignorant whether my letter had reached its destination; but recollecting then that I had other friends in the Assembly, I procured half a sheet of paper, which I tore into three pieces, on which I wrote three notes, and addressed one of them to the President (Hérault de Sechelles); another to M. Lafont Ladebat, who had displayed so much talent, honesty, and courage, during the sitting of the Legislative Assembly, and whose colleague and particular friend I had been at the academies of Bordeaux;* another to the mother of two young persons, whose early studies I had directed, and who regarded me, the mother as her most tender brother, and the children as their father. These three notes were the last adieux of an unfortunate man, who saw himself on the point of being dragged to death,—the last cry of a dying man, who called to his assistance the sympathetic souls by whom he knew he was tenderly loved.

The Assembly was no longer sitting; but an obliging and compassionate doorkeeper was still in the hall. My note was delivered to him. He ran immediately to the house of the President, who forthwith repaired to the Committee of Public Instruction. M. Lafont Ladebat could do nothing. He thought of Chabot, and went to his house; described to him the dreadful situation in which I was; told him how short a time there was to save me; and demanded, what he had never demanded of this monster for himself, the life of his friend Sicard. The female to whom I had also written, and whose name cannot but adorn this melancholy history, Madame d'Entremeuse, was absent: the eldest of her two daughters received my note, and fainted on perusing it; but the danger to which the Abbé Sicard, her father, her friend, was exposed, restored her to her senses. She flew to the house of M. Pastoret,* deputy, to whom

* He was banished after the eighteenth Fructidor, but returned to France, and was head clerk in the ministry of the interior.—*Note of the Editors.*

I was known. Upon arriving, she had not courage to speak, but fell down in a swoon, with my note in her hand. It was read. M. Pastoret quitted his dinner, and went to the Committee of Instruction, of which he was a member. He prepared, in conjunction with Hérault de Sechelles and Romme, who had been called thither, a decree, which a second time ordered the Commune to hasten to my assistance. By this decree, the committee claimed me as one of its most interesting adherents. I ought not to forget the effect which the note I had written to her mother produced on the heart of young Eleonore d'Entremeuse. It had given her a death-blow. Alas! after having languished more than a year, in inexpressible sufferings, she perished, at the age of nineteen, leaving me eternal regrets. The remembrance of so many virtues, united with all the charms of youth, will follow me to the tomb; and will shed over the sad life which I owe to that pure, noble, affectionate, and tender soul, a bitterness that would render it insupportable to me, had I not a thorough conviction that this young and lovely creature has only quitted this deplorable life to receive, in a better, the reward of her virtues. †

The order of the Committee of Public Instruction was sent to the Commune, who, upon receipt of the former decree, which I before mentioned, had passed to the order of the day. They were now going to do the same, and the second decree would have had no more success than the first, if there had not been in the council a man of Bordeaux, named Guirant, who requested to be charged with the execution of both. It would even have been too late (for then it was six o'clock in the evening), if at four o'clock, the period fixed by the assassins for my execution, a storm of rain had not dispersed the group, and preserved me from their fury.

At seven o'clock I saw the doors of my prison open again; it was another preserver, who, by virtue of the decree of the

* Afterwards created the Marquis de Pastoret, a peer of France.—*Note of the Editors.*

† Since this relation was penned, we have learnt that the young person did not die. Her restoration, and the preservation of her health, were the result of a long voyage, which her mother made her take. She afterwards resided in the Isle of France.—*Note of the Editors.*

Legislative Assembly, and of the order of the Committee of
Public Instruction, came to restore me to liberty, and present
me to the National Assembly. He took me by the arm, and,
under his safeguard, I passed through the midst of those who,
during the three preceding days, had massacred so many victims
in that court which was formerly consecrated to meditation and
to silence. Upon my appearing, all the clubs, the reeking
sabres, the pikes, and other fatal weapons, were immediately
elevated in the air; and had not the municipal scarf rendered
them motionless, I should have experienced a thousand deaths
in passing through this crowd of ferocious cannibals. At this
moment *Chabot* was in the tribune of the Abbaye, endeavouring
to interest in my favour those who had demanded my head.
I got into a coach with the municipal officer, and with *Monnot*,
—that Monnot whose name, rendered sacred by gratitude, will
doubtlessly pass to posterity with those of the martyrs of those
days of execrable memory,—I arrived at the National Assembly.
All hearts waited for me, and universal applauses announced
my arrival. All the deputies hurried to the bar where I was,
in order to embrace me. Tears flowed from all eyes, when,
inspired solely by the most imperious sentiment, I returned
thanks to my preservers, in the following speech, which being
the sudden expression of my gratitude, I could not preserve,
but was reported in the *Moniteur* of the time, and in all the other
newspapers.

SICARD.

*Extract from the Moniteur of the 4th September,* 1792,
*six o'clock in the evening. No.* 250.

Some municipal officers presented themselves at the bar, and
one of them addressed the assembly thus:—

Legislators, the prisons are empty; innocence has escaped the
sword of the vengeance of the people; guiltless citizens were in
a state of arrest, their heads were threatened, and they appealed
to us. We flew to their assistance; we dispersed the bayonets,
and a tri-coloured ribbon was sufficient to stay an armed populace.—*(Cheers.)* The life of Abbé Sicard, teacher of the deaf
and dumb, was threatened; he was at the committee of the
Quatre Nations; we claimed him, he was delivered to us, and

we brought him to the bar of the National Assembly. Behold him. I have yet to add, that his colleague, who had been arrested with him, is likewise liberated. The brave citizens of the section Quatre Nations have accompanied them hither, assuring us that they would defend them against all violence.

*Abbé Sicard.*—Legislators, I come to express before you the lively gratitude with which I am penetrated for the interest which you have taken in my imprisonment, in inviting the Commune to provide for my safety. I return thanks to M. Monnot, who saved my life, and to the commissaries of the Commune, who have evinced so much care and activity in preserving from the fury of a misled populace, myself and my colleague, whom you see before you; but,—I mourn while I say it,—you do not here behold a man, the memory of whom will always be dear to me, and whose loss I deeply deplore: it is *M. Laurent,* who was thrown with me into prison; he was massacred by my side. . . . Legislators, suffer me to weep for him. None can repair the loss which I have experienced in the death of my friend. The only consolation which you can still give me,—the only one which I claim from you, is to restore me to my family, to my children. Never did a word hostile to the cause of liberty escape my pen; and yet seals, insulting to a patriotic soul, have been placed upon my papers. No, he who has sworn, with fulness of heart, submission to all your laws,—he who has sworn to die for them,—ought not to be treated like an enemy of liberty. Fathers of your country, teach Europe that you, the fathers of our country, know so well how to repair the evils of the old regime, that the very men who are the victims of it are forced to cherish and to defend it.—(*Cheers.*)

*The President (Hérault).*—Those who have so well merited of the country, by preserving a man so valuable to society, have their recompense in their own hearts. The Assembly will take your request into consideration; in the meantime, it invites you to take your seat in the midst of the legislators who have had the glory and the happiness to restore you to your fellow citizens.—(*Cheers.*)

*M. Chabot.*—I come from the section of the Quatre Nations. It is the section in which the vengeance of the people has been exercised with the utmost fury these several days, and is the most populous section of Paris. In arriving amongst the citizens of that section, I read to them the decree which you had passed, and added that it was time to put an end to their vengeance. Immediately all the citizens swore that not the least violence should be again committed; they have taken a resolution to acknowledge no other authority but that of the National Assembly, and have decided that all others should act under its order; they have taken the oath before me to maintain liberty and equality, and to die, if necessary, for the National Assembly. I demanded the liberation of the Abbé Sicard, and the Abbé Sicard was free before I finished speaking. I claim, in the name of the section of the Quatre Nations, that the Abbé Sicard be restored to his pupils.

This proposition was decreed.

*To the Citizen* SICARD,* *Teacher of the Deaf and Dumb.*

Citizen,

The recital of the dangers which you incurred on the 2nd and 3rd September is so interesting to history, that it is important nothing should be wanting to its authenticity. I entreat you, then, to add to it the order of the section of the Arsenal which you merely allude to; and, if I am not deceived, there are also several other anecdotes which I have heard you relate *vivâ voce*, which would not be indifferent for the history of those unfortunate days, and of which you ought not to deprive the readers of the *Religious Annals*. It is through the medium of this journal, that I venture to address my request to you. I am, fraternally, etc.

*Reply of the Citizen* SICARD *to the request which was addressed to him in the preceding No.*

I am asked for a faithful copy of the resolution of the pretended section, styled the section of the Arsenal of Paris, mentioned in the Relation of the Events of the 2nd, 3rd, and 4th of September, 1792.

* The foregoing relation having appeared in the *Religious Annals*, Abbé Sicard received, some days afterwards, the following letter, which made him decide on adding some explanations and details to the recital which he had written.—*Note of the Editors.*

I must intimate, in the first place, how this copy came into my hands, and all that I have learnt since, relative to this deed of darkness.

After my escape from the prison of the Abbaye, and my restoration to liberty, my first care was, to go to the Commune of Paris, to procure the removal of the seals which, on the day of my arrest, had been placed in my apartments. It will be difficult for any one to conceive how eager I was to be restored to my pupils, and to go and resume labours so dear to my heart. Commissaries were granted to me, and two others of the section were appointed for the same office. One of the latter was the very person who had taken to the Commune and to the Abbaye the famous resolution. This man had been present several times at my lessons; he had manifested the utmost interest and esteem for me; and it is almost impossible to conceive how, with any honesty, this man would have accepted such an infamous mission, if one did not know that weakness sometimes does as much evil as wickedness, from its want of courage to resist. This man, in beholding me again, threw himself on my neck, and confessed to me his fault: "I have been," he said, "the accomplice of your assassins. It has not been by my consent if the man I esteemed the most has not been included in the general massacre which has caused so much bloodshed. I myself carried to the prison where you were waiting for your doom, the *resolution* which was intended to provoke the assassins to butcher you; and yet I had been a hundred times the witness of the miracles, of the beneficence, you daily wrought in your school. But I saw I was undone if I had refused to serve the hatred of the perse-cutors of the priests; and I had not courage to resist. To-morrow I will deliver to you one of the copies of the resolution."

He proceeded to remove the seals. I felt the happiness of being restored to my pupils. "Have a care," said this com-missary, who knew the revengeful spirit of my persecutors of that period, "have a care, and do not follow the inclinations of your heart; do not yet lodge at your own residence; they cannot pardon you for having escaped from the steel of the assassins. They would come even into your retreat, and would punish you for it by murdering you."

I followed this advice, and retired into a distant section, to
the house of citizen Lacombe, a celebrated watchmaker; but
more celebrated, however, by his courage and his virtues. He
had been seen, during my imprisonment, when there was so
much danger in claiming the release of a priest, going, at the
peril of his life, to demand the liberation of the teacher of the
deaf and dumb. It will be a matter of some surprise, without
doubt, that it should have been a watchmaker who saved my
life, and also a watchmaker who offered me an asylum, in
which I found, with the most virtuous couple, all the consolation
of which my dejected mind had so much need. It was there
that I received the first visit from that valued pupil, whom I
had named my legatee, at the time when, on the eve of receiving the fatal blow, I delivered my watch for him into the
hands of the commissary. What an affecting interview! Massieu
in the arms of his instructor, his father, and his friend! . . . . .
Massieu! That ardent soul united with mine; our hearts beating
against each other! This unhappy young man had passed
without food and without sleep all the days in which his master
had been surrounded by dangers. Another day, and he would
have died of grief and hunger. What a moment was that in
which he beheld me again, after having wept so much and so
bitterly over my fate. . . . What touching signs he made me!
. . . . What a scene for those who were witnesses of it! . . . .
Who would not have been affected by it. . . .

The commissary of the Arsenal kept his word. He brought
me a collated copy of the resolutions, which is subjoined:—

" *General Assembly of the 1st September, 1792.*

" Upon the representations made by several members:—

" 1st. That the Abbé Sicard, teacher of the deaf and dumb,
arrested as a *non-juring priest*, was upon the point of being
liberated, on account of the utility which, *it is pretended*, he is
of in his institution.

" 2nd. That his liberation would be so much the more dangerous, as he possesses the guilty art of concealing his disaffection
to the nation under the appearance of patriotism, and of
serving the cause of the tyrants, by silently persecuting those
of his fellow citizens who shew themselves favourable to the
revolution.

" The Assembly has resolved to make the following demands :

" 1st. That the law be executed, *in all its extent*, towards the Abbé Sicard.

" 2nd. That he be superseded by the learned and modest Abbé *Salvan*, second teacher of the deaf and dumb (inheritor, like many others, of the sublime method invented by the immortal Abbé de l'Epée), who has taken the oath, and is approved of by the National Assembly.

" Finally, that copies of the *present resolution* be carried to the executive power, to the Committee of Inspection, to the *Council of the Commune*, and to the *register office of the prison*, by M. Pelez and M. Perrot, commissaries named to that effect.

(Signed) " BOULA, *President,*
" RIVIERE, *Secretary.*"

I could not mistake the author of this paper, in which so much precaution had been taken, in order that I might not be able to escape death. A paper had been clandestinely communicated to me a month before, in which, amongst other expressions, were the following:—" M. Sicard ought not to be so very difficult in granting what is required of him, He ought not to forget that, not having taken the *civic oath,* he might *be replaced by the learned and modest Salvan, inheritor, as well as himself, of the sublime method invented by the immortal Abbé de l'Epée, and who has taken the oath.*"

I shewed this document to my worthy coadjutor Salvan, whose honesty was so well known to me. Indignant to see his name in this base warning, he went to complain of it to him whom we suspected of having written it. The accused stoutly denied that he knew anything about it; but since that period, there has been found a minute of it written entirely with his own hand, in the papers of the revolutionary committee of the section, without finding it written upon any of the registers. The reason of it is, that at that time, when the general sitting of the sections was terminated, a handful of scoundrels made resolutions in the name of the whole Assembly, and had them executed, without their being known to any but those who had formed them, and by those who were the unfortunate victims of them. The one in question would never have been known, but for the extreme good-nature of the man who had carried it to the prison, and the injudicious conduct of the author, who forgot to take away the guilty minute of it.

I forgot, in my relations of the 2nd, 3rd, and 4th of September, some facts which deserve to be known. An individual, to whom I have related them, has more than once requested me to publish them, and they are here subjoined:

I have said, that the *ladies* of the neighbourhood of the Abbaye repaired in crowds to the scenes of horror which took place in that wretched inclosure. It may be imagined what kind of *ladies* these were. Well, these same *ladies* sent a request to the Committee where I was, that they might be allowed the pleasure of seeing, perfectly at their ease and comfort, the *aristocrats* massacred in the court of the Committee; and in order to gratify this request, a small lamp was placed near the head of each body, and immediately the *ladies* had the enjoyment of this execrable illumination.

In the middle of the night the murders took place: Billaud de Varennes learnt that the assassins robbed the prisoners, after having killed them: he repaired to the court of the Abbaye, and there, upon a raised place, he spoke thus *to his labourers:*

"My friends! my good friends! the Commune sends me to you, to represent to you that you *dishonour this noble day.* It has been stated that you rob these *rascally aristocrats,* after having done yourselves justice upon them. Leave, leave all the ornaments, all the money, and all the effects they have upon them, to contribute towards the expenses of the great act of justice which you exercise. Care shall be taken to pay you, as has been agreed upon with you. Be noble, great, and generous, as the profession which you fill. Let all in this great day *be worthy of the people,* whose *sovereignty* is committed to you."

Manuel also, a few minutes before, in the middle of the Rue St. Marguerite, in front of the large prison, and just at the moment when the assassins had commenced, had thus spoken to the same people:

"French people, in the midst of the legitimate revenge which you are going to exercise, do not let your axe strike all heads indiscriminately. All the criminals which those dungeons inclose are not equally guilty." And this Manuel is the same whom a worthy man endeavoured to justify lately on the subject of these slaughters! This speech, heard by several persons worthy of credit, being compared with that which, two days before, I had heard myself in the prison at the mayoralty, can there remain any doubt of the duplicity of that great criminal, who has expiated upon a scaffold both the crimes of that day of horror and all the blasphemies which he had vomited forth in the commune against religion? Doubt not that this promise, which Billaud de Varennes gave to the murderers, was made and fulfilled. Yes, the unfortunate wretches who shed so much blood, in those days of desolation and of mourning, received their salary, as it was promised to them. Lists have been found, both of the names of those who received the price of innocent blood, and the names of those who paid them. We yet read these names, written with blood, upon the registers of the section of the Jardin des Plantes, on those of the Commune, and on those of the section of L'Unité. I have less reason to doubt of it than many others, as one of the commissaries of this section, who was forced, under pain of being killed upon the spot by the assassins, to contribute to their payments, told it himself to me. Yes, they received their wages; and, good God! what wages were they? The unhappy beings, pursued by remorse, meeting everywhere the accusing voices of their countrymen, have fled Paris. Some have joined the armies, hoping to find *comrades* there. Miserable wretches! they deceived themselves in their idea of French soldiers. They have been recognised, and have only met with avengers. A few only now remain, whom the scaffold is waiting for. They are pursued at length by national justice, whose sword has only been suspended thus long that retribution might the more effectually overtake the guilty.

SICARD.

# DECLARATION

OF

## CITIZEN ANTOINE-GABRIEL-AIMÉ JOURDAN

LATE PRESIDENT OF THE DISTRICT OF THE PETITS AUGUSTINS,
AND OF THE SECTION OF THE QUATRE NATIONS

IST FLORÉAL, YEAR III

# DECLARATION

## CITIZEN ANTOINE GABRIEL AIMÉ JOURDAN

THE Section of L'Unité, late of the Quatre Nations, having desired me to communicate to it what I know respecting the memorable days of the 2nd, 3rd, etc. of September, 1792, I am anxious to fulfil its wishes; but I must premise that I shall speak only of the facts of which I was an ocular witness.

At that fatal period, I was President of the Civil and Inspecting Committee of the Quatre Nations. The invasion of the Prussians, who were advancing upon Châlons, had created great alarm through Paris. A hundred thousand inhabitants of this vast city were preparing to march against the enemy, and to expel them from the territory. On Sunday, the 2nd of September, the Committee of the Section of the Quatre Nations was engaged in a permanent sitting. About one o'clock in the afternoon, in order that the public business might suffer no delay, I proposed to my colleagues to arrange, that one half of us should take our dinner while the other half remained and prosecuted the business of the committee. I myself went at three o'clock.

On my return, I learnt that, during my absence, assassins had massacred several individuals, who had been brought from the prisons of the mayoralty in hackney coaches.

I will not give details of these earlier horrors, for I did not behold them; but there yet remain in the section the greater part of my former colleagues, who were witnesses of what passed: amongst others, citizen Monnot, the preserver of the Abbé Sicard, teacher of the deaf and dumb; citizen Maillot, painter, Rue St. Benoist, who preserved a native of Metz, named Dubalay, who knew me, and who made an appeal to me. The citizen Maillot had recourse to a stratagem, as ingenious as it was generous, and succeeded, during the space of fourteen hours, in hiding this person from the assassins, although he was under their eyes; and he finished by withdrawing him from their fury in their presence.\*

About seven o'clock in the evening all was tolerably quiet. I took advantage of this period to attend to some very urgent personal affairs, and returned about nine o'clock. On entering into the court of the church of the Abbaye, I saw a multitude of men and women collected together, and heard reiterated shouts of *Vive la Nation!* in the midst of which arose the most frightful howlings. This tumult was occasioned by prisoners who were being dragged from the Abbaye into the large court of the garden, and who, either there or on the way, were inhumanly struck down by sabres.

The door of the committee was in the great court of the garden. I advanced to it, and was suffered freely to pass under the cart gateway, which separated the two courts. On entering into this court, I perceived a troop of armed individuals, unknown to me, who were pitilessly murdering all the unfortunate victims who were led towards them. The court was strewed with about a hundred dead bodies. But what was

---

\* We must not forget to mention an instance of courage and presence of mind which has few equals. While the massacres were going on at the Abbaye, a watchmaker demanded powers from his section to go and claim two young people. He repaired into the den of the assassins, waded through blood, and trampled over throbbing limbs. "Art thou tired of life?" said one of the executioners to him, taking him by the collar. The desire of doing a good action gave nerve to this estimable man. "I require to speak to the president." He was suffered to enter. "What art thou coming to do here?"—"I come to claim two young people of my section: here is my authority?"—Who are they?"—"So and so; are they living?"—"Yes; why are they here?"—"For a trifling quarrel, which had no serious result."—"Wilt thou answer for them?"—"I answer for them with my head."—"Well, here is paper, sign; but take care of thyself." The registers were examined; and very fortunately the bill of commitment did not state the cause of aristocracy, or the bail would have perished. The prisoners arrived. "Here," said the president to him, "behold them.—Go."—(Extract from the *Spy of the French Revolution.*)

This honourable action consoles one a little for other sanguinary deeds, and reconciles us, for a moment, with humanity.—*Note of the Editors.*

still more horrible, was to behold inanimate bodies, which had
been placed around tables covered with bottles of wine, and the
glasses dripping with the blood with which the hands of the
cannibals drinking out of them were still reeking.

To reach the committee it was necessary to ascend five
steps: they were also covered with dead bodies, over which I
was obliged to stride. I found in the committee-room several
of my colleagues stupefied with horror and alarm, and assisted
them to do the little good the fury of the people would permit
us. We found means to preserve several unfortunate beings.

About midnight, the painful and horrible sensations which I
every moment experienced, joined to the vapour from the human
blood that flowed so near us, affected my head so much, that
I was taken extremely ill. I sought in vain for a jug of water,
and, being unable to obtain it, I thought to go to my own
house, which was close at hand, at the corner of the Rue
Taranne, and I went out for that purpose.

Upon coming up to the cart gateway. I was challenged by
about a dozen National Guards, who were stationed there, but
whom I had not observed upon entering. They levelled their
pieces at me, as I approached. I was more surprised than terrified; the prospect of death occasioned no fear, so familiarized
had I become with the grim monster. I moved towards the
National Guards, and coolly raised up their muskets, and lifted
them over my head. In the commander I recognised one
Leprince, formerly a hair-dresser, and who, I believe, was an
officer of the police. I asked him if he did not know me:
"Yes," said he to me, "I know that you are our president;
but our orders are to let every one enter, but to suffer no one
to depart."

"Who gave you such orders?"

"The battalion commandant."

"I am much astonished that he has given you such orders,
without speaking of it to the committee. Where is he? Seek
for him."

"We have not seen him since he placed us here, about five
or six hours ago. We are completely worn out with horror and
fatigue."

I entered again into the large court, to seek for the battalion

commandant, but could not find him. I then returned to the
citizen Leprince. "I have not seen," I said to him, "the commandant; he is probably at the general assembly (it was held
in the great church): let me pass : if I find him, I will make
him relieve your post."

A passage was made for me, and I went into the church ; I
twice went around the assembly, but did not see the battalion
commandant. My indisposition increased, and I decided upon
going home. On leaving the church, I was stopped in the
court by a crowd of spectators, who were gazing on a victim
whom the assassins were leading to death, dragging him by the
feet, and hacking him at the same time with their swords.

I then beheld two Englishmen, one on each side of the
double ranks, opposite to each other. They held bottles and
glasses in their hands. They offered the assassins wine, and
pressed them by lifting the glasses to their mouths. I heard
one of these murderers, whom they wished to constrain to drink,
say to them, "D——n! let us alone; you have made us drink
enough,—we do not wish for any more." I remarked, by the
light of some torches which surrounded the victims, that these
two Englishmen were in long coats, which hung down to their
heels. He by the side of whom I stood appeared to me to be
a man of about thirty-eight, about five feet four or five inches
in height, of a ruddy complexion; his coat was of bright green,
inclining to olive. The other one was thinner; his coat appeared
to me to be of a deep slate colour. I knew that they were
English, because I heard them speak to one another, and,
although I do not know their language, I am sufficiently familiarized with the sound of it, to know it from any other, and to
judge of the accent. I went to my own house, where I took
some cordial waters, and passed the rest of the night in a dreadful situation, which continued for nearly six weeks, and at last
ended in a spitting of blood and apoplexy, the consequences of
which I shall feel for the remainder of my life. I made an
effort to return to the committee the next day. In the course
of the morning, seven or eight of the assassins came to demand
their wages from me. "What wages?" said I to them. The
tone of indignation in which I asked this question disconcerted
them. "We have passed," said they, "one day in stripping the

dead; you are just, Mr. President, you will give us what you please." Citizen L—, one of my colleagues, was by my side. I proposed to him to give a crown (three francs) to these mons- ters, that we might get rid of them. "It is not enough," replied citizen L— to me; "they would not be satisfied."

At the same moment, citizen Billaud de Varennes, then munici- pal officer, came in; he made a long speech, to prove the utility and necessity of all that was passing, and concluded by telling us, that in coming to the committee he had met several of the labourers (this was his expression), who had toiled all the day, and who had requested their wages from him; and that he had promised them we would give them a louis each. I then started up with warmth, and said to him: "Where do you suppose that we shall get these sums? You know as well as we that the sections have not any funds at their disposal?" He was thunderstruck for a moment, but afterwards observed to me, that it was necessary to apply to the minister of the interior, who had funds set apart for this purpose.

Citizen L— observed to me, that he was to dine with the minister of the interior that day, and offered to speak to him on the subject. I accepted his proposal, and gave him imme- diately, in writing, an authority to demand of the minister a sum of 3,000 francs, the disposal of which the section of the Quatre Nations would be accountable for.

Citizen L— reported to me, that the minister had replied to him, that he had no funds destined for such purposes, and that the section must apply to the municipality.

When the *soi-disant* labourers returned, I communicated to them the reply of the minister; they went the next morning to the municipality, and only succeeded in procuring a hearing be- tween eight and nine o'clock in the evening. It was observed to them (according to their own statement) that it was very astonishing that the section of the Quatre Nations should refuse to pay them, as they had especial funds for the purpose.

These people returned to the committee; I had just dissolved the sitting, and we were going out. They were furious, and I saw that we were on the point of being massacred. Happily, citizen C—, one of our colleagues, saved our lives, by giving them at once some assignats, which he had upon him, and by inviting them to follow him to his house, where he would give them the residue of what they demanded.

Most probably these labourers informed those who had worked in the other prisons, that a louis *per diem* was given by the Committee of the Quatre Nations. The next day, a considerable number came to demand their wages. Fearing that some sinister occurrence might take place, I determined immediately to proceed to the Commune, and have an explanation with the municipal officers. I could not succeed in getting into the large hall, it was so full of people. I then thought it advisable to address myself to citizen Tallien, who was then secretary of the municipality. I explained to him the motive that led me thither. He answered, that the affair did not concern him, but the *Committee of Execution*. I confess that I could not refrain from shuddering at this word *execution*. Citizen Tallien perceived it: "It is not what you probably conceive it to be," said he to me: "It is a committee established to pay the expenses ordered by the municipality." He offered me one of his clerks to conduct me thither.

On reaching this committee, which was composed of four or five members, I inquired what plan we were to pursue; and stated that we were besieged by a multitude of these labourers, who openly threatened us; that, in fact, we should be forced to abandon the committee of the section. The president asked me if there had not been assignats and money found upon those who had been killed. "How!" I exclaimed, "are the unfortunate victims to pay their executioners? But even if we should wish to dispose of these sums, we cannot, as they have been put in a bag, on which we have placed the seal of the section, and a dozen of the people have also put their seals upon it." The president replied, that these people were very honest; and added that, the day or the day but one before, one of them had presented himself to their committee, in his jacket and clogs, all covered with blood; and presented to them, in his hat, twenty-five louis d'or, which, he said, he had found upon a person whom he had killed; and that the Committee of Execution had been so struck with this act of probity, that it had given the man ten crowns, to buy him a coat and a pair of shoes.

One of the commissaries, who was sitting on the left of the president, said to me: "Is it true that there have been some persons preserved at the Quatre Nations?"

"Yes, there have been several preserved."

"How many?"

"Not as many as I should have wished."

"What is that you say? Do you know that, if those scoundrels had had the upper hand, they would have murdered us all?"

"I know not what they would have wished to do; but all I know is, that when my enemy is down, I give him a helping hand to raise him up again, and I do not assassinate him."

"Oh, ho, Sir! learn, with your fine sentiments, that these people knew the number of their victims, and that, if any of them are missing, the head of the president of the Quatre Nations answers for it."

"I understand. Well! I have sworn to die at my post, if it be necessary; my post is the arm-chair of the section of the Quatre Nations; and I shall always be found there; but if they come to assassinate me, do not think that I will suffer myself to be butchered like a sheep, as all these unfortunates were; be assured that it shall not be with impunity."

In uttering these words I placed my hands upon some pistols which I had in my pockets. The president endeavoured to pacify me, by telling me that we might send all the labourers there, and that the Committee of Execution would see and satisfy them.

I here finish my declaration; the rest relates only to the accounts which were rendered at that time; these and the vouchers the section possesses.

I will now make a few observations which naturally arise upon the perusal of my declaration.

It cannot be denied that the day of the 2nd September is much more disgraceful to France than that of St. Bartholomew, as the latter was the work of the court only of that period, whereas the former appears to be wholly the work of the people. The honour of the French people requires that this foul stain should be washed away; and I think that my declaration discloses the means of doing it, and points out the thread of that infernal plot. There is every reason to believe, that the English government was the mover and instigator of all the horrors which have covered France with mourning.*

Let us call to mind that, at the commencement, the English people were enthusiastically in favour of our revolution. The cabinet of London feared that the English might imitate our example: and it was therefore its policy to make war with us, and to draw us into war with all the world; but the greatest difficulty was to get the consent of the English people to raise the necessary supplies. Let us likewise recollect, that it was at the very moment when the news of the events of the 2nd of September reached London, that the English demanded war against us. There is, therefore, every reason to think that the cabinet of London had promoted the massacres of that day; this suspicion becomes a certainty, if we turn our attention to the two Englishmen of whom I have spoken in my declaration; I am certainly not the only one who saw them; it would be easy to question all the male and female inhabitants who dwell around the Abbaye, and who were in the court of the church on the 2nd of September, about eleven o'clock of the evening, or near midnight. The lemonade-manufacturer, and the wine-dealer, who lived in Rue Saint Benoît, opposite the door of the Abbaye, might likewise be questioned. I presume that they were the individuals who furnished the Englishmen with the wine and liquors which they gave the assassins. Perhaps it may be said that the crime of two isolated individuals does not prove that the English government was their accomplice. This would show little knowledge of the cabinet of London and its execrable policy.† Let us not forget that it was precisely at that period,

* What a striking instance is this of national vanity! It is hardly necessary to refute the calumny for the English reader.—*Note of the Translator.*

† We will not find fault with these words, *execrable policy;* it was the language of the period. We will only remark, that they would not be too strong, if the allegation which the passage contains could be proved. But it would require a more imposing authority, a combination of more numerous testimonies, a burden of irresistible proofs, in order to give weight to this accusation, which, if it were true, would, in fact, deliver up those whom it aims at, to the *execration* of mankind. History must, so far, suspend its judgment. The revolution which plucked Charles I. from his throne, was not marked by less fury than that of which the ill-fated Louis XVI. was the victim. Seas of

that it succeeded in stimulating the people, by inspiring them with horror at our proceedings. But there is yet another fact with which all Paris is acquainted, and which perfectly coincides with that of which I have spoken. After the execution of Louis XVI., an Englishman gave a white pocket-handkerchief to the executioner, to steep it in the blood of the King. A few days afterwards, this pocket-handkerchief was hoisted on the Tower of London. Immediately the English people became like elephants, rendered furious when the colour of red is shown to them,* and loudly demanded the annihilation of France. If these two facts be compared, they will form a sort of connection which may tend to discover the truth. It would be easy to ascertain who the Englishman was who gave his pocket-handkerchief to the executioner; perhaps he may be one of those who excited the massacres on the night of the 2nd September.

Why did the executioner take this pocket-handkerchief? Why did he steep it, and why did he return it to the man? It is for the constituted authorities to pursue and discover the conspiracy. I am convinced that they are as jealous as I am of the honour of the country, and that they will unfold to the eye of the whole universe, as well as to posterity, the source whence all these frightful crimes have sprung; they will purify the French nation from a stain which, without that, would be indelible.

Signed, JOURDAN.

blood have flowed in both nations; but their long enmity has not given them a right to accuse each other mutually of the excesses and horrors that sully their history; and, notwithstanding the revenge which England, in 1792, had it in her power to take for the American insurrection, nothing demonstrates that she exercised against France such cruel reprisals.—*Note of the Editors.*

* As we are ignorant whether this fact is correct in itself or not, we will not examine into the inferences that might be drawn from it.—*Note of the Editors.*

# THE

# INCARCERATION

## AND THE DREADFUL

# TERRORS OF BEAUMARCHAIS

## EXTRACT OF A LETTER

### FROM

## BEAUMARCHAIS TO HIS DAUGHTER

# A

## LETTER FROM BEAUMARCHAIS

## TO HIS DAUGHTER.*

. . . . . . On Wednesday, the 8th of August, 1792, in the morning, I received a letter from a gentleman, who gave his name without any mystery, informing me that he was anxious to acquaint me of an urgent and important affair which nearly concerned me, and requested an interview. We met as he desired, at an appointed rendezvous; and he then apprised me, that a band of thirty robbers had formed a project to come and pillage my house, on the night between Thursday and Friday; that six men, in the uniform of National or Federal Guards, were to call and demand, in the name of the municipality, an entrance into my doors, under pretence of searching for concealed arms: the whole were to follow, armed with pikes, and wearing red bonnets, as assistant citizens; and they were to close the gates after them, and take out the keys, in order to prevent, as they would pretend, the crowd from getting admission. They designed to shut up my servants in one of the subterranean apartments, threatening to murder the first who should utter a syllable. They were then to ask me, with their bayonets directed to my breast, where I had placed the eight hundred thousand francs, which they believed, said my informant, I had received from the National Treasury. "In fine," added the worthy individual, "they have let me into the plot, swearing

* The witty author of the *Barbier de Seville*, and of the *Marriage of Figaro*, has *himself related* his incarceration, in the interesting memoir which is hereafter given. We have deemed it desirable to preface this relation with a letter, which Beaumarchais wrote to his daughter a few days before his imprisonment. This letter touches upon facts which relate to the history of the times.—*Note of the Editors.*

to assassinate him who shall betray them. Here is my name, my profession, my abode; take your own precautions, but do not expose my life as a recompense for the momentous intelligence which my esteem for you has constrained me to give you."

After I had cordially thanked him, I wrote to M. Pétion, as first magistrate of the city, to demand a safeguard. I delivered my letter to his porter, and had received no answer from him, when the disturbances commenced, which greatly increased my alarm.

Saturday the 11th, about eight o'clock in the morning, a man came to inform me, that the women of the Quai de St. Paul were about to conduct the people to my house, stimulated by the false information that there were arms in my vaults .... On receiving this intimation, I opened every thing in my residence, secretaries, cupboards, chambers, and closets; in a word, every place where anything could be hidden, and resolved to yield both my person and my house to the severe scrutiny of all the people whose visit had been announced to me: but when the multitude arrived, the noise and cries were so loud and boisterous, that my anxious friends would not allow me to go down, but all advised me to save, at least, my person.

While the people were struggling to open the iron gates, my friends forced me to escape by the upper end of the garden; but a man had been placed there as a sentinel, who cried out, " Here, he is making his escape." I deliberately walked on, and he ran by the boulevard to give information to the people, who were collected at my gates. I redoubled my steps; but the women, who are ever far more cruel than the men in these dreadful atrocities, when once they yield to their passions, pursued me.

Certain it is, my Eugenia, that thy unhappy father would have been torn to pieces, had he not the advantage; for no search having yet been made, nothing could have removed from their minds the idea that I was escaping, conscious of guilt. This was the result of my weakness in following advice dictated by fear, instead of coolly remaining, as I had intended to do ....

I had entered the house of a friend, whose door was immediately closed again, in a street which, forming an angle with that in which the cruel wretches were running, made them lose all traces of me, and from which I heard their cries.....

While I was enclosed in this impenetrable asylum, thirty thousand persons* entered my house, where, from the attics to the cellars, locksmiths and masons were at work, forcing the cupboards, examining the vaults, and sounding all around them, raising the pavement, even at the bottom of the *commodités*, and making holes in the walls, while others dug all over the garden, all passing backwards and forwards through the apartments; but some amongst them declaring, to the great regret of the thieves, who were there in hundreds, "If nothing be found here which has relation to the object of our researches, the first who shall touch the smallest article of furniture, or remove even a straw, shall be hanged without mercy, and then cut to pieces by us . . . ."

At length, after seven hours' most rigid examination, the crowd dispersed and went away, by the order of some chief, who directed their movements. My servants swept out heaps of dirt from the house, but nothing of any kind was missing. A woman plucked a wall-flower in the garden, for which she received twenty blows as a punishment; and she even narrowly escaped a ducking in the basin surrounded by poplars.

I returned quietly home. It appears that the attention of those who searched was carried so far, that they had a *procès-verbal* (a written statement), bearing at least a hundred signatures, which attested that they had found nothing suspicious in my possession.

I now come to the dreadful night which I have already mentioned, the fearful particulars of which I shall give you.

As we walked in the garden towards dusk, in the evening of the day which had already been so terrifying, one of my friends observed to me, "I really think, Sir, that, after what has happened, there can be no danger in your passing the night here." To which I replied, "Doubtless not; neither can there be any if I go and pass it elsewhere: it is not the people that I fear, for they have had their suspicions removed; but the intimation which I have received of an association of robbers to pillage

---

* The number certainly appears an extraordinary exaggeration; but it is possible that as many might enter in succession, within the seven hours' search. —*Translator's Note.*

me, one of these nights, makes me apprehend that, in the crowds
which gained admission into my house, they may have studied
the means of entering it by night; for, it seems, dreadful menaces
were heard amongst those who entered. Perhaps, indeed, there
may be some who are already concealed here. In fact, I have
a great inclination to go and pass a comfortable night with our
good friend in the Rue des Trois Pavillons. It is certainly
the most quiet street; go, Francis, go and prepare everything
for me."

I supped with my daughter; but, fortunately for me, did not
eat much. I then left the house in darkness, in the direction
of the Rue des Trois Pavillons, carefully observing, from time
to time, whether any one was following me.

My servant Francis having returned to my own residence, the
door of the street being well barred and closed, and a domestic
belonging to my friend remaining in the house with me, I
yielded myself to sleep with confidence. At midnight, the valet
entered my room in his shirt, full of alarm. "Get up, Sir," he
cried out to me, "get up; all the people are come to seek for
you; they are beating at the door to break it open; some one
at your own residence has betrayed you; the house is going to
be plundered." In fact, they were striking at the door in a
tremendous manner. Only half awake, the terror of the man
restored me, however, to my presence of mind. "One moment
only, my friend," I said to him; "fear acts upon the judgment,"
I put on my great-coat (forgetting a waist-coat) and my slippers,
and then inquired from the servant "if there was any outlet
by which I could leave the house." "None, Sir; but hasten,
for they are about to break open the door. Heavens! what
will my master say?" "He will say nothing, friend, for I am
going to give up my person, in order that they may respect
the house. Go and open the door; I will descend with thee."

We were both agitated. While he was going down, I opened
a window which looked into the Rue du Parc Royal. Upon
the balcony there was a lighted vase, by means of which
I saw, through the blinds, that the street was full of people.
The foolish desire which I had felt to leap through the window,
was at once extinguished by what I then beheld. I descended,
trembling, to the kitchen, at the bottom of the court; and,

looking through the window, I at length saw the door open.
Men with blue coats, bearing pikes, and others with only their
waistcoats on, entered, while the loud cries of women were
heard in the street. The servant came back towards me to
seek for several candles, and said to me, in a stifled voice,
"Alas, Sir, sure enough it is you they want to find." "Well,
they will find me here."

In the kitchen there was a sort of office, with a large cupboard
for the porcelain, the doors of which were open. As the only
asylum, and as my last refuge, thy poor father, my child, placed
himself standing behind one of the folding doors, supported
upon his cane, the doors projecting in a singular way, which
it is impossible to describe. The search then commenced.

Through the grated windows which looked into the court, I
saw the candles move about, rise, descend, and pass through
the different suits of apartments, and I heard footsteps immediately
over my head. The court was guarded, and the street-door
open. Stretched out on tiptoe, and suppressing my breath, I
endeavoured to bring my mind into a state of perfect resignation,
and at length succeeded in recovering my coolness. I had two
pistols in my pocket, and debated mentally for some time
whether I ought, or ought not, to use them. The result of
my reflections was that, if I made use of them, I should immediately
be cut to pieces, and should expedite my own death, by depriving
myself of the last chance of calling out for assistance, and
perhaps obtaining it, by mentioning my name, on my way to
the *Hôtel de Ville*. I was wholly unable to divine the cause of
these excesses, after the visit to my house. I determined to
suffer all, and was calculating possibilities, when, the light making
a turn below, I heard some one draw the door close, and I
judged that it was the worthy domestic, who, perhaps, in passing,
had imagined that he could thus remove for a moment the
danger which threatened me. The most perfect silence prevailed.
I perceived, through the staircase windows of the first storey,
that they were opening all the cupboards; I then fancied that
I had discovered the meaning of the enigma. The robbers,
I mentally exclaimed, have been at my house, and have forced
the servants, under pain of assassination, to confess where I am;
terror has made them speak. The depredators have arrived

here, and, finding the house as valuable for plunder as mine, they reserve me for the last, convinced that I cannot escape.

My wretched thoughts then reverted to thy mother, thyself, and my poor sisters. With a deep sigh I said to myself: My child is in safety; my age is far advanced; my life is of little moment, and this event will only accelerate the course of nature by a few years; but my daughter, her mother, they are all in safety. Tears trickled down my cheeks; but, consoled by these reflections, I began to meditate on the close of my life, which I imagined was just at hand. Then, feeling my mind relieved, after so many mental struggles, I endeavoured to become indifferent, and to think of nothing. I gazed, as it were mechanically, on the lights passing to and fro: the moment approaches, thought I; but yet I contemplated it like one exhausted, and whose ideas began to ramble without a fixed object; for I had remained four hours standing in this sad condition, which was at a subsequent period changed into one still more wretched. Finding myself weak, at length I sat down upon a bench, and there awaited my fate, without further alarming myself. In this reverie of melancholy fancies, I heard a loud noise, which approached the place where I was; I arose in haste, and, by a sort of mechanical impulse, I placed myself again behind the folding-door of the cupboard; a cold sweat stood upon my forehead, and produced a complete exhaustion.

I saw the servant coming towards me, in his shirt, with a candle in his hand: "Come, Sir, you are asked for."

"How! you wish then to give me up? I will go without you. Who asks for me?"

"M. Gudin, your cashier."

"What is that you say of my cashier?"

"He is here with these gentlemen."

I then imagined it was all a dream, or that my tottering reason was deceiving me in the objects presented to it. My hair streamed with perspiration, which trickled down my face. "Go up," said the servant to me, "go up; it is not you they seek: M. Gudin will explain all."

Being totally unable to attach any connected meaning to what had struck my bewildered ear, I followed the man, who lighted me up to the first story. There I found M. Gudin, in his uni-

form of the National Guard, armed with his musket, accompanied by other individuals. Astonished at the sight, "By what
chance," said I to him, "are you here?"—"By a chance as
strange as that which conducted you hither on the same day
that an order was given to visit this house, in which information
was given that there were arms concealed." No longer finding
it necessary to exert my strength, I felt it gradually diminish,
and at length it entirely forsook me; I sat down upon the bed
on which I had slumbered before the noise commenced, and he
imparted to me what follows:—

"About eleven o'clock in the evening, feeling some anxiety
to know if our neighbourhood was guarded by the patrol, I
took my military coat, my sword, and my musket, and went
down into the streets, notwithstanding the advice of my son.
I met one of the patrol, who, recognising me, asked me if I
would go with them, observing, that I should be better with
them than being all alone. I accepted the offer so much the
more readily, as the gentleman whom you see there in the
uniform of the National Guard is the dealer in lemonade who
lives opposite your windows; in a word, it is M. Gibé."

On my honour, my dear child, I felt it necessary to rub my
forehead, in order to procure the assurance that I was not
dreaming. "But how is it," said I to M. Gudin, "if it really
is you who are speaking to me, that you have left me four hours,
almost in the agonies of death, without having come to console
me!" "I shall astonish you much more," replied Gudin, "by
my recital, than I have done by my presence. I saw them
quicken their paces, and thereupon observed to these gentlemen: 'It is not thus that one patrols.' 'For which reason we
are not patrolling, but are going to make a capture,' was the
rejoinder. I saw them arrive at the Rue du Parc Royal,
and my heart began to palpitate when I felt that we were so
near you. In turning into the Rue des Trois Pavillons,
upon arriving at this habitation, the word was given: 'Halt here,
and surround the house.' I mentally exclaimed, 'Great God!
by what strange fatality do I find myself with those who have
come to arrest M. de Beaumarchais?' I likewise fancied I must
be in a dream. I contained my feelings, however, as well as I
was able, in order that I might see how matters would terminate.

The servant opened the door, and almost dropped down upon finding me amongst these gentlemen. He fancied that the treason, which he suspected in your servants, had extended to me, and stammered from his agitation. With a loud voice, the order which had been given by the section, to come and search here, on suspicion that there were arms concealed, was then read." "Well, then," said I to him, "why did you not hasten and take pity on me in my distressed situation?" "My terror was even augmented," replied Gudin. "After I heard the order read, my tongue was less inclined to perform its office, and I was still more alarmed, not knowing, Sir, whether there were or were not arms; but presuming, with extreme apprehension, that if, unfortunately, any were found, you would become a victim, in consequence of having enclosed yourself here, I beheld, in idea, the frightful relation there was between this night and the visit which had just been made to your residence. During the course of the search, I found at last an opportunity of whispering to the servant—'Is your master's friend in the house?' 'He is,' was his answer. A few moments afterwards, I inquired from him where you were. 'I really do not know,' was his reply. He could not remove to any distance, as he was lighting those who were engaged in the search, and they did not lose sight of him; I stole away, without a light, to the chamber where your bed was. I sought you, groping about, both upon it and underneath, and calling upon you in a low voice. But you were elsewhere, and I did not know where to find you. At length, the search being finished, and feeling assured that calumny had once more missed her mark, I communicated to these gentlemen by what chance you had been concealed in the apartment of the master; and their astonishment has at least equalled our alarms. God be thanked, the evil is past; go to bed again, Sir, and endeavour to sleep, for you must have need of it."

Then, all the patrol having entered into the chamber, I said to the commissary of the section, or district: "You here behold me, Sir, under the safeguard of friendship; I cannot better pay for the asylum which it has given me, than by requesting you, in the name of my friend, who is an excellent citizen, to render your examination as severe as the people made it yesterday at my house, and to draw out a *procès-verbal*, in order that his safety may not again be compromised by infamous calumnies." "Sir," said the commissary to me, "our *procès-verbal* is closed, and your friend is in safety."

These gentlemen went out, and told the people in the street, that the house was pure. The women, however, enraged that nothing had been found, pretended that the search had been badly managed, and declared that they would go and find the hiding-place in a few minutes. They wished that the house should be entered again, but the commissary opposed it, and had the door abruptly closed. Thus my anxieties finished for the time; but the perspiration which flowed from my pores, exhaustion, and weakness, completely overpowered me.

I learnt, the following morning, that some old men, much attached to this quarter, which had never before been disturbed, on hearing the dreadful uproar, were seized with affright, and leaped over the walls; and that, passing from one garden to another, they went and roused some ladies in the Rue de la Perle, entreating them, having nothing on but their shirts, to shelter them from death; one of the individuals had broken his leg.

Alarm had spread around throughout the neighbourhood, and thy father, who had the greatest reason for apprehension, was, perhaps, the only one who finished this disturbed night in his bed.

# THE INCARCERATION AND THE DREADFUL TERRORS

OF

# BEAUMARCHAIS

I HAD drawn up a long memoir for the National Assembly, from whom I demanded an inquiry relative to a purchase which I had made of 60,000 muskets, then deposited in Holland; and was just getting it transcribed, when some officers came, on the 23rd of August, 1792, at five o'clock in the morning, in a most outrageous manner, to arrest me, and to place the seals of the government on the different repositories of my house. I was dragged to the office of the mayor, where I remained standing, in a dark passage, from seven o'clock in the morning until four in the afternoon, without any one speaking to me, except those who had arrested me. At eight o'clock they came and said to me, "You must remain here; we are now going, as we have a receipt for having delivered you."

Very well, thought I within myself; here I am like a beast in the market-place: the drivers have got their acquittance, and depart; and, as for me, well bound, I wait for the butcher who may purchase me.

After remaining nine hours upon my legs, in anxious expectation, some one came to fetch me, and conducted me to a bureau, called the Bureau of *Surveillance*, of which M. Panis was president—that person began to question me. Surprised that no written notes were taken, I made a remark upon the subject; he told me that this was only a summary examination, and that more form would be employed after the seals were removed from my house. What I ascertained for a certainty was, that clamours had been raised against me in the Palais Royal, on the treachery with which I refused to bring into France 60,000 muskets, which they had, it was alleged, paid me for in advance, and that I had public accusers. "Name them, I entreat you, Sir; or else I will point them out myself."—"Well," said he, "a M. Colmar, member of the municipality; a Monsieur Larcher; and several others." "Larcher," I exclaimed, "ah! do not proceed further. Only send for a portfolio which I have put aside, under a private seal, and you will there discover the black ingratitude of this Larcher, and of one Constantini, with several others, as you have intimated, whom it would be too tedious to name," "Your seals will be removed, and we shall see," said M. Panis; "in the meanwhile, go and sleep at the Abbaye." I went thither, and was lodged in the same room as the unfortunate beings. . . . . who were soon afterwards butchered.

The next day, 24th, in the afternoon, two municipal officers came to fetch me from the Abbaye, that I might be present at the removal of the seals, and the taking of the inventory of my papers. The operation lasted all the night, until nine o'clock the following morning; I was then conducted to the mayor's office, where the same dark passage received me a second time; I remained until three o'clock in the afternoon, when I was again ushered into the Bureau de Surveillance, still presided over by M. Panis. "I have had an account rendered," said he, " of the examination of your papers, and find that on that score you merit nothing but praise; but you have spoken of a portfolio on the affair of those muskets, which you are accused of dishonourably retaining in Holland; those two gentlemen (pointing to those who had accompanied me and removed the seals) have seen that portfolio, and they even tell us that we should be astonished at it." "I am eager, Sir, to open it for you, and here it is." I took the vouchers one after another, but had not got half through with them, when M. Panis exclaimed: "Gentlemen, it is pure, it is pure! do you not think so?" Every one in the office repeated: "It is pure!" And they further added, that it was necessary to give M. Beaumarchais an honourable attestation of his patriotism and his purity, and to make him an apology for the chagrin which had been occasioned him, the fault of which must be attributed to circumstances. A M. Bercheret, secretary, whose benevolent looks consoled and interested me, was writing out this attestation, when a little man with black hair, turned-up nose, and a frightful countenance, went and whispered to the president. Shall I mention him to you, my readers? It was the great—the just, in a word, the merciful Marat!

He went out. M. Panis, rubbing his forehead with apparent embarrassment, said to me, "I am much grieved at it, Sir, but I cannot restore you to liberty. There is a fresh denunciation against you."

"Tell me what it is, Sir; I will clear it up instantly."

"That I cannot do; a word, a single gesture, to some of your friends who wait for you without, would be sufficient to destroy the effect of the search which is about to be made."

"Mr. President, let all my friends be sent away; I will remain a prisoner in your bureau until the search be ended; perhaps I can furnish the means of shortening it. Only tell me what is the matter in hand."

He took the advice of the gentlemen present; and after having required my word of honoûr, that I would remain in the bureau, and not speak to any one, until they should all return, he said to me, "You have sent five trunks of suspected papers to the house of a president's wife, No. 15. Rue St. Louis au Marais: the order is given to go and seek for them."

"Gentlemen," I replied, "listen to my answer. I give these five trunks and their contents, if any such exist, to the poor; but I declare to you, that there is no trunk belonging to me in the house which you have named. There is only a packet of mine in the house of one of my friends, in the Rue des Trois Pavillons: it contains title-deeds of property, which I deposited there on receiving information that my own house was to be plundered on the night of the 8th or 10th of August, of which I gave intimation to M. Pétion. While they are seeking for the five trunks, you can send for this packet, which will be delivered to you on the production of this order, by the servant of my friend; and I freely permit you to examine it on its arrival. Another trunk of papers and old registers were stolen from me the same day that I deposited this packet with my friend: order this to be cried, gentlemen: I cannot go further than this." They did as I requested. The attestation was given to me, and signed by each of the gentlemen in attendance at the bureau; but it did not contain the examination of the trunks and the packet.

These gentlemen then went to dinner, and I remained prisoner in the office, with a single clerk, to whom the care of it was confided. As they were just going out, a man very much heated, wearing a scarf, entered, and said, that he held in his hand proofs of my treason, and of the abominable design which I had formed of delivering sixty thousand muskets, for which I had received payment, to the enemies of my country. He was like a madman when he learnt that I had received an attestation to the contrary. It was M. Colmar, who had been anxious to deprive me of the contract for the muskets, and who moreover had been my accuser.... He uttered the bitterest invectives against me, observing, that it would cost me my head. "I am very willing," I rejoined, "provided you be not my judge."

They departed, and I remained, sadly reflecting on the singularity of my fate. My packet arrived, but there was no news to be heard of the five trunks. Will the reader credit, that I stayed there thirty-two hours, without any one returning? The young man of the bureau, on going to his rest, told me, that he could not leave me alone in the bureau during the night. He therefore removed me into the dark passage; and, had it not been for the compassion of a servant, who threw me a mattress upon the ground, I should have died there from fatigue and cold.

At the expiration of thirty-two hours, no person having yet returned, some of the municipal officers, compassionating my distressing situation, consulted together, and said to me, "M. Panis does not return; perhaps he is indisposed. In examining the trunks at the house of the president's wife, where eight or nine of them were found, it has been discovered that they contained old clothes belonging to certain nuns, to whom she has given an asylum. We know that you are innocent of every thing that is imputed to you. We must wait the re-assembling of the Bureau to clear you, but we have determined to permit you to go and rest at your own house. To-morrow morning your packet will be examined, and you shall then have a complete certificate."

Turning to my weeping servant, I ordered him to go and

prepare me a bath, for I had not slept for five nights, nor taken any rest. He hurried away, and I was sent after, accompanied, however, by two gendarmes, who were to guard me through the night.

The next day, I despatched one of them, to know if the Bureau had at length assembled, in order that I might receive the desired certificate. He shortly afterwards returned with other guards, and a rigorous order to conduct me to the Abbaye, with directions to confine me in a solitary dungeon, and an express prohibition not to suffer me to speak to any one whatever from without, except by special permission in writing from the municipality. I found it difficult to curb the despair of my domestics, but consoled them as well as I could, and was led to prison, where I met with Messieurs d'Affry, Thierry, the Montmorins, Sombreuil, and his virtuous daughter, who had immured herself with her father in this disgusting place; Abbé de Boisgélin; Lally-Tolendal; Lenoir, treasurer of the charities, an old man of eighty-two; M. Gibé, notary: in fact, there were in all a hundred and ninety-two individuals heaped together in eighteen small rooms.

An hour after my arrival, I was sent for, by an order from the municipality, into the gaoler's apartment, whither I repaired. There I found M. Larcher, the associate of Constantini, and several other individuals, to whom allusion has already been made. He came to renew the kind proposals which he had already made at my own house, for the purchase of all the muskets that I had in Holland: and I should take in payment, said he, the eight hundred thousand francs which I had just received from the treasury. Upon this condition I should be released from the Abbaye, and should have a perfect attestation.... After a moment's silence, I coldly replied to this man, "I transact no business in prison; go and state to the ministers who send you, and who know, as well as myself, that I have not touched a fraction of the eight hundred thousand francs which you speak of; a ridiculous idea, which has been circulated in order to have a pretence for plundering me on the melancholy night of the 10th of August." "You have not received eight hundred thousand francs within the last fortnight?" said he, in rising from his seat. "No," I replied, turning my back upon him. He then advanced to the door, and hurried away; and I have not since seen him.

On my return into the room where the other prisoners were, I related to them all that had just taken place, and I perceived that I was the only one in whom it had excited surprise.

One of these gentlemen said to me, "The enemies have taken Longwy; if they succeed in entering Verdun, terror will get possession of the people, and our tormentors will profit by it to work our destruction." "I see too much probability in the idea," I returned, with a bitter sigh.

The next day, the following note was sent to me in prison: —"Colmar, a municipal officer, the same who stated in your presence that he had proofs against you, is the cause of a new order, which keeps you still imprisoned. We are promised that your case shall be attended to without delay.... Write in energetic terms to the Committee of the Mayoralty, which I shall not quit."

This note, from my nephew, was delivered to me by the gaoler, to the honour of whom, I must say, that he alleviated, as far as possible, the fate of all his prisoners.

I asked permission of my companions of misfortune to write a memoir to the Committee of *Surveillance* of the Mayoralty. M. Thierry lent me paper, M. d'Affry his portfolio, to serve in lieu of a desk; and young Montmorin, seated on the ground, supported it while I wrote. M. Lally-Tolendal was arguing with the Abbé Boisgélin; M. Gibé watching me writing; M. Lenoir, upon his knees, was at fervent prayer; and I occupied myself with my petition . . . . .

On the subsequent day, the 29th of August, about five o'clock in the evening, we were gloomily moralizing. M. d'Affry, that venerable old man, had left the Abbaye the evening before. A turnkey came and called out to me, "M. Beaumarchais, you are inquired for." "Who asks for me, friend?" "M. Manuel, and several municipal officers." He left us, and we mutually gazed upon each other. M. Thierry inquired if he was not one of my enemies. " Alas! " I rejoined, "we have never seen each other; it is dreadful to commence our acquaintance thus, and the omen is a terrible one. Has my hour then come?" My companions cast their eyes upon the ground, and remained silent. I quitted

them, passed on to the gaoler's room, and exclaimed, as I
entered, "Which of you gentlemen is Manuel?" "I am that
person," said one, advancing forward. "Sir," I observed to him,
"without knowing each other, we have had a public dispute
about my taxes. Not only, Sir, have I punctually paid them,
but I have also paid those of several other individuals who had
not the means of doing it themselves. My case must indeed
have become very serious, to induce the procurator syndic of
the Commune of Paris to leave his public affairs to occupy himself with me." "Sir," said he, "far from leaving them, it is for
the purpose of attending to them that I am now in this place;
and is it not the first duty of a public officer to snatch from
prison an innocent man who has been persecuted? Your accuser,
Colmar, is proved to be a villain; his section has deprived him
of the scarf of which he was unworthy, and driven him out of
the Commune. I believe he is now in prison. It is in order
that I may make you forget our public disputes, that I have
obtained permission from the Commune to absent myself for an
hour, for the purpose of liberating you. Leave this place at
once." I threw myself around his neck, without being able to
utter a single word; my eyes alone were the interpreters of my
soul, and must have been most expressive if they portrayed all
I felt . . . . . Never shall I forget this man, or that happy
moment* . . . . . I departed.

On Sunday, the 2nd of September, having no reply from the
minister Lebrun, of whom I had earnestly desired an audience
upon my affair of the muskets, and learning that a free departure
from Paris was permitted, I went to dine in the country, about
three leagues from the city, designing to return in the evening.
At four o'clock, some one came to inform us that the city was
closed again, that the tocsin was sounding, the general alarm
beating, and that the people were furiously rushing towards the
prisons, to massacre their melancholy inmates. Then it was
that I exclaimed, in the height of enthusiastic gratitude, "Oh,
Manuel! Manuel!" . . . . .

---

* This is one trait more of virtue to be noted down in the life of Manuel,
whose conduct, as has been proved by the memoirs on the massacres of September, presents an inconceivable mixture of good and bad actions.—*Note of
the Editors.*

My friend invited me to accept a bed with him. At six o'clock, in the evening of the following day, a commandant of the National Guards of the environs came and whispered him, " It is known that you have M. de Beaumarchais in your house; the butchers missed him last night in Paris; they are to come *hither to-night* to carry him off, and perhaps I shall be obliged to repair to the spot with all my troop." " I will inform him of all this," returned my friend; and he immediately came to me in the garden.

I saw him approaching with a pale and dejected countenance, and he falteringly gave me the melancholy information. " My unhappy friend," said he, "what can you do?" " In the first place," said I, " I shall quit your house, in order that it may not be plundered. If they should seek for me here, say that a party came to fetch me, and that I have set out for Paris; farewell. Take care of my servants and my carriage; and I will go and seek my wretched fortune. Let us not say another word: return to the drawing-room, and do not speak again of me." Upon this I opened a small gate, and walked straight across the tilled lands, avoiding all the public roads. During the night, I walked three leagues across the country in the rain, and in the morning found an asylum among some worthy people, from whom I disguised nothing. They welcomed me with such kind and touching hospitality, that I was affected by it even to tears. Through their means, by the most circuitous channels, I got news from Paris. I learnt the massacres were still continuing . . . . . . I wrote to the minister Lebrun.

I know not whether it was the lofty words which I repeated in my letter of " Memoir to the National Assembly, in which I should retort the wrongs I had suffered upon those who had rendered themselves guilty of them," which secured me at length, on the 6th of September, the following note from the government officers, in the name of M. Lebrun: " The minister for foreign affairs has the honour to request that M. de Beaumarchais will come to-morrow, Friday, at nine o'clock in the morning, to the hotel of that department, in order to finish the affair of the muskets. The minister desires that the whole may be arranged before ten o'clock, a.m."

Owing to the circuitous channels by which anything could

be conveyed to me, to prevent my being traced, this note did
not reach me till the following day at nine o'clock, which was
the hour of the rendezvous that M. Lebrun had appointed, and
it was therefore impossible to attend to it, as I was five leagues
distant from Paris, and could only go thither on foot.

One thing particularly struck me in this note: it may be they
had strongly suspected that, being concealed out of Paris, I
should not go in open day and expose myself to be assassinated ;
that therefore, *if the affair was not completed, they would say it
was my fault*, in consequence of my neglecting the meeting
which had been appointed to arrange it definitively.

I immediately replied to M. Lebrun, entreating him to alter
the hour for the conference, and to fix it for ten o'clock in the
evening, in order that I might arrive with less danger of losing
my life than I should incur in broad daylight.

My letter was delivered; and the minister sent a verbal
message by his porter, that he should expect me the next day,
Saturday, precisely at nine o'clock, p.m.

I calculated that it would take me four hours to reach Paris,
and set out at four o'clock in the afternoon of the 8th of
September, from the house of the good people, who wished to
conduct me, which I refused, fearing that we should be remarked.

I arrived alone, my strength completely exhausted, wet through
with perspiration, a beard of five days' growth, my linen dirty,
and wearing my great coat, just as I departed from prison. At
nine o'clock precisely I was at M. Lebrun's door. The Swiss
told me that the minister, having business then on hand, had
deferred the intended interview till eleven o'clock that night,
or the following morning, at my own option. I desired the man
to tell him that I should return at eleven o'clock, not daring
to show myself in the day time.

I could not remain at the minister's, where some one might
see me, and noise abroad my return. I went out, but knew
not where to go, or what to do, until the hour of rendezvous.
The fear of being recognised by some incendiary amongst the
patrol made me resolve to conceal myself upon the boulevard
amongst some heaps of rough stones, where I sat myself down
upon the ground. I could not help admiring the contrast
between the past and this strange asylum, in which fatigue threw

me into a sound sleep; and had it not been for a noise which was made near where I was, about eleven o'clock, I should have been found there the next day.

I heard the hour strike, and hurried away to the office for foreign affairs . . . . O God! judge of my distress, when the Swiss told me that the minister was gone to bed, and that he would expect me at nine o'clock the following morning. "You did not, then, tell him?"—"Pardon me, Sir, I did tell him." "Give me some paper quickly." I endeavoured to smother my grief, and wrote a brief letter, reminding him of the danger I feared in showing myself during the day, and requesting a meeting on the morrow, at night-close.

The time which was occupied in copying it enabled me to send for a hackney coach. I arrived again at my temporary abode after midnight, discharging the coach at five or six hundred paces distant from it, in order that he might not discover who I was. In entering the house again, I had great difficulty in restraining the joy which I felt in seeing myself still in the land of the living. I urged my kind friends to secrecy* . . . . . . . .

---

* Here ends this part of the Memoir of Beaumarchais. He returned several times to the minister Lebrun's, without being able to terminate the affair which called him thither. He departed for Holland, and afterwards went over to England, with the firm resolution of returning to imprisonment at Paris, thinking his means of justification unquestionable. "If I be massacred, National Convention," exclaimed Beaumarchais, "do justice to my child; at least suffer her to glean after me, where she ought to have reaped."—*Note of the Editors.*

# HUMANITY TRAMPLED UPON

## OR THE

## DREADFUL SUFFERINGS OF A PRISONER

BY JOSEPH PARIS DE L'EPINARD

# HUMANITY TRAMPLED UPON

*etc. etc.*

DURING the horrible reign of the tyrants who desolated France by their depredations and their fury, my name stood upon the fatal lists of proscriptions which the inhuman proconsuls drew up in the departments. My death had been determined upon, and I was sent to Paris, in order to be slaughtered by the assassins of whom Robespierre had constituted a tribunal.

I arrived at the Abbaye, that frightful prison, the walls of which were yet tinged with the blood of the unfortunate victims who were massacred on the 2nd and 3rd September, by the contrivance of Danton, aided by the infernal genius of Fabre d'Eglantine. I was searched with the utmost care, stripped, and cast into prison, where despair seemed to have fixed her gloomy abode. A worm-eaten table, disgustingly filthy, a heap of old chopped straw, and a wretched truckle bed, held together by a sort of girth half torn, formed the whole of the furniture of my new abode. I wished to sleep; but swarms of vermin attacked my feeble limbs, and gave me the most excruciating pains.

Twenty-four hours had passed, and my prison door remained motionless on its heavy hinges; the death-like silence was at length suddenly interrupted by the arrival of a terrific gaoler.

"Here," said he, with a harsh voice, "I have brought thee a pitcher full of water: thou wilt be able to drink to the health of thy friends; here is likewise a piece of bread; this is not very dainty fare, but what wouldst thou have, brother?—We live in a time of penitence."

I mechanically turned my eyes towards the pitcher, and observed that the spiders had formed their webs in the inside;

and, as to the bread, it was so dirty, that I fancied it must have been picked out of the common sewers. I could not fix my gaze on the gaoler, so strongly was my imagination impressed with the idea that I beheld in the man one of those executioners whose features the sublime Rubens has portrayed in his Descent from the Cross. I shuddered with terror; but, after recovering my coolness a little, I ventured to implore, with tears in my eyes, that, as a special favour, he would have the humanity to get my den cleaned out. I entreated him to procure me a rude chair, to support my emaciated body, a pen and ink, paper, and candles.

"Thou art in solitary confinement, and canst have nothing of what thou askest," replied the gaoler, and immediately the dreadful bolts were drawn upon me with a creaking noise which vibrated to the depths of my soul.

Behold me, then, consigned to the most overwhelming reflections, alone in my misfortunes, with an eternity of grief opening before my gloomy fancy. Two days I remained without a visit from my terrible gaoler, who at length appeared, bringing some bread, the appearance of which was little calculated to excite appetite. I could not help expressing my disgust, upon which he told me, that if I would not satisfy myself with dry bread, he would bring me whatever I should demand, and that with money there was good eating to be had below. I thanked him for his offer, and repeated, that I required nothing from his kindness without payment, but that I would give the world if he could procure me a chair, pens, ink, paper, and candles. The brute replied, that I might have all these things as soon as I had been examined.

I had remained three days without tasting food, and a burning fever was preying upon my frame: every hour seemed hastening my destruction: in a word, my situation was so deplorable, that I succeeded in softening the iron heart of my keeper, and he appeared affected with my fate. I had effected a prodigy, and he went to the head gaoler, to whom he doubtlessly drew a faithful picture of my wretched condition, returning shortly afterwards to inform me, that, as a signal favour, I had obtained permission to leave my dungeon. I attempted to walk, but my legs and my whole body sank under me. By the assistance of my guide, I was removed into a kind of hall or saloon, decorated with the produce of the spoils of the victims who had been huddled together at the Abbaye.

When I had arrived before the head gaoler, the despot stammered out a few broken sentences, but he was almost dead drunk. "Oh, ho," said he to me, "thou art not then accustomed to prisons .... I am keeper,—I am recorder,—I am magistrate,—I am everything here .... My people have informed me that thou hast refused to eat..... As was my duty, I have apprised the committee of it, and their reply was, 'Well, he must either be left to perish, or be conducted to the Bicêtre.' ... At once decide: eat, or do not eat, it is all the same to me." He drooped his head for a moment, then, raising it again, exclaimed, " Listen to me: I have a good cook in my kitchen; everything can be found in my larder,—every thing that can be desired,—(then, as if he would congratulate himself on a flight of wit)—with money be it understood .... From whence dost thou come, and what are thy pursuits?" On my answering that I lived at Lille, he added, "Aye, aye, I know that city .... I was there with Caumartin. (It was natural enough he should be acquainted with it, for he had been that person's footman.) But, zounds and the d—l, thou smellest of fever! go along ... pugh."

He called the turnkey, who took me up and placed me on his back, in which way he was bearing me towards my dungeon, when some unfortunate prisoners, who had heard the broken sentences of the gaoler at the door of the hall, which remained ajar, stopped me and said, "How, citizen, do you suffer yourself to be thus cast down! In the name of Heaven, we entreat and conjure you to take some food."

There is solace, then, even amidst the most overwhelming sufferings! Gratitude choked my utterance; I endeavoured to give vent to the grateful sentiments which swelled my bosom, but my voice expired in a copious stream of tears, and I could only convey, by gestures, how deeply I was touched and affected by their expressions of sensibility.

My companions in misfortune removed me from the shoulders of the turnkey, and carried me into the hall, where their urgent solicitations, and their pressing entreaties, forced me, after eight days of actual fasting, to take some nourishment.

Life having become an insupportable burden to me, I wished
to die, and hoped that, by eating, and eating plentifully, I might
bring on a fit of indigestion which would put an end to an
existence that was hateful to me. My extreme weakness, and
the raging fever which was operating on me, seemed to promise
a speedy arrival at the port I ardently wished for. I therefore
ate voraciously, and, full of the assurance with which I had just
flattered myself, I was once again plunged into my dungeon;
but what greatly surprised and grieved me was, that I felt no
ill effects from what I had done, and was forced, in spite of
myself, to enter, as it were, into life again.

The next day my keeper made his visit earlier than usual;
I was indebted for this attention to the entreaties of the feeling
individuals who had been interested by my situation. About
two o'clock the turnkey came for me, and led me to the hall.
Being ordered into close confinement, I had the severe mortification of not beholding again my benefactors. Notwithstanding
the most fervent prayers and supplications, which I made to
those around, I was not permitted to enjoy a second sight of
them; I learnt, however, that the interest with which I had
inspired them had lost none of its warmth, and that they were
constantly anxious to receive intelligence of me.

After my second meal, I was wholly abandoned to myself for
fifty hours. When I complained to the turnkey of this rigorous
neglect, he appeared astonished. These gentlemen, it seemed,
enjoyed, every ten days, a holiday, during which they went to
ramble through the city. In the absence of my turnkey, I had
been forgotten by his companion; and this was the cause of the
mistake. Fearing that I might complain to the head gaoler, he
hurried away to fetch me my dinner.

The following day I experienced, on the part of this man, a
striking change of temper: his manner was threatening, and,
after some altercation which arose between us, he attempted to
strike me with the bunch of keys which he held in his hand.
Upon this I felt my blood rise, indignation gave me strength,
the quarrel increased, his arrogance became extreme: I darted a
bottle at his head, and, taking advantage of the stupefaction which
the blow occasioned, threw him upon the steps of the staircase.

The noise of our struggle drew all the turnkeys to my dungeon. They uttered a torrent of abuse against me, and loaded me with menaces and curses: not one, however, dared approach; and, after a fresh volley of imprecations, they retired.

This adventure excited a bitter feeling of revenge against me, and my tormentors made me feel the cruel effects of it, during the space of ten whole months that I was incarcerated in this infernal prison.

Finding it impossible to convey intelligence of my situation to my wife, I had recourse to invention, which seems to be the science of misfortune. I manufactured ink out of rust, some coal that I had found in a heap of filth, and the black dust which I scraped off the walls and the door; stalks of straw, which I had cut with my teeth, were to serve for pens, and a few scraps of paper which I had discovered amongst the straw, were to supply the place of a better material for registering my thoughts. I was about to make use of my invention, when I perceived a nail in the wall, which I pulled out and employed in drawing blood from my body; with this ink it was, that I hastened to sketch to my wife the picture of my deplorable situation.

I was ignorant of any mode by which I could have my letter sent to her; the anxiety, however, which I felt to communicate my feelings to her, wrought, in an extraordinary manner, upon my imagination, and I was in hopes to find means to secure the wished-for object. At one time I thought I had obtained it: the prisoners, in order to satisfy the calls of nature, ascended as far as the third door of my dungeon; the two other doors had not been closed, and I had an opportunity of conversing with one of my companions in misfortune. I entreated him to send to the post the letter that I would then convey to him under the door; but, upon my attempting to do this, the door was so thick, that, from the smallness of my note, he could not receive it on the other side, and, consequently, was unable to render me the service which I requested.

In despair at the ill-success of my first scheme, I suffered my tears to flow unrestrained; at this instant my ear was struck by a hollow sound, which proceeded from the prisoners in the room underneath my dungeon, who were striking the ceiling. I answered them with the heel of my boot, and afterwards raised a square of the pavement and dug into the cement, in order that I might be able to establish a mode of communication with my neighbours; but the floor was so thick, that I was obliged to renounce this hope.

In the evening, the prisoners with whom I had wished to communicate, again visited the conveniences, and one of them suggested to me the idea of hanging out of my window, at night, a piece of string, and that they would attach paper, pens, and ink to it, and that I could also adopt the same expedient for conveying my letter to them, and soliciting the little services which they were in a condition to render me.

I eagerly adopted the plan which had been just pointed out. I tore some strips from my quilt, and formed a sort of cord of them, which I suspended through the bars of my window. Upon a concerted signal, I drew up my cord, and had the inexpressible pleasure to find an ink-horn, and some pens and paper, attached to it.

I congratulated myself on the success of our happy invention; I poured out my thoughts in delightful freedom, conversed upon the paper with my wife, and felt the course of my sorrows suspended. I waited the approaching night with that impatience which can be better felt than expressed; darkness at length spread forth her friendly shroud, and I despatched through my window a letter, which contained the liveliest expressions of gratitude to my kind neighbours, and enclosed a note addressed to my wife.

The note reached its destination; but the answer, which was received at the Abbaye, raised the most furious storm against me. A detachment of turnkeys, preceded by the gaoler and his wife, suddenly entered my dungeon, searched all around it, and tumbled every thing about, without addressing to me a single word. If their tongues were silent, yet their looks were furiously expressive, indicating clearly the rage which they felt in having derived no benefit from their careful search. I had safely concealed from discovery the instruments of my correspondence, in the hole which I had formed in the floor, and which I had artfully covered with the square that had been displaced. The disappointment of my inquisitors, who were furious that they had discovered nothing, broke forth in menaces and invectives of the most gross and brutal description. The gaoler held in his hand my wife's letter; I rushed upon him, tore it from his grasp, and thrust it into my bosom; fury sparkled in the eyes of my tormentors, who uttered the most horrible imprecations. Collecting all my strength, I entrenched myself behind the door, and, as the gaoler was advancing towards me, I rushed upon him, seized the tyrant with a vigorous arm, and succeeded in rolling him back upon the staircase. It was a repetition of the scene which had passed a few days before between me and one of his satellites. Alarm spread abroad immediately through the house, like a devouring flame extending to every part of an edifice. The prisoners called aloud for help, and cried out that they were on the point of being assassinated; at length, after heaping the vilest abuse upon me, they closed my door, and I was left alone in my melancholy habitation.

I fully expected that the act of violence which I had committed would be a signal for the cruellest revenge on the part of the gaoler and his turnkeys; but what was my surprise, when I was asked whether I wished to take my meal in my own dungeon or below! The invitation appeared so extraordinary, that I kept silence. The gaoler's wife came herself, escorted by three turnkeys and four dogs. She was no longer haughty nor arrogant, as she had been in the morning; but, softening her tone, she kindly told me, that what had happened arose solely from a want of a proper understanding. She enlarged upon her own humanity, and entreated me, as a favour, to forget everything that had occurred, adding, with an air of benevolence, that, although I was condemned to solitary confinement, she would take upon her, unknown to her husband, to allow me to write to my wife, provided I limited myself solely to mentioning what related to my wants.

I heartily subscribed to this unhoped-for concession; I represented to her, that for ·three weeks I had not changed my linen, and that I was devoured by vermin, entreating her to procure me the means of providing for wants which were of the most rigorous necessity. The officious wife of the gaoler brought me paper, pen, and ink, herself; I scribbled a few lines to my wife, which were taken to her residence, and, a few hours afterwards, I received a packet of linen.

I continued daily to take my meals in the hall, or in the apartment of the gaoler's wife, until two other prisoners came to share the horrors of my dungeon. My new companions were an agent of a commissary of police, and a clerk of the War Office. The latter remained during the space of six weeks. The cause of his incarceration was this:—The deputy Chabot having seen him give his arm to one of his (Chabot's) mistresses, he denounced him as a suspicious character, and caused him to be thrown into prison. The punishment of this lascivious monk put an end to his imprisonment; his deliverance was claimed by the young people of his section, to whom he was given up.

Until their arrival, I had not been able to obtain the favour of having my dungeon cleaned out, or of being supplied with light; my two fellow-prisoners, more fortunate than myself in this respect, enabled me to enjoy the double advantage. At this time I ceased going down to the hall. The dinner of these prisoners was more plentiful than mine, yet they paid nothing. I inquired from them the reason of this extraordinary privilege; they answered, that the nation defrayed their expenses; and they were not a little astonished on being informed that four francs were extorted from me, for a miserable beverage which they called *Bouillon* (broth or soup), for a very small piece of detestable bread, and a bottle of vinegar, which was designated wine.

My companions wrote to their relations, in order to procure themselves an ordinary somewhat more plentiful than that of the prison. They obtained their liberty some time afterwards, and the separation was to me heart-breaking. I sank again into a state of dejection, and limited myself to my solitary meals, for which the same system of extortion was pursued, without my being permitted to breathe a syllable of complaint.

Two other citizens were thrown into my dungeon, and took the place of those who had been so happily released. They were municipal officers of the Commune of Paris. One of them inquired how I was supported in the prison; and when I had given them the same details which I had furnished my former fellow-prisoners, they raised their hands and eyes as it were towards heaven, stamped on the floor, and exclaimed in a rage, "that I ought to enjoy fifty sous per day, a sum which the nation granted to each prisoner of the Abbaye, and that what I had been made to pay was a manifest robbery."

"In that case," I replied, "they rob me with impunity of four francs a day, which I have paid during the three months and a half that I have been buried here, excepting a few of the first days, in which I took no food."

Dinner was brought for three. The two municipal officers desired to speak to the gaoler's wife, having no idea of paying, as I had done, four francs a day. The cunning wife took care not to make her appearance. The next day the same request was sent to her, and answered in a similar manner. She preferred giving up what I was wont to pay her, to exposing herself to humiliating reproaches.

I then lived in the same manner as my companions of misfortune; but this state of things did not long continue, for they were removed from my dungeon,* and I again experienced the bitterness of grief and of solitude. The only solace which I experienced in my torments was obtaining every four days a very small candle, upon paying for it.

My food was always execrable, and very insufficient for my wants. All the subsistence which I received during the day was a decayed herring, or a piece of wretchedly cooked meat, scarcely two ounces in weight, which more resembled human flesh than the flesh of an ox. The idea will never be removed from the minds of those who were confined in this abominable prison, that human flesh was eaten in it. I was one day informed that the commissaries were about to visit my dungeon, and I took care to place my portion of food before them. One of them, barbarous as they were, drew back with an emotion of horror, and could not refrain from saying, in the presence of myself

* My two companions were called before the revolutionary tribunal. Our farewell affected us even to tears, which did not cease, on my part, until I learnt that they had had the signal good fortune to be acquitted. One of them, named Jobert, was afterwards guillotined, as member of the rebellious municipality of Paris; and the other is citizen Moille, the father of four young children, an excellent husband, a virtuous citizen, and a well-educated man, whose society was much courted. He has constantly taken a share in my sufferings, and has aided me to support them—in alleviating them by all the services which it was in his power to render, and particularly by sending me books from his library.

and his companions, to the gaoler, who took great care to accompany them, "that men should not be fed in that manner." Notwithstanding this reproach, I perceived no change in my unfortunate situation; it served, on the contrary, to embitter the minds of my keepers against me. What gave rise to the belief about the meat among the prisoners was, that it often happened during the night that groans were heard, which seemed to be stifled by tortures, and by a rattling noise in the throat, indicative of death.

The cold was already very severe, and I demanded wood for a fire, which was refused me; the consequence was, that an obstinate cough was added to my other sufferings, and did not give me any respite either night or day. It was so violent, that the prisoners who were confined beneath me, and even those on the other side of the court, complained that I prevented them from sleeping.

By dint of earnest entreaties, I succeeded in obtaining a stove; but I only received a single stick out of a faggot, not more than two inches in diameter at the utmost, and for which they made me pay twelve sous. My chest was greatly weakened, and the efforts which I made in coughing occasioned a *very copious spitting of blood;* and, to crown my misery, I was attacked by a dreadful dysentery. I fell into a state of weakness, which threatened speedy dissolution: existence became an intolerable burden to me, and I resolved to get rid of it: all my imagination was centered in this wished-for object.

A copper candlestick was one of the articles of furniture in my prison. I procured myself some vinegar, with a view of preparing verdigris with these materials. I filled the grooves in the bottom of the candlestick with the liquid, left it to dry, and afterwards scraped off the poisonous composition with the point of the nail which I had used for bleeding myself, when I wrote the first time to my wife. I had already collected a strong dose of poison, when my project was discovered. I had left the candlestick upon the table: the turnkey, wishing to place something upon it, upset the liquor upon my napkin, which immediately assumed a green colour. The turnkey appeared much surprised, and addressed several questions to me, to which I made no reply. He contracted his eyebrows, murmured between his teeth, took away the candlestick, and left me in a state of profound stupefaction.

After this adventure, my gaolers evidently mistrusted me. The same day they gave me three Hungarians as companions, prisoners of war, one of whom was an officer, another a trumpeter, and a third a hussar. They all spoke German; but the officer and the trumpeter knew Latin, and we managed to understand one another in that language.

This accession of society was some alleviation to my fate. Misfortune makes men confiding and tender. After mutual communications as to the causes of our detention, these compassionate soldiers, more occupied with my sufferings than with their own, were eager to lavish upon me all the attentions which they had in their power. They assisted me to clear my bed from the filth and from the vermin which infested it: they even became the support of my weakness, in those necessities in which fainting nature is repulsive to herself. The services which I received from these generous men will always be present to my recollection.

In the meantime, my condition daily grew worse. Preyed upon by the bitterest anguish, I asked for the assistance of a physician, which was refused: all the remedy which it was thought proper to supply me, was a piece of liquorice-root, of which I made a cold beverage. I had no fire to boil it: the merciless prudence of my gaolers would not grant me even that trifling aid.

Nearly ten months had I thus struggled against death, and seen robust health gradually exhausting itself in this tedious state of agony, when one morning, about two o'clock, we heard the door of our dungeon open with a loud noise, and saw four grenadiers enter, their drawn swords in their hands, followed by a crowd of turnkeys, and after them came several men, who called themselves municipal officers, wearing their scarfs. At the sight of this terrible apparition, we thought that a new September was about to commence, and that our last hour was come. The young trumpeter fell down upon his knees on his bed, clasped his hands, and implored pardon. The officer and the hussar rose upon their seats; and, as for me, having recovered from my first emotion, and endeavouring to collect

the little strength that remained in my frame, I put myself
in a state of defence.   My blood boiled in my veins, and
I was determined to sell dearly the breath of life which still
animated me; but what was it in the power of an unfortunate
being, unarmed and weakened by sickness, to do against ten or
twelve armed officers, whose every look and movement inspired
terror and the certainty of death ?   My hostile attitude intimidated
them, however, to such a degree, that they instantly disappeared.
A moment after, a municipal officer ventured to enter, having
previously taken the precaution to decorate himself with his
scarf.   His first object was to remove my apprehensions, by
assuring me, that it was only my assignats which were wanted.
I peevishly threw my portfolio towards him, and lay down
again, after having signed some register which he presented to
me.   I requested in vain that he would give me an acknowledg-
ment for the assignats, and I could only secure a promise that
every ten days there should be advanced, of my money, fifty
livres, and that it should be punctually paid to me.   The fifty
livres, and my portfolio, I never received.

Some days after this scene, a tipstaff came to conduct me to
the Palace of Justice, where I was to undergo my first examination.
I arrived in the presence of the judge, who questioned me on
my name, surname, age, and condition.   My replies convinced him
that I was not the accused whom he had to interrogate, and
he was going to send me back to the Abbaye.   But I used
such urgent entreaties, and described so energetically my situation,
and the nature of the frightful dungeon which I had just quitted,
that I obtained permission, as a favour, that I might be conducted
to the Conciergerie.   Alas!   I was ignorant that I was merely
changing one tomb for another.

In descending the great staircase of the palace, I tried to
prevail upon the constable who conducted me, to give me a
place amongst some honest persons; the man, with cold *naïveté*,
replied to my request, that nothing was easier than to grant
my desire, all the individuals who were confined in that prison
being respectable persons.   "What," said I to him, "and some
of them are guillotined every day!"—"Aye, that is true enough ;
but here people are guillotined for opinions.   Rogues and robbers
are at La Force."   I was about to indulge in fresh questions;

but the fatal gate half opened, and I was precipitated into this new abyss.

A gloomy dungeon was likewise here destined for me; with much difficulty I succeeded in securing admission into a sort of hall, somewhat less horrible, called the *chauffoir* (warming-place). On payment of twenty-five livres, I was furnished with a folding-bed and a mattress, at the foot of which was a tub to serve as a close stool for twenty individuals. My state of weakness obliged me to remain in bed until my removal.

Good God! to what a spectacle was I the witness during the three days and a half that I spent in this prison! At the Abbaye, I drank, unmixed, of the cup of my own misfortunes; but here I daily had the sorrows of others present to my view. I beheld wretched beings heaped *pêle-mêle* upon rotten straw, exposed to the vermin, to the rats and mice, which devoured even the very shoes upon their feet, merely because they could not pay for a miserable bed and mattress, which often served only for a single night. Some of those unhappy beings died in my presence, the victims of such barbarous treatment. It was necessary to avoid any expression of pity for their hardships; for pain of death was pronounced against every one who should dare to bestow the least mark of compassion upon them.

Every evening there was delivered, through an aperture, the decrees of accusation against the victims destined for the sacrifice of the morrow. The distributors, in the ebullitions of their ferocious gaiety, called this communication the evening paper. It was often impossible for the accused to read their fate, for want of light. But what need was there for reading them? In seeing one, all were known; for the formula, the principal accusers and the witnesses, were the same for each. The name alone of the victim was peculiar to him. The difficulty afterwards was to convey extracts of these death-warrants to their friendly defenders. The gaolers required as much as fifteen livres for performing the commission. If it happened, by chance, that there was an identity of name, the keepers would not give themselves the trouble of seeking the individual whom it had been intended to accuse. "Well, well," said they to the ill-fated individuals whose evil star had destined them such an unlucky present, "take it at all events; whether it be to-day or to-morrow, still it is neces-

sary that thou shouldst undergo the trial." A female monster
governed this gloomy den, the walls of which were yet reeking
with the blood that had been shed on the 2nd and 3rd September. Woe to the prisoner who had offended this Megara, or
refused to suffer her to strip him.* I have been assured, that,
connected in interests with Fouquier, she paid him twelve thousand livres every ten days, on the produce of the shameful robberies to which the unfortunate prisoners were subjected. If
the fact is true, one may form an idea of what Fouquier must
have derived from other prisons.

After the lapse of four days and three nights, I was transferred
to the national hospital (the Hôtel Dieu). A few hours were
sufficient to enable me to appreciate justly my new abode.
Gratings, bolts, trap-doors, and mason-work which served to
obstruct free ventilation, gave it the appearance of a bastile. It
was easy to judge that it was hypocrisy alone which could adorn
with the name of National Hospital this disgusting asylum of
misery. Five or six persons died in it daily; and I have seen
individuals who were perfectly well in the evening, and who
ate their suppers with a good appetite, stretched out the following day upon their death-beds. I was placed in a hall, where,
in less than ten hours, three unhappy wretches expired before
my eyes. It would have required more than indulgence to at-
tribute all these events to natural causes. The idea of poison
presented itself to my imagination, and filled my mind with the
most gloomy apprehensions.

In the morning I had to endure a visit from the physicians
of the house. Although firmly resolved not to take any of their
prescriptions, yet I could not dispense with submitting myself to
the formality. They felt my pulse. I spat blood, and an op-
pression at my chest almost stopped my respiration and even
prevented me from remaining in bed. They ordered me to be
bled, and to be dieted strictly with *tisane* (a decoction of herbs)
as a medicine. God knows what result would have been produced
by following this receipt.

The first night of my entrance I had become acquainted with
one of the medical officers, whose mild physiognomy inspired
me with confidence.—This worthy man, whom I have infinite

* Vide note at the end of this volume.

pleasure in offering to public esteem, was called Bayard, chief surgeon of the section of Indivisibility, Rue St. Louis au Marais. He had what was called a department in the hospital, that is, one hall, or large chamber of invalids, under his inspection; I applied to him in the cruel anxiety occasioned by the prescription and visit of the physicians. I informed him of the regimen which had been prescribed. He did not think proper to increase my alarms, by informing me of the danger which I should incur in executing what had been ordered for me; but contented himself by having me placed in his department. Every attention was there bestowed upon me, and he visited me three or four times a day, and often in the night. I remained for a length of time in a condition which made him fear for my life. As soon as he discovered reasonable ground for hope, he told me that I should infallibly have been undone, if the prescription of the doctor, as far as regarded bleeding, had been carried into execution. He advised me to procure certain syrups, which he indicated, and which were not to be found in the hospital; at first I dared not confess that I was without money. His kindness, however, rendering me less timid, I hazarded the confession, and told him that I had no means of sending my letters; that the gaoler of the Abbaye, in which prison I had been kept in the closest confinement for ten whole months, had entered my dungeon one night, with an armed escort, and carried off my portfolio. I entreated him to inform me what steps I should take to recover it, and he kindly undertook to execute the commission for me; until the success of which, he offered me the loan of whatever should be necessary, and used every possible delicacy to engage me to accept his offer, and to avoid hurting my pride. A short time afterwards, he succeeded in delivering to me a parcel, which my unhappy wife had sent at a venture: for, during more than four months, I had found it impossible to give her any information of my movements; but, notwithstanding all his address, he could not obtain the restoration of my portfolio, or of any of my other things, which remained in the hands of the gaoler's wife of my first prison.

During these transactions, the individual whom circumstances had rendered so valuable to me was ordered to leave the hospital, the victim of some infamous manœuvre. His departure left

me in the most complete despair. I will not speak of my grief
and my regrets: they were shared by all my companions in
misfortune. From a convalescent state, I became again danger-
ously ill, and the relapse was still more dreadful than the first
attack had proved. Bleeding was again spoken of; but the observations of Bayard had rendered me suspicious of the operation, and I refused without hesitation. However, as they threatened to bind me, in order to make me undergo the operation,
and, as I had seen similar cruelty exercised towards others, a
fear of the same fate made me adopt the prudent resolution of
entering into an understanding with my surgeon. He was a
prisoner, like myself, who had voluntarily undertaken to attend
to the sick, without any other reward than the consciousness of
being useful; I prevailed upon him to place upon my arm a
ligature stained with blood. This excellent young man, who knew
that I was inscribed upon the list of proscription, did not hesitate
to favour my stratagem. The next day, at the visiting hour,
the physician, satisfied that I had been bled, did not fail to
express his opinion that I was materially better.* He declared
that it was necessary to open the vein again, and that the oper-
ator must not be sparing in the blooding, as the results were
obviously so beneficial; it was observed, that I had such a copious perspiration, that the attendants were obliged, for eight days
successively, to change every hour my shirt, the sheets, and
even the mattress; such was the material improvement which
the physician had remarked in me since my pretended blooding.
I recovered, however, by slow degrees; but was indebted for
my almost miraculous escape to a robust constitution: indeed, all
the energy of nature was requisite to enable me to resist, for so
long a period, evils without number, joined to the horrible stench
of the dead bodies, which could not be removed fast enough;
the dying and the dead surrounding me, as well as pregnant

---

* We cannot refrain from citing an example of the interest which was felt in
the fate of these unfortunate beings, and of the regret which their death excited:
one day, at the Conciergerie, the head doctor approached a bed, and felt the
pulse of the sick man. "Ah," said the doctor, "he is better to-day." "Yes;
doctor," replied the superintendant; "but this is not the same: the invalid of
yesterday is dead, and this has taken his place." "Oh ho! that is another affair;
well, well, let the vegetable decoction be made."—*Note of the Editors.*

women in the agonies of accouchment, and others who had already been delivered four-and-twenty hours and were still neglected. It might have been supposed that the tormentors had taken a pleasure in assembling, in this narrow space, the most terrible images of death. Every hour messengers came for such of the victims as were designated for the sacrifice of the day. They were thrown upon hand-barrows, and thus carried to the tribunal.

The extreme heat of the summer greatly increased the number of the sick, and it was at last resolved to remove a part of them to another hospital, which should serve as a branch of the other. The house of the former bishopric was fixed upon for this establishment. No sooner were the new arrangements made, than as many of us as could bear the removal, were hastily huddled together in the new hospital, and I was one amongst the number. Shortly afterwards, some of the prisoners from the Conciergerie, who had been seized with an epidemic disorder which had broken out in that prison, were also removed thither. Prudent regulations were at first adopted to arrest the spread of the contagion. They were followed, it was said, for a few days; but, though the fact was posted up at the corners of the streets of Paris, I am a witness that the regulations were soon neglected. Medical attendants were also appointed. Théry, member of the Committee of Health, a creature of Robespierre, from the same province, and his faithful coadjutor, was placed at their head. The best remedy which could be hoped for from this new doctor was the being deprived of his prescriptions. Fortunately, his reign was of short duration, for he was named, by his execrable protector, secretary of the committee, and was obliged to quit the hospital. It may easily be conceived that his departure was not regretted.

The second doctor was Naury, an ignorant man, pitiless in his system of phlebotomy, and extremely avaricious; he was a friend of Fouquier, and member of the Select Jacobins, and consequently walked in the same path with his colleague Théry. And, finally, the third was that Bayard who had acquired so strong a title to my gratitude. My joy was inexpressible, when I saw myself once again under the care of this tender-hearted man. Indeed, he was esteemed as the tutelary angel of the prisoners, and was admirably seconded in his humane efforts by his wife and daughters. I have been assured that they bestowed the most assiduous care on the female prisoners, and poured the balm of consolation into their wounds.

Théry having entirely abandoned the hospital, the day which followed his departure was a complete holiday for the prisoners. Providence had delivered them from one of their chief tormentors. In fact, it has been proved, that in the space of two months, either from ignorance or rascality, more than sixty individuals, most of them farmers, perished under the hands of this wretch. The sick who were under his care barely amounted to that number; but, in proportion as death carried them off, they were immediately replaced by others taken from different prisons of Paris. By this means Théry always found his advantage. Those whom their happy star led into Bayard's department experienced a very different fate. I can aver, that during five decades (fifty days) I did not hear of the death of a single individual in his ward. To Théry alone had death confided his scythe. I am not the only one who has done justice to Bayard; as many prisoners, in memoirs written in their own justification, have taken delight in extolling his name and declaring their gratitude.

The hospital of the bishopric daily received a considerable increase of patients from the Conciergerie, and the other prisons. Fouquier appointed, as a substitute for Théry, a man named Enguchard, who had been driven out of several hospitals, particularly that of Compiègne. His face, his manner of dressing his hair, his deportment,—everything about him, except mustachios, announced one of those hussars who are sometimes exhibited at our theatres for the public amusement. The ruffian had undoubtedly his orders to employ *poison*, as Carrier had to employ the *drowning*, and Collot the *firing* system, on their victims. His grand remedy was bleeding again and again,— eternally bleeding. He it was whom I deceived at the national hospital, with a ligature stained with blood.

Enguchard and Naury soon leagued together to procure the dismissal of Bayard, whose humanity contrasted too strongly with their cruelty. They therefore procured Quinquet, the apothecary, as an auxiliary, another Jacobin, with a Jesuitical face, well worthy of forming the third in the sanguinary triumvirate. The great cause of their hatred against Bayard was the attention which they saw him take that his patients should not be gorged with drugs before he had carefully examined them. He even assumed a kind of authority to prescribe the same precaution to them; and in this manner he acted several times with regard to myself. By this it may be perceived, that these reptiles had just cause of grievance against their too virtuous colleague.

Decrees of accusation daily arrived in this anticipated sepulchre. Death was the order of the day, under every form, and in every mode. Bayard frequently refused to deliver up to the messengers of crime the victims which the tribunal demanded; and sometimes he appeared before the judges himself to certify their unfortunate condition, and the absolute impossibility that they would be able to argue a single word in their own defence. Out of a hundred instances which I could mention of the individuals who owed their lives to Bayard, I shall select the following as the most striking:—The municipality of Sédan, consisting of seventeen fathers of families, having more than eighty children, masters, most of them, of the principal trading establishments of that city, were guillotined, without one exception, on the 10th Prairial. The attorney of the Commune was at the hospitals, and was sent for five times in succession. The barrow was before his bed, upon the last occasion, to carry him to the scaffold, when Bayard arrived, who refused to give up the sick man; and, in the contest, he exclaimed, "If they are so much athirst for blood, let them guillotine me!" The name of the citizen in question was Veyrier, and he is now free. I have lived a long time in his society, in a state of reciprocal friendship.

I must relate another fact, which will not less interest feeling hearts in favour of Bayard. The amiable sex, which is so well qualified to soften the cruelty of the most ferocious, found no favour in the sight of Fouquier. Pregnant women, who have so many claims to individual and national regard, were remorselessly dragged before the bloody tribunal. The officers one day came to execute a sentence of this nature in the presence of Bayard, who courageously started up, opposed the barbarous measure, and hurried *to the council himself*, to plead, with all the energy of true feeling, the cause of the unfortunate creatures who were summoned to undergo their cruel fate. Supported by the authority of all the colleagues of medicine, he proved, that a woman who declared herself pregnant ought to be believed upon her word; and that the medical attendants could not definitively pronounce upon her state of pregnancy until the lapse of four or five months. The council was forced to pass a decree conformable to the decision of the faculty, which was never further attended to.

The calumnies of the three monsters to whom we have alluded had the effect of obtaining the dismissal of Bayard, who was obliged to leave the hospital, and was replaced by Enguchard. The former horrors of the place were immediately renewed: dead bodies were every moment moving through the halls; the fatal barrows appeared again; the dying were borne away, without shame or pity, to the scaffold; women in a state of pregnancy, or whose accouchment had taken place only a few hours before, were dragged to the tribunal; hemlock, and other poisons, were freely administered to the miserable beings who were already marked with the seal of death, and sinking from inanition.

There are persons whose feeling natures will not suffer them to reconcile the idea of these horrible poisonings and who will reject, as the fruit of an excited imagination, what I here allege, but I beg them to call to mind the anecdote of the bloodings; to which I will add, for their scrupulous meditation, a fact, the truth of which I can testify.

A man of the name of Blamont, quarter-master of a battalion in garrison at Landrecies, my companion in misfortune, suffered from a most severe disease. He was restored to life almost miraculously; but the wounds which had been left in his legs by issues, not healing for want of the necessary remedies, he ventured to complain somewhat too bitterly to the doctor. Immediately a potion was ordered, which shortly threw him into the convulsions of death. In vain did the unfortunate man, agonized by the most burning thirst, call for some refreshing beverage: he was obliged at last to have recourse to the jugs of diet drink, belonging to the sick around him, and it was only by the utmost care that he was enabled to recover from this horrible state, the future consequences of which were alarming attacks of fainting sickness.

I do not hesitate to declare, that after the retreat of Bayard, and of Rey, the house steward, the basest crimes were perpetrated in the hospital, a few of which I will narrate.

A woman condemned to death was confined while Bayard remained: he concealed the child, in order to screen her, at least for a time, from the greedy impatience of the executioners; but he was barely gone out of the apartment when, upon the information of the nurse, the unhappy victim was added to the hecatomb.

A girl of seventeen years of age, under condemnation, declared herself pregnant, and was conducted, after her sentence had been read, to the hospital. She received the customary medical visit; and on the report of Enguchard and of Naury, that she was only seeking to gain time, she was guillotined the next day.

A young Polish princess, a perfect Venus in loveliness and beauty, who was evidently pregnant, indulged her just resentment, and reproached the gaolers with their assassinations and their crimes. These monsters, without a particle of indulgence for her despair, or her situation, denounced her to the public accuser, and she was led to the scaffold.

On the 7th and 8th Thermidor, eight women, blooming in youth, beauty, and ingenuousness, were likewise condemned. They declared themselves in a state of pregnancy, and were taken to the hospital. The next morning they were submitted to a humiliating examination, and, in the afternoon, seven of them lost their heads upon the scaffold.

Amongst the latter was the Princess of Monaco. I shall never forget the heart-rending spectacle which she made me witness. She advanced from the female wards with a firm step, not evincing the least emotion but that of indignation against her assassins. On her passage she thus addressed the prisoners whom she met:—"Citizens, I advance to my death with all the tranquillity which innocence inspires; I wish you all a happier fate." Then, turning towards the infamous keeper, who was dragging her to the cart, she drew from her bosom a packet containing some of her beautiful hair, and said to him, as she delivered it into his hands, "I have a favour to ask thee; wilt thou grant it?" The man having promised he would, she continued, "That is a packet of my hair: I venture to implore this from thy compassion; I claim it in my own name, and in the name of all those who hear me: send the packet to my son, it bears his address; dost thou hear me? Swear to me, in the presence of these worthy beings, whom the same fate is waiting, that thou wilt render me this service, the last which I ask from man." Afterwards, addressing one of her female attendants, who was included in the same proscription, but whose dejection presented a striking contrast to the firmness of her mistress:—"Cheer up, my good creature! Crime alone should display weakness." All the prisoners, with aching hearts, melted into tears; and, although such horrible scenes were necessarily familiarized to us, yet never was afternoon more gloomy and miserable.—Twenty-four hours later, however, the 9 and 10 Thermidor, brought safety to many trembling wretches who had made their account with death. But let us continue our gallery of melancholy pictures.

A married woman of the name of Quétineau, whose husband died upon the scaffold, had a miscarriage, owing to her extreme dejection of spirits. Twelve or fifteen hours afterwards, she suffered the same fate as her husband.

Soon after my arrival at the hospital, a surgery was begun to be formed. By chance I was one day on the staircase, at a short distance from the medical attendants, who were conversing on the subject. Quinquet, the apothecary of the house, observed that many things were yet required to complete the surgery; "but I hope," added he, "that they may guillotine a few apothecaries, in order that nothing may be wanting to finish it." This piece of wit was received by bursts of laughter. I was affected, and walked towards the garden, with a gloomy countenance and tears in my eyes. I was met by some of the prisoners, who accosted me, and inquired the subject of my sadness, which I, shuddering, mentioned to them, repeating what I had heard, at which they recoiled with horror.

I could write volumes, were I to relate all the tales of grief which I witnessed, or which were imparted to me. I am well aware that there are some which appear inconceivable, and which are deemed improbable. But I here accuse, openly and publicly, in the presence of my country, which has been disgraced by their conduct, these horrible cannibals: I challenge them to pursue me by the law: and, if I do not support every fact by authentic vouchers, by irreproachable witnesses, let the sword of justice strike; I consent to be punished as a vile calumniator.

An unforeseen circumstance occasioned my removal to the College of Plessis, called, doubtlessly in derision, the Prison of Equality; I was carried off with a great number of others, and the event proved more fortunate for me than I could have hoped. In the morning visit I had been ordered certain medicines, which it was intended to force me to take the following day; it was a bitter revenge which the doctors and the gaoler wished to take, for some cutting reproaches which I had addressed to them a few days before, in a fit of despair, occasioned by the gaoler who had got possession of a letter from my wife to me, and I accordingly made severe complaints. Indignation carried me beyond my natural character, and I represented to him the difference between his past condition and his present trade, a trade which degraded him below the reprobates whose crimes he promoted. I was not even satisfied with this explosion, but wrote to Fouquier. This was at least the fiftieth letter, and in it I did not express myself with more circumspection than before. I told him that, since I was one of the victims destined to glut his thirst for blood, I preferred assassination, or a death upon the scaffold, to the slow poison which his agents daily insinuated into my veins. My letter was directed to the *public exterminator*, flattering myself that this singular address would secure its perusal; for I had received no answer from those which I had previously written to him, either to solicit a speedy trial, or to demand the restitution of my portfolio and other effects. From all appearance, it was this letter which was communicated to Dr. Enguchard, and which drew from him an abundant dose of abuse, with the certainty of being poisoned the following day.

Fortunately, Fouquier claimed me as his prey, and I was transferred to Le Plessis, in order to wait there for the first vacant place in the Conciergerie. I should not assuredly have languished long in my new asylum, if the day of national retribution had been more distant.

A great many of my companions, as ill as myself, were plunged into the same bastile. They assigned us for our abode a part called the Souricière. We there found at least a hundred unfortunate beings just arrived from the provinces, who had been waiting, for twenty-four hours, their turn to be searched, robbed, registered, and afterwards immured in their respective dungeons. As for us, not quite so hardly dealt with by fate, we were removed, at the end of about two hours, and placed in corridors, without beds or mattresses. All my clothes were wet with perspiration. I changed my linen, and then laid myself down upon the floor.

On the following day, the prisoners of the other quarters came eagerly to pay us a visit. They amounted to nearly nineteen hundred, sad successors of the collegians, and unfortunate usurpers of the classes. Old men of seventy, with hoary locks, were seen in the sixth class; while deaf and dumb children, women, and girls, filled the benches of rhetoric and philosophy. These whimsical changes might have afforded matter for humorous remark, if one could have laughed under such serious circumstances.

I was fortunate enough to be recognised by a number of the prisoners, and formed more particular relations with my former friends. An individual from Amiens, the father of six or seven children, who had served me generously at the hospital, threw his arms around my neck; and seeing that I was without a lodging, and that I might probably wait long before I procured a bed, he led me to his chamber, in which he was one of six who occupied it, and forced me to accept his bed, lying himself upon the floor. This kind being prepared to continue towards me the same services which he had rendered me at the hospital; but the next day proved a happy one for him, for he unexpectedly gained his liberty, after having been immured in dungeons more than twelve months. My regret on parting with him was alleviated by the satisfaction I felt in beholding the termination of his misfortunes.

I cannot enlarge upon this prison, as I was so happy as to remain in it too short a time to collect much information. I shall content myself with a few words respecting the gaoler Haly. I have been apprised that, before he exercised his noble calling, this worthy minister of Fouquier gained a livelihood by travelling about with an African menagerie. Thus, we perceive, it was amongst ferocious beasts that Haly served his apprenticeship to the trade of gaoler. He possessed more than one talent, being an adept at conspiracies. No one denounced with more audacity, nor played the part of false witness with more *sang-froid*. At the time of my entrance into Le Plessis, fifteen or sixteen prisoners were on the point of being carried to the scaffold, victims of his depositions, and would have lost their heads, had not Fouquier himself been arrested. Haly had made confidants of certain robbers, whom he sent amongst the prisoners to espy their conduct, and afterwards to act as accusers and witnesses. A defect of memory, or want of order in the registers, caused the stratagem to be detected. A list of proscription was drawn up, upon which the names of a number of prisoners were inscribed. It happened that, amongst these pretended conspirators, many had already been guillotined; others had been transferred to different prisons, and some had at length been liberated. Similar mistakes were not unfrequent. In this prison, as well as at the Conciergerie, individuals were called upon to have their chains removed, who had already been guillotined. One day, more than eighty orders for liberation were sent to the gaoler by the Committee of Public Security, and it was discovered that sixty-two of those for whom they had been intended had been destroyed by the tribunal. Some of Haly's agents of accusation, having said too much, were guillotined; but he retained his place.

At length the memorable period of the 9th and 10th Thermidor arrived. The fears which we had at first conceived were converted into exclamations of delight and joy, when we heard of the signal victory gained by the National Convention over the execrable faction which had filled all France with bastiles and scaffolds, and deluged her with blood. We sought for assurances of our absolute resurrection from a condition more deplorable than the grave itself. Romantic from our altered feelings, we hugged each other in mutual embraces; and the excess of our emotions almost stifled us. All we could do was to indulge in fresh embraces, and to raise our eyes with gratitude towards heaven. It will readily be conceived, that those who were placed over us as a guard were not unconcerned spectators of our transports. Dismayed and confounded, the pallid hue of death appeared upon their countenances; but yet they lost none of their cupidity. We paid as much as 150 livres for a paper which contained a relation of the most prominent events which had just occurred.

Our liberation took place some days afterwards: for mine, I was indebted to the representatives Legendre and Bourbon de l'Oise.*

---

* The *History of the Prisons* contains the following note on the recital which has just been completed:

"The reader must have seen, with surprise, in this heart-rending relation, the manner in which the prisoner expresses himself on the subject of the female gaoler, who must then have been Madame Richard, a woman whose humanity has been praised by all who have known her. It may be presumed, that the author of this recital, confined in a dungeon from the commencement at the Conciergerie, imagined that she resembled most other female keepers."—*Note of the Editors.*

# MEMOIRS OF A PRISONER

BY

RIOUFFE

# MEMOIRS OF A PRISONER

*etc., etc.*

I was arrested at Bordeaux, on the 4th of October, 1793, at three o'clock in the morning, a few days before the entrance of the lieutenants of the conqueror of the 31st of May.

I had never in my life appeared before any magistrate; I had never been cited before any tribunal; and I think I may say that my independence had been, until then, as great and as complete as any individual had ever enjoyed. I actually had no idea of the nature of a prison or of fetters. Being since cast into dungeons, in the midst of a crowd of unfortunate creatures, I have often reproached myself for having never suffered my thoughts to dwell upon these receptacles, in which the laws of society confine those violators of social order whose sacrifice is necessary to its safety, and which have been also filled with thousands of the victims of tyranny. It was in this state of primitive independence, if I may so express myself, that I was suddenly plunged into captivity, and loaded with irons. My situation at first appeared to me like a dream,—I expected every moment to awake and find myself at liberty.

A Spaniard had been arrested at the same time with me. He had come into France in pursuit of liberty, under the guarantee of national faith. Being persecuted by the religious inquisition of his own country, he had fallen, in France, into the hands of the political inquisition of the revolutionary committee. I doubt whether there ever existed a soul more strongly or more sincerely imbued with a love of liberty, or more worthy of enjoying it. It was his fate to be always persecuted for that sacred cause, and yet his love for it increased. To relate my own misfortunes is to relate his: our persecution proceeded from the same causes:

the same irons chained us to the ground, the same dungeon inclosed us, and the same unhappy fate appeared to await us. At the moment when we were made prisoners, a municipal officer accompanied the band. I relate this circumstance, because I have not since seen a magistrate of the people; nor have my eyes since rested upon the national scarf, a consoling badge, which at least recalled the idea of a civilized country. It was to this band of ruffians that Frenchmen were abandoned. I was indignant enough on my own account at the conduct of these wretches, but was much more so when I beheld, in the midst of them, the representative, Duchâtel, with his head uncovered, pressed by the questions of these satellites . . . . . . They had the impudence to interrogate him . . . . . . I felt as if I beheld the whole French nation outraged in his person. At the end of three hours, after a short examination, we were informed that Duchâtel, the Spaniard, and I, were to be immediately sent forward to La Réole, to undergo an examination before some other authorities.

A confused noise of arms now arose, and I beheld Duchâtel led before me, his hands loaded with irons, and his body fastened with a rope, which was held by a gendarme: this unfortunate young man restrained the tears of indignation which sparkled in his eyes; he advanced with head erect, and a courageous and undaunted air; his character of representative was traced upon his forehead, in features the more noble, from a conviction that his rank was now despised; intrepidity breathed so strongly in his countenance, he appeared so determined and independent, that the gendarmes were in alarm throughout the entire journey, though his hands and feet were ironed, and his body fastened by a dozen ropes, both inside and outside the carriage. He now crossed, with a majestic air, the long corridor of the prison, and a part of the public square, and the very men who conducted him seemed ashamed at the idea of descending from the ranks of French citizens to play the part of sbirri to the tyrant.

We were each of us thrown into a carriage; the people kept silence, the women wept, a high degree of interest was painted in every countenance; it was a mystery, a secret of the government. We at length set off; our escort was magnificent: three berlins with six horses, outriders before, behind, and at the

doors of the carriages, this will give some idea of the ceremonies
which were exercised on these occasions. It was the day of
the *fête des chars*, and we recruited, near the gates of the town,
a large number of Sans-culottes, to whom their comrades cried
out to follow us on horseback: "*Take a horse*," said they, "*the
nation pays for all.*"

I had four citizens in my carriage, without reckoning those
who were on the coach-box, and on the roof: I spoke to them
with frankness and warmth upon several subjects; they did not
refuse to listen to me, but how could my knowledge of these
matters be equal to that of citizens who were sent down expressly
from Paris to introduce the real system of politics into Bordeaux
and who, as if by magic, had rendered the greater part of the
porters and messengers of that town so powerful, that they
arrested the rich inhabitants, and so independent, that they
travelled by post?

At our first pause, in order to take supper, I could not restrain
my indignation: the Spaniard and I were not bound; but
Duchâtel was, and strange hands performed the functions of his
own, which were tightly confined with handcuffs. An innocent
man, a representative of the people,—any man in such a state
thus insulted and abused, made the blood boil in my veins. I
read in his eyes, the most expressive I have ever seen, all that
passed within his soul; I was seeking in his looks a signal for
resistance, which would infallibly have caused the three to be
massacred. A bitter smile played upon his lips, and despair
was in his heart. While expressing myself forcibly against the
indignity with which he was treated, I seized, without perceiving
it, a bottle, in the attitude of a person who intended to throw
it. Nothing more was necessary: three gendarmes immediately
seized me, as if by an insensible manœuvre. In about a quarter
of an hour I was tied hand and foot, like my unhappy companion of misfortune, and continued so during the remainder of
our journey to Paris. The leader of the escort that accompanied
us was a complete Jacobin in his appearance, with curly black
hair, a bilious complexion, and hanging jaw, an enormous belly,
and the mysterious air of a satellite of Lenoir or Sartines.
Liberty had not given him an exalted idea of the dignity of
man, or he would not thus have outraged us. It is probable,

also, that he had never studied the principles of tolerance in
Voltaire; he had always in his mouth the words *Montagne,
Sans-culottes*, or *Jacobins*, just as a parish beadle uses the words
*Lutheran, Pope*, and *assembly of the faithful;* it seemed that these
words were all he knew respecting the revolution. His costume
was in perfect accordance with his character: he wore the
mustachios, the large sabre, the pistols at his girdle, the new
pantaloons, and all the insignia and medals of his order, and I
dare say all his civic cards and certificates were perfectly *en
régle*. It was by his order that I was bound, and I testified
my resentment by a volley of sarcasms. "Monseigneur le Jacobin,"
said I to him, "you who are crowned with a red bonnet, in
virtue of what article of the rights of man do you load a French
citizen with irons?" He answered, in a serious tone, that there
were no longer any monseigneurs. He was enchanted to see that
I was an anti-jacobin. This discovery entirely freed him from
any species of remorse; and this was the only fruit I reaped
from my harangue. He turned his attention towards the prey
which principally occupied his thoughts, namely, the representative.
It is by such Vandals that France has been overflowed with
blood for upwards of a whole year. Upon our arrival at La
Réole, he locked me up alone in a dungeon, under pretence of
my having mutinied. I had a fresh altercation with him upon
our passing the Garonne, and was strongly tempted, while crossing it, to go to the bottom of the river to seek for truth, in
company with a rascal of a Biscayan, who discussed most warmly
the subject of the rights of man with me, whom he held
chained.

When I was left in these subterranean vaults and the enormous bolts were drawn upon me, with a noise before unknown
to my ears; when I found myself alone, sequestered from all
nature, and deprived of the cheering light of day, I paid the
common tribute which we all owe to humanity. I remembered
all the objects of my affections, and I wept. These were the
only tears I shed during my long course of adversity. I bade
a last adieu to all that my heart held dear; and since that
moment my eyes have remained tearless. There are certain
tender chords in the heart which cannot be touched without a
painful vibration. I endeavoured to escape from the feelings

which I could not subdue; and I considered myself, during my confinement, as a man already doomed to certain death. The subaltern agents had disappeared, and a degree of good treatment, and even of humanity, was again shown me. In two days after our arrival, the Spaniard and I were removed to a house of Benedictines, which was used as a barrack, and were there confined in separate chambers. Through the bars of the window of my apartment I enjoyed the view of an immense valley watered by the Garonne. I again beheld trees, fields, and the magnificent spectacle of nature, and enjoyed them with all my heart, as a view which I was about to lose for ever. The guards, and appearance of everything around us, belonged exclusively to the military. Upon our examination a few days before, we had passed through a file of soldiers, who guarded a narrow, long, and dark passage, by which we reached a badly lighted chamber, in which the representatives were seated. I was asked but few questions at this time, and those with a sort of kindness, which however seemed to me forced, and with the true tone of an intendant naturally polite, but already grown old in the exercise of despotic power. The general of the revolutionary army had come for me, accompanied by a few soldiers, to conduct me to the club, which was held in the room under mine;—he appeared to me on that day to perform precisely the same office that I have since seen executed by the under turnkeys at the Conciergerie. During my imprisonment I used sometimes to see, at a distance through the trees, the representatives of the people riding about, followed by the revolutionary general and his aides-de-camp. I was not sorry to see the sword thus give precedence to the toga; but I could not help comparing this state of power with the dogmas of *sans-culotterie*.

We were at length sent to Paris, under the guard of two gendarmes, who made a speculation of us, and famished us during our journey. Duchâtel was with one gendarme in the first carriage, and the Spaniard and I with the other gendarme in the second. In consequence of their cupidity, we performed the journey without once getting out of the carriages, or taking any rest, and were forced to remain for a hundred and forty-nine hours seated in the back of a very inconvenient cabriolet. Upon stopping at the relays, we succeeded in having our carriages placed fronting one another, so that we were able to see each other, which gave us some consolation. Duchâtel even made some jokes upon the fate which awaited him.

While we were changing horses at one post-house, Duchâtel learned that one of his colleagues was in the inn. He requested to see him; but the only answer was, "I have not time, I am at dinner." I shall not endeavour to recall to my recollection the name of this individual: it was to his unfortunate, suffering, and fettered colleague, that he made this unfeeling reply. He may probably be one of those who have usurped the sovereignty of the nation, but he was certainly not a man worthy of his post.

I owe a short digression upon the conduct of one of the gen-darmes, for the instruction of those who so carelessly confide the existence of their fellow-citizens to the hands of mercenary agents. It will be seen how nearly allied is the abuse of authority to the right of exercising it, and how great should be the wisdom and the skill of the rulers of a nation whose particular failing is ostentation, and a wish to appear beyond its sphere.

This gendarme had originally been a cook at Agen, and was anxious to show himself in all his splendour in the place where he had once acted in so inferior a situation. He made us go a round of forty leagues expressly to gratify his vanity, that all Agen might behold him disposing of the revenues of the state, and leading citizens in chains. This man was really one of the most vaunting and malicious wretches I have ever seen. He had one of those broad flat foreheads, upon which are engraven, in conspicuous characters, the word *impudence*. He never failed, at any of the military posts, to call out the national guard, who advanced their heads into our carriages, and pryed into them with as much mystery and precaution as if Pitt and Cobourg at least were inside. If a free government could consistently admit of gendarmes, they should at least be organized expressly for it. I have seen the roads covered with women, with iron collars round their necks; men chained three by three; and others running along tied to the tail of a horse; and all for having been *brissotines*, *rolandines*, or *modérés*. Humanity has been more degraded in France during one year (l'an 2 of the republic), than it has been in Turkey for a hundred years. My only reason for dwelling upon these matters is to show the necessity of inciting in the people a respect for themselves, and for the dignity of man.

It was upon our arrival at Agen, in the very inn in which he was formerly a servant, that our gentleman particularly endeavoured to attract the general notice. He went and came, and visited the carriage every moment, and without the smallest necessity; he made signs to the citizens, and appeared as triumphant as if he had brought a dozen Austrians, made prisoners with his own hand. He left us for three hours exposed to the burning heat of the sun, and to insults of every description. I became the principal object of their attack, because my eyes were lighted up with indignation; and my features must doubtlessly have assumed that sinister expression which lurked in the looks of the clubists who visited us, with their badges at their button-holes, the sacred cap on their heads, and imprecations in their mouths.

The illustrious cook at length put the finishing stroke to his glory. He opened a passage for himself through the crowd, crying, *take care*, and made his appearance with two farriers. He then, in the presence of all Agen, ordered them, in a commanding voice, to rivet on the legs of the Spaniard and myself a bar-shot of eighty pounds' weight. These two balls were ostentatiously produced, and first exhibited to the people. Our hands being tied, and our bodies bound with a triple rope, did not appear to him sufficient precautions: we were loaded during the remainder of our journey with this weight of iron, which was so heavy, that, had the carriage fallen on one side, we should inevitably have had a leg broken. They were so extraordinary and uncommon, that they astonished, at the Conciergerie in Paris, some of the turnkeys who had been in office for nineteen years. It was to the vanity of the illustrious cook that the Spaniard and I were indebted for this treatment. Nothing could be added to the barbarity of that which the representative of the people had experienced since the commencement of the journey. How often did I not beg pardon of the Spaniard, in the name of the French nation, for the indignities which were heaped upon him!

We arrived at Paris on the 16th of October (old style). Here a new scene begins to open. Behold us three cast into that abyss of the living, into the *Conciergerie* of Paris, still dyed with the blood of the victims of the 2nd of September, and in which the revolutionary tribunal, by its conduct, exceeded all former instances of ferocity and crime. We were carried to all the prisons of Paris, one after another, from the *Luxembourg* to *La Force*, and from *La Force* to the prison of *L'Abbaye*, and from thence to the Conciergerie, where we were at length received. Upon our arrival we were carried into the first ward-room, and a blacksmith was sent for to unrivet my irons, and those of the Spaniard. Those of Duchâtel were fastened with screws. I was first put into an arm-chair; but this posture not appearing convenient to the workman, I was stretched on the ground, where I lay like an animal offered for sale,* and exposed to their insulting ridicule. The operation being finished, I endeavoured to rise; but not being aware of the exhaustion of my strength by my long journey (I had remained, as I have already mentioned, a hundred and forty-nine hours in the carriage, without a moment's change), I could not support my steps. No hand was held out to assist me. I was pushed about from one to another like a drunken man who is made the sport of the mob. This treatment drove me to despair: I cursed the human race, and fell flat upon the earth. Yes, my mind must be strong, since it has not sunk under such trials. Oh, dignity of man, first basis of liberty, when wilt thou be respected! I was soon separated from my companions, and plunged, under the pretence of secrecy, into the most loathsome dungeon in the prison. I there found some robbers and an assassin, who thought himself a considerable gainer in prolonging his miserable existence in such a den by means of an appeal to the Court of Cassation, which was not attended with success. In the evening three gigantic turnkeys, followed by enormous dogs, came to visit us. My wretched companions hastened to meet them; they were, in fact, the only beings through whom they kept up any communication with the world. It was by the flame of their torches, which shed a light through this cavern, into which that of the sun had never penetrated, that I was able to see, both by what sort of men I was surrounded, and the nature of the habitation which had fallen to my lot. It

---

* This alludes to the practice in France of tying the legs of the calves, and laying them for sale upon the ground.—*Translator.*

was at the utmost not more than twelve feet square. My
companions were to the number of three. One of them, who
was condemned to death for murder, was an old robber of
fifty years of age, named Pantin, quite mutilated and disfigured
by crime, lame, and blind of an eye, with his face all scarred
and covered with hanging wrinkles. He had powerful arms,
and shoulders of an extraordinary breadth. The seal of homicide
was stamped upon his person from head to foot. His voice
was hoarse and frightful.

The second was a money-broker, a fabricator of forged assignats; a degraded being, who had not even the spirit which often
remains in the mind of a robber. His entire appearance was
false and crafty. He seemed more formed for the base office
of a spy than for robbery. He pretended to have no money,
in order that he might live at the expense of others. What he
had he spent alone, and ate the product in secret. His mean
and hypocritical supplications, his begging habits, and his selfish-
ness, were enough to rank him, if possible, as much beneath
the murderer himself, as Barrière is beneath Robespierre. His
other comrades saw his meanness, and treated him contemptu-
ously: they reproached him for his want of good-fellowship, and
often endeavoured to teach him by force of blows. When Pantin,
so celebrated for his long sufferings, and his labours more numerous than those of Hercules, said to him, in his hoarse but
powerful voice, "You are not fit to live with honest fellows,"
he made no reply; and if Pantin's lessons became a little too
warm, he only wept, and called for mercy. I here forcibly
learnt that cowardice and avarice are the basest, the most hateful
of vices; and I took such an aversion to this wretch, that I was
ready at every moment to join the others against him. The
union of the cavern, the services of fraternity, and a certain
air of independence, maintained, in the heart of Pantin, and
of some of his class whom I have seen, some of the characters
of its primitive essence. This wretched publican, this false
coiner, who would also have robbed on the high road, had
he had the courage to do so, had none of these qualities, and
appeared formed of the vilest materials. He would even have
robbed his companions, but for Pantin; who, as the depository
of the grand code of laws to be observed among thieves, said,

that it was not allowed to *work* in prison. Zeno dictated his precepts with less austerity.

The third was a young man, whom libertinism had led on to crime, in which he now seemed to find an irresistible charm. He was not entirely deficient in education. He had been, when very young, the secretary of Diétrich, who, for being too virtuous, had perished on the same scaffold to which this young man was led, a short time after, to suffer for his crimes. The prison had often been his dwelling: he was incarcerated, on this occasion, for forging assignats, and this time was the last. He was a second Pylades. The name of one of his friends, who had been arrested as his accomplice, was incessantly in his mouth. He spoke of nothing but the happiness of sacrificing his own life for his. This friend, on his part, provided carefully for all his wants. The same scaffold saw them both perish.

Such were the individuals whom I discovered around me, and with whom I had been associated, because I was suspected of being a *brissotine*. They were clothed in rags, and their professions were written in their features. The turnkeys treated them with a degree of kindness, but with an air of protecting superiority. As for my part, I remained in silence, stretched upon my filthy dunghill. A turnkey shook my leg with one hand, and then let it fall, and with the other passed a candle backwards and forwards before my face. I have since learned that such was the manner of their making themselves acquainted with a new-comer. I said, " If your office gives you a right to treat me with this indignity, you are right to do so," and then turned my back upon him. During the thirteen days that I remained in this dungeon, I did not again open my lips to them a single time.

During all this time, in which I have had occasion to see several robbers, I scarcely ever knew one of them feel any other remorse than that of having let himself be taken. I learned from their own lips several of their exploits, which were often rendered bloody by assassination; and it was always with bursts of laughter that they related them. I there learned, what would scarcely be believed, if we had not since seen it proved before a jury of the revolutionary tribunal, that one of their comrades, who was executed at the age of twenty-two years, had already assassinated sixty-three persons. I ascertained, from their conversations, while I feigned to sleep, that they were connected with all the robbers in Paris; among the rest, with those of the garde-meuble, and that, if the law had not overtaken them, they would have committed new murders, which they meditated even while in irons. As for the young man, he was truly black with crimes, and had committed murder, but without being discovered. Their gang was principally recruited by money-brokers and sharpers; they were constantly sighing after a life of activity, and I have often heard them envy the fortune of some of their comrades, whose names they mentioned, who lived retired in the country upon the fruit of their undiscovered crimes. These men generally take up their residence in the villages near Paris; they keep up a regular correspondence, and will often go sixty or a hundred leagues upon an expedition. The corruption of their morals is beyond conception, and a contempt for the laws of social order has been preceded in their minds by a contempt for the laws of nature. Speaking without prejudice, they are certainly most dreadful wretches. Incest and atheism are words which they pretend have no real meaning.

One of their stratagems is, to enrol among their ranks a number of young lads, of an agreeable countenance, and these Ganymedes, the children of Mercury, opened to them, at night, the doors of the man whose depraved inclinations were not proof against the beauty of a beardless face. They were almost all partial to an aristocratic government, but the cause of this preference was entirely in reference to their own pursuits, and the reason of it was, that in the new state of things, they were tried by juries whom they found it difficult to deceive. I could not refrain from laughing upon seeing them strike their foreheads in a passion, and exclaim, with an oath, *If they had been able men, we should have got out of the thing*. They had a perfect knowledge of the laws which concerned them, and particularly of their ambiguities. But the sense and reason of a jury were not dazzled by the false lights of chicanery, in which they were more skilled than many of the lawyers. They were particularly attached to the old bar, under which they had fought their first battles, and to the old Parliamentary perruques, whom they had more than once defeated. Pantin always spoke in the highest terms of the old magistracy.

The cunning of these men was surprising. There were few among them who had not escaped several times from prison. They themselves told me, that in 1791 and 1792, they found means of forging charity tickets, and even assignats, in their very dungeons, and afterwards putting them in circulation. They made use of a nail, or of the tongue of a buckle, to engrave the plates, and, in order to procure a light, they pressed the oil out of their salad, and unravelled the cotton of their shirts, which they wove into wick. They informed me that their wives managed to get these forgeries out of the prison as they were made, and to sell them to the amount of a hundred francs' worth a day: in fact, these men appeared to me to be, to their fellow-creatures, what the wolf is to domestic animals: they entertained the greatest contempt for the *révolutionnaires*, the name which they gave to those who were arrested for political causes, and looked upon them as men without cunning, without invention, without courage, and only likely to cause the failure of any enterprise.

Notwithstanding their politeness, and even their friendship towards me,—notwithstanding their entire confidence, I was overwhelmed with melancholy, in the midst of these robbers. I could find no connection between my pretended *girondisme* and their crimes. Deprived of light—the air charged with a most loathsome smell—covered with filth—confined in a hole only twelve feet square, in which seven of us were often heaped together, and those the very refuse of mankind—my wretched situation may be easily conceived. I was regularly informed by the new-comers of what was passing at the *Bicêtre*, and at the great and the little *Force*, and of all the petty robberies that took place; but I was in complete ignorance of what was going on in the rest of the world. I was kept in the most rigorous confinement, without any news of my companions in misfortune, and without even being examined. I had at first recourse to my imagination, but it no longer worked up any flattering ideas; I endeavoured to call to my recollection the enchanting beauties of nature, and to embellish my reveries with the charm of her pictures, but she was deaf to my voice. Despair took entire possession of my soul; I almost entirely abstained from taking any nourishment, not that I had made up my mind to die, but because I found, in the coolness of my blood, a patience and a resignation which I could not have drawn from all the lessons of Seneca or of Epictetus himself. If I did not court death, I at least acquired its immobility; I remained without feeling any pain for forty-eight hours, lying on the same side: on the contrary, when I ate, as was the case on the day I regaled my companion Pantin, my blood resumed all its activity; I was again seized with rage, and suffered the torments of hell. An excessive abstinence reduced me into a sort of torpid state, which was not without its advantages: I felt myself approaching towards the grave by the easy road of sleep and stupefaction, I advanced like an indolent traveller, and knew that it depended upon myself to arrive at the end of my journey when I pleased.

About eleven o'clock one morning the bolts resounded, the four or five doors which it was necessary to open in order to reach our dungeon, creaked upon their hinges, and were thrown open with a loud noise; the door of our cell was opened, and Lebeau, the keeper of the prison, made his appearance. He came in person to lead me to be examined. One of his children, who had come along with him, drew back at the sight of our dungeon, and exclaimed, with the simplicity of his age, " *Oh papa, what a horrid place a dungeon is!* Lebeau himself, a good and tender-hearted man, kept at some distance, and turned aside his head, less to avoid breathing the pestilential air which issued from it, than to avoid beholding so deplorable a sight. Pale and exhausted, with a long and filthy beard, and my clothes covered with the chopped straw which had composed my bed for thirteen days, I departed for the examination-hall. I sustained a long interrogatory, and was not treated with the indulgence that was due to the state in which I was. I did not return any more to my cavern, and I am happy to inform my readers that, in a few months afterwards, Fouquier-Tinville caused all the robbers and murderers to be removed from the Conciergerie, and had that prison reserved exclusively for the honourable, the talented, and the enlightened. My dungeon was suppressed, as being too unwholesome.

I was confined in another part of the Conciergerie. I quitted the den of crime more lightly chained, and entered the temple of persecuted virtue.* Vergniaux, Gensonné, Brissot, Ducos, Fonfréde, Valazé, Duchâtel, and their colleagues, were the inmates whom I found installed in my new dwelling. During the whole year that I inhabited that prison, I never ceased to behold the shades of these great men hovering over my head, and reanimating my courage. A sentiment of admiration soon gave way to that of gratitude. I learned that it was to the solicitations of Ducos that I was indebted for my release from the dungeon,—that is to say, for my life, a burdensome present, it is true, in those disastrous times, for which, however, it was most grateful to me to be indebted to that amiable and interesting young man! He had met me once before in the world, and he then received me like a brother.

Curiosity will be awakened at the mention of these celebrated names, but I have but little means of satisfying it; I arrived among them two days before their condemnation, and as if to be a witness of their death. France and all Europe are acquainted with the particulars of their trial, if that name can be given to the most atrocious proscription; it was all through a most solemn violation of every right, even of that of defending themselves. †

All these powerful champions, who united among themselves alone almost all the eloquence of the nation, were dragged into the arena; chained down in every limb, restrained from making use of their strength. Vergniaux alone let one spark of his talent escape with that flexibility of organ which forces its way to every heart; all eyes wept, tyranny grew pale, and forced from the tribunal the decree which sealed the glory of the proscribed and the infamy of the proscribers.

They were all calm and unostentatious, and not one of them allowed himself to be deceived with hope. Their souls were elevated to such a height, that it was impossible to address to them the commonplace expression of ordinary consolation.— Brissot, § serious and thoughtful, had the air of a sage contending

* Riouffe occupied No. 13 in his new dwelling; we have placed at the end of the work a short fragment, in which he gives a sketch of what occurred there.—*See Note* E.

† Upon his sentence being pronounced, Lasource cited to his judges this saying of one of the ancients:—"I die at a moment when the people have lost their reason; you will die the day they shall have recovered it."

§ See his letter to Barrière, Note F.

with misfortune; and if any uneasiness was, at intervals, painted in his countenance, it was easy to see that his country alone was the object of it. Gensonné, collected within himself, seemed to dread the idea of soiling his mouth by pronouncing the names of his murderers; not a word escaped him respecting his own situation; his only thoughts were for the happiness of the people. Vergniaux at one moment grave, and the next less serious, cited for us a number of humorous verses with which his memory was adorned, and sometimes gave us the enjoyment of listening to the last accents of that sublime eloquence which was already lost to the universe, since the barbarians had prevented him from speaking. There was a certain divine expression in the eyes of Valazé; a calm smile of serenity hovered over his lips; he indeed appeared to taste the sweets of his glorious death. I could not help saying to him, " Valazé, how happy you are at the idea of so glorious a death, and how grieved you would be, had they not condemned you!" On the final day, before he departed for the tribunal, he turned back to give me a pair of scissors which he had about him, and said, "It is a dangerous weapon; they fear lest we should make an attempt upon ourselves." The irony, worthy of Socrates, with which he pronounced these words, produced on me an effect which I could not then account for; but when I learned that this modern Cato had stabbed himself with a poniard, which he had concealed under his cloak, I was not surprised, and imagined I had foreseen it; he had concealed this poniard from their researches, for the persons of all were examined like the meanest criminal, before ascending the scaffold. Vergniaux threw away some poison which he had preserved, and preferred to die along with his colleagues.

The two brothers, Fonfréde and Ducos, formed a detached group in this gloomy picture, as if to inspire a more lively and a more tender interest. Their youth, their friendship, the gaiety of Ducos, unclouded even in his last moments, the graces both of his mind and figure, increased the detestation of the crowd at the fury of their enemies. Ducos had sacrificed himself for his brother, and had surrendered himself to partake his fate. They frequently embraced each other, and seemed to acquire fresh strength in their caresses. They were about to leave all

that can render life dear, an immense fortune, and beloved
wives and children, and yet they did not cast their looks
backwards, but kept them firmly fixed on their country and on
liberty.

Once only, Fonfréde took me aside, apart from his brother,
and indulged in a torrent of tears at the recollection of those
names,—which almost break the most stoical hearts, the names
of his wife and of his children.  His brother perceived him:
" *What ails you?*" said he to him.... Fonfréde, ashamed at
being seen weeping, checked his tears: "*It's nothing; it is he
who speaks to me.*" .... He thus threw upon me the blame of
what he believed a shameful weakness.  They once more
embraced, and resumed all their strength.  Fonfréde dried up
his flowing tears; his brother restrained his, which were ready
to flow; and they both, once more, became true Romans.  This
scene passed about twenty-four hours before their execution.

They were condemned to death on the night of the 30th of
October (old style), at about eleven o'clock.  They all received
the same sentence; we had in vain hoped that Fonfréde and
Ducos might be saved, and they themselves probably entertained
some hopes.  They did not forget to give us the signal which
they had promised.  This was a patriotic song which they
simultaneously broke out into, and all their voices were mingled
in a last hymn to liberty; they parodied the song of the
Marseillais:—

> "Contre nous de la tyrannie
> Le couteau sanglant est levé," etc.

All this dreadful night resounded with their songs, which they
only interrupted to speak of their country, and to listen to an
occasional sally of Ducos's.

At the side of the Conciergerie, to which I was now removed,
was the prison of the women, separated from that of the men
by an iron grating.  The men communicated with them through
this barrier, and through the two windows of the ground-floor,
which opened upon the court of their prison.  It was there that
I saw an innumerable crowd of victims, of all ages and conditions,
heaped up together.  The blood of the 22nd was still smoking,
when the wife of Roland arrived.  She maintained the most perfect
calmness, though well aware of the fate which awaited her.

Without being in the flower of age, she was still full of charms, extremely tall, and of an elegant figure, with a most intelligent countenance; but her sufferings and long confinement had left traces of melancholy upon her features, and had cooled down her natural vivacity.

The day on which she was condemned, she had dressed herself in white, and with unusual care. Her long black tresses fell down in folds as far as her waist. She would have softened the most ferocious heart, but these monsters had none. Besides, she made no efforts to do so; she had merely chosen this dress as a symbol of the purity of her soul. After her condemnation, she crossed back into the ward-room with the quick step of a satisfied mind, and made us a sign that she was condemned to death. Being joined in the same sentence with a man whose courage was not equal to hers she succeeded in inspiring him with firmness, by such charming and unaffected gaiety, that she frequently forced us, melancholy as we were, to smile.

Upon arriving at the public square, where she was to undergo her sentence, she saluted the statue of liberty, and pronounced these memorable words, *Oh liberty! how many crimes are committed in thy name!*

A short time after the death of the charming and unfortunate wife of Roland, I pressed in my arms Girey-Dupré and Boisguyon, who had just arrived from Bordeaux, bruised and lacerated by their irons. I shall not speak here of the courage of Gornay; I will only say, that he died without bestowing a thought upon his fate.*

About the same time the doors of the prison closed upon Bailly, the creature of the revolution, who had been the most loaded with honours, but was now doomed to suffer the most cruel torments. He underwent all the fury of the populace, of which he had been the idol, and was shamefully deserted by the people who had never ceased to esteem him. He died, like that just man, Plato, or like our Saviour, in the midst of ignominy. They spat upon him; they burned a flag under his face; several wretches gave him furious blows, in spite of the executioners, who were themselves indignant at this inhuman treatment. He was literally covered with mud, and was kept in

* *Vide* Appendix, Note G.

tortures for three hours, while his scaffold was erected amidst a heap of dirt and filth. To add to the horror of his situation, a chill rain fell in torrents; and his hands tied behind his back, he was compelled to bear the taunts and outrages of the multitude: he occasionally begged for the close of his sufferings; but his request was uttered with the calmness of a philosopher. To a man who addressed him, ".You tremble, Bailly!" he replied, "It is with cold, my friend."

Another personage, whose name has not been made known, although it belongs to history at least as much as those of the deputies whom I have mentioned, was L'Admiral. I know not under what colours this man's character has been painted. The following are the particulars of my knowledge respecting him, the truth of which I can certify.

Upon his arrival at the Conciergerie, preceded by the report of the attempt he had made upon Collot d'Herbois, the turnkeys rushed upon him, as they would have done upon Damiens or Ravaillac. Was it not, in fact, against one of the kings of the Committee of Public Safety, that the attempt had been made? They overwhelmed him with reproaches and questions. Firm and unshaken in the midst of their abuse and insults, he replied:— "Though I should tell you the motives which have induced me to execute such a design, you would not understand me."

They placed in the dungeon with him a prisoner who had been sentenced to the galleys for robbery, and was respited, on condition of performing the meanest offices in the prison. He was placed with L'Admiral as a *mouton*, that is to say, as a spy; but he could draw nothing out of him, except that he had wished to serve his country.

These facts have been related to me by a woman, who, though a Robespierrist, was put on her trial, and sentenced along with him, for having purchased some furniture from him, about four months before. There was no other relation, no other connection whatsoever, between them. However accustomed we may be to these unexampled traits of barbarity, we still cannot help feeling astonished at them.*

* The following fact is equally characteristic of the times, and will serve to prove that Robespierre's example did not want imitators. It refers to a young man who was arrested at Brive, by the orders of one Desprez, a furious Jacobin.

The trial of the girl Renaud, who accompanied him to the scaffold, was no less horrible and atrocious. This young girl, who seemed to have a degree of disorder in her ideas, had not the smallest intention of killing Robespierre: she had no offensive weapon whatsoever on her person. Her opinions, it is true, were false; but what relation is there between opinions and the scaffold; yet she was arrested and plunged into prison. It would seem as if they endeavoured to invent new tortures, to prove to the tyrant how sacred were his days. Every one belonging to this unfortunate young girl was doomed to perish,—her father, her relations, her friends, her acquaintances; her brothers, who had shed their blood upon the frontiers, were brought to Paris, loaded with chains, expecting to lose its last drop on the scaffold, and, if they escaped, it was only because their assassins, being too eager for the destruction of their family, had not the patience to wait for their arrival. Sixty persons, whom Renaud had never seen, who were as innocent as herself, and the greater part of whom had been in confinement for six months, accompanied her to the scaffold, covered with red shirts as accomplices. The house, the entire street in which she lived, were directed to be razed to the ground. If we examine the conduct of that senate which disgusted Tiberius by its meanness, we shall find nothing in it marked with such ferocious adulation. This conduct of the government of that day and of the revolutionary tribunal, surpasses anything that Tacitus has related: as they gave the example of the greatest ferocity, so they gave that of the vilest servility.

Before the memorable twenty-second Prairial, many unfortunate individuals, while their examination was going on, had overheard their death-warrant drawing out in an adjoining room. Before that day, they always insulted, in the most barbarous manner,

---

For ten years back, says the author of this recital, he had not resided at Brive; upon the suppression of the Court of Aids, in which he was employed, he had attached himself to the person of a friend whom he met with in the neighbourhood of Tours. Being upon the point of marrying in that country with a rich and lovely woman, he came to Brive to make arrangements with his family, provided with a passport and regular certificates. Desprez having met him in the street: "Friend," said he, "be it known to you that your countenance displeases me, and that I will, in consequence, send you this very evening to prison, to keep company with your cousin Faurie:" which was accordingly executed.

the accused, whom they loaded with insult and every species of outrage, and left exposed to the ridicule of the mob. The modesty of the most virtuous and respectable women was called in question, and forced to blush at the disgusting insinuations of the debauched wretches, who were frequently inebriated while sitting on the bench. I have already mentioned, that there was a forger of assignats among these judges, but they were all of the same description; and, if we were to enter into an examination of this common sink, we should find it composed of men already marked by the hand of justice. Coffinhal and Dumas' were among the judges previous to that period, and they only waited for the signal of the law of the twenty-second to give vent to their fury.

The furious rage of these monsters was seconded from without. Never had a body of cannibals more zealous or more numerous providers. New victims were incessantly arriving. It seemed as if their blind fury was particularly directed against the weakest and most amiable. The loveliest, the youngest, and the most interesting females, were dragged in crowds into this receptacle of misery, whence they were led, by dozens, to inundate the scaffold. The depraved wretches, not contented with treating the sex with the grossest insult, continued to vow towards it the most implacable hatred. Young females, far advanced in pregnancy; others, who had just become mothers, who were still in that state of weakness and paleness attendant upon their situation; others, whose milk had stopped, either through fear, or because their children were torn from their breasts, were daily and nightly precipitated into this abyss. They were dragged from prison to prison, their hands loaded with irons. Some of them had collars round their necks. Some of them fainted on their entrance, and were carried in the arms of the turnkeys, who laughed at their terrors; others wept; and some were in a state of stupefaction, which deprived them of the use of their senses. Within the last month, particularly, the work of destruction went on with dreadful activity. The bolts were at work both night and day. Sixty persons arrived in the evening on their way to the scaffold, and were replaced on the following day by a hundred others, who met with the same fate.

Victims were thrown into the Conciergerie from all parts of

the country. It was filled incessantly by the crowds sent from
the departments, and was emptied as soon by the daily massacres, and the transfers to other prisons. The turnkeys, who
were charged with the announcement of the sentences, went
about in the middle of the night, from cell to cell, to execute
their office. Thus, the daily distribution of these death-warrants,
which were destined for sixty or eighty persons, filled with terror
the hearts of at least six hundred. The prisoners, when roused
from their sleep by the frightful and insulting exclamations of
these ruffians, expected to hear their own sentence. The regular
gradation which took place in the massacres taught me to appreciate fully all the depth of that line of Racine's —

> "Et laver dans le sang vos bras ensanglantés."

They began by heaping fifteen persons together in the fatal
cart. They soon put thirty, and at length went as far as eighty-
four: and the day that the death of Robespierre rescued the
human race from their fury, they had everything prepared for
sending a hundred and fifty persons together to the place of
execution. An immense aqueduct had already been dug in the
*Place St. Antoine*, for the purpose of carrying away the blood,
and, I tremble as I mention the dreadful fact.... the blood of
the unfortunate victims was spilled each day in buckets, and
four men were occupied, at the moment of execution, in emptying
them into this aqueduct.

It was about three o'clock in the afternoon that these long
processions of victims generally came down from the examination-
hall, and crossed, with slow steps, through the long vaults, in
the midst of the prisoners, who ranged themselves in a line to
see them pass. I have seen forty-five magistrates of the Parliament of Paris, and thirty-three of the Parliament of Toulouse,
walking forth to death with the same air with which they formerly followed in the public processions. I have seen thirty
farmers-general pass by with a calm and firm step; and five-
and-twenty of the first manufacturers of Sedan, who, while
marching to the scaffold, lamented over the thousands of labourers
whom they were going to leave without food. I have seen Beysser,
the terror of the rebels of La Vendée, and the numerous gener-
als whom victory had just crowned with laurels; yes, I have

absolutely seen these men led to the scaffold, like droves of
cattle to the slaughter-house.   Not a single complaint issued from
their mouths: they advanced in silence, and seemed to avoid
looking up towards heaven, lest their countenances should express
too much indignation.

These bodies of victims, to which they gave the name of
*batches*, were composed of men the most diametrically opposite
in principles and parties.   Thouret walked side by side with
d'Eprémenil; *   Chapellier with the ci-devant Duchess of
Grammont.   Entire generations have literally been swept away
in one day.   The venerable Malesherbes, † upwards of eighty
years, was dragged to the scaffold, at the head of his whole
family.   He perished together with his sister, his daughter, and
his son-in-law, and the daughter and son-in-law of his daughter.
Madame de Montmorin was accompanied by her son.   Four of
the Briennes suffered together.   In other *batches* all that was
lovely was united in a body.   Fourteen young girls of Verdun,
who appeared like virgins dressed out for a public fête, were
led out together to the scaffold.   They disappeared on a sudden,
and were mowed down in the spring of their youth.   The
women's court had the appearance, on the day after their death,
of a parterre stripped of all its flowers by a storm.   I have never
seen any occurrence which caused so much despair amongst us
as this unexampled barbarity.

* Chapellier said to d'Eprémenil, "Monsieur d'Eprémenil, they give us,
in our last moments, a terrible problem to solve."—"What is the problem?"
"That of ascertaining against which of us the shouts will be directed when we
shall be in the cart."—"Against us both," replied d'Eprémenil.

† This old man, who was respected by all Europe, received in his last moments the homage which is due to virtue.   It was not forgotten that the first
use he had made of his power, when minister, was to give liberty to a number
of citizens, and to lighten the sufferings of the unfortunate who were condemned
to imprisonment.   A citizen having perceived him in a distant corner at the
bottom of the infirmary, threw himself at his feet, with tears of commiseration
and respect.   "I have taken it into my head to turn wicked in my old days,
and to have myself put in prison," said the venerable Malesherbes, raising him
from the ground.   He retained his serenity, and even an air of gaiety.   Upon
reading his act of indictment, he said, "I wish it had even common-sense."

Upon descending the staircase, on his way to the tribunal, he made a false
step.   "That is an unlucky omen," said he; "a Roman would have returned
home."

Twenty women from Poictou, the greater part of whom were
peasant girls, were also butchered together. I still behold these
unhappy victims, lying in the court-yard of the Conciergerie,
overwhelmed with the fatigue of a long journey, and sleeping
on the .pavement. They were all executed a few days after
their arrival. At the moment of her mounting the scaffold, they
tore, from the breast of one of these unfortunate females, the
child she was suckling, and which was, at that very moment,
imbibing a nourishment of which the executioner was going to
destroy the source. Oh! her piercing cries of maternal despair
were dreadful. Several of the others died in the cart, on the
way to the scaffold, but their dead bodies were guillotined. A
few days before the 9th Thermidor, I saw other women dragged
forth to die, who had actually declared themselves pregnant! ...
And those who acted thus were men, were Frenchmen, to whom
the most eloquent philosophers have been preaching humanity
and tolerance for sixty years back .... If a stop had not been
put to this deluge of human blood, I· have no doubt that we
should soon have seen men voluntarily precipitate themselves
under the edge of the guillotine. As Fréron has observed, the
first of human feelings, the love of life, was already extinguishing
in every breast.* I have seen more than ten women, who,
not wishing to take poison, cried out *Vive le Roi*, and by that
means furnished this abominable tribunal with the sure means
of terminating their days; some of them not wishing to survive
a husband, others a lover, others from a disgust of life, but
scarcely one of them through royalist fanaticism. These unfortunate women were of the most indigent class; some of the lowest
description of prostitutes, but still rich with all the charms of
youth and beauty. Upon the passing of the law which forced
all the nobles to leave Paris in three days, I saw arrive, among

* The following is an instance of this disgust ·of life; it is extracted from a
work which we have already quoted :—

"A poor man, impatient that his turn had not arrived, wrote a letter to the
public accuser, dated as of *the second year of persecution*, in which he called
down curses on the tribunal, and demanded a king and the *ancien régime*. Upon
being summoned to a secret examination, he was asked if he recognised the
letter. "Yes," answered he; "it is I who wrote it; and the proof is, that here
is a copy of it," added he, drawing a paper from his pocket. The unfortunate
man was despatched on the following day.

several others, a young woman, who had not taken any food since she had heard of this law.  Born in opulence, she had with difficulty found, for a year back, in the work of her hands, the means of providing for her existence: this law deprived her of every resource: she had now no consolation but death, which she came to demand, by denouncing herself.  Her extreme paleness, caused by her sorrows and her want of food, did not deface the traces of virtue, youth, and beauty, from her countenance. Her misfortunes were not yet at their height: she had still to learn that an adored husband, whose fate she was ignorant of, had perished on the scaffold a few days before.  On reading her act of accusation, she learned that she was a widow . . . . The poor sufferer soon rejoined her husband in a better world!

If in the midst of so many desolating scenes some particular misfortunes inflicted poignant wounds on the heart of the sufferers, so, in the midst of the general courage, some particular actions shone with a bright refulgence.  This epoch, which affords examples of every crime, offers also proofs of the sublimest virtue.  Several young waiting-maids chose to die along with their mistresses; and, while treachery and espionage were striking a mortal blow at the root of the public morals, these females perished by their noble devotion.  A nun refused to save her life at the expense of a trifling falsehood.  The ci-devant Marchioness of Bois Bérenger, and her sister the Countess of Malézy, conducted themselves with all that heroism which is so admirably described in the *Almanach des Prisons*, article *Luxembourg*.  All these women were very young, and of the most interesting appearance.

The ci-devant Marchioness of Bois Bérenger never left her mother for a moment, but watched and tended her with such anxious care, that one would have said that the maternal feeling had passed into the heart of the daughter. *

* The following affecting trait of filial piety is equal to any we have met with:—" A young girl, upon her unfortunate father's being ordered to the Conciergerie, travelled two hundred leagues on foot to follow him.  She accompanied the cart in which he was tied along with his companions.  The unhappy girl went into each town to prepare his food, and to beg a covering, or at least a little straw for her father to repose on in the different prisons at which he stopped.  She did not quit him for a moment, until the prison of the Conciergerie separated her for ever from her wretched parent.  Habituated to the art of

The Countess Malézy said to her father, "I will cling so close to you, my father, and you are so good a man, that the Almighty will let me pass with you, notwithstanding my sins." This lady was one of the most interesting creatures I ever beheld.

All these ruined families, happy at dying together, became closely united in every thought, persuaded that they would again meet each other, and that this passage from a world in which they were persecuted, to another, where they would be happy, was a desirable change; that to die was to close their eyes, in order to open them shortly again to eternal light, and that they would at length find true equality in an asylum of peace, where titles were unheeded, and no longer the excuse for murder and persecution. But how stormy and terrible was their passage before arriving at this wished-for harbour!

moving gaolers, she endeavoured to excite the pity of the murderers of Paris. She watched every morning for three months at the doors of the elder members of the Committee of Public Safety. For three months she obtained nothing but perfidious promises, insulting refusals, and even menaces. Her father at length appeared before the judges. The execrable Dumas prevented this unfortunate man from proving that he was taken for another person. The daughter endeavoured to make the cries of nature be heard: she was dragged away with violence. This heart-rending sight the father witnessed; and he went to the scaffold with the dreadful thought that his daughter was now left destitute in the world, a prey to despair and to all the horrors of indigence.—*Note of the Editors.*

# HISTORICAL SKETCH

OF THE

# PRISON OF SAINT LAZARE

FROM ITS OPENING UNTIL THE 9th THERMIDOR

(27th July, 1794)

WHEN ROBESPIERRE WAS EXECUTED

Containing Anecdotes of each of the Members of the Revolutionary
Committee of the Bonnet Rouge (Red Cap), and of
the Prison of the Rue de Sèvres

By * * *, PRISONER IN BOTH PLACES

# HISTORICAL SKETCH

*etc., etc.*

O~N~ the 26th of October, 1793 (O. S.), about eight o'clock in the morning, I beheld two men, whom I had never seen, enter my house. By their ferocious looks, and the clubs which they carried, I suspected they were messengers of a revolutionary committee; and the result proved that my suspicions were correct.

One of them was agent of the revolutionary Committee of the Bonnet Rouge (Red Cap), * and the other † of the Contrat Social (Social Contract). They requested me to follow them to the Committee of the Contrat Social, where my presence was required. I obeyed; but, upon arrival at the committee-room, no one was there; and the same men ordered me to follow them to the Committee of the Bonnet Rouge. I concluded, from that moment, that I was going to be put under arrest; yet I confess it did not give me any uneasiness at the time. My conductors addressed several questions to me upon the road, all equally insignificant.

We arrived at the place where the last-mentioned committee was held, when I was placed under the guard of an armed force; and, half an hour afterwards, I was withdrawn, and led back to the Contrat Social, without having been seen or interrogated by any one. I was not more fortunate here than before; for the same individuals, who had left me in the ante-room of the committee, came back for me, to conduct me to my own house; and there they declared that they had come to arrest me, and put the seals upon my papers.

In vain I inquired the cause of my arrest: brutal abuse was the only reply I received; and the tears of my wife seemed still further to irritate the monsters.

The placing of the seals became a matter of great difficulty

---

* Rénaud, a cobbler.　　　　　　† Potat, also a cobbler.

for them, as it was necessary to draw out a procès-verbal upon the occasion; and they could neither of them write, or at least could not do more than sign their names.

They called to their aid a man as ferocious as themselves, the registrar of the justice of peace of the Contrat Social, a man of the name of *Robert*.

The latter, struck by the neatness of my furniture, imagined I was rich, and spoke of appointing two guardians of the seals. His design was just on the point of being accomplished, when I obtained permission, by giving a candid statement of my circumstances, that the guard should be confided to my cook.

When the affair was ended, they tore me from the arms of my wife, and I was conducted back again to the Contrat Social, and thence to the Bonnet Rouge, remaining at each place in the ante-rooms of the committees.

I here waited patiently, in the hope that the committee would examine me as to my offences, and would acquaint me with the motives of my arrest, by the procès-verbal, which I thought it their duty to prepare of the circumstances; but my expectation was illusive; for, an hour afterwards, a man of the name of Lebrun, whom I knew from his having been discharged from the situation of adjutant of the battalion of the Bonnet Rouge, decided on my fate, by ordering me to be carried to the barracks of the Rue de Sèvres, until further orders.

On my arrival at this place, I was presented to two men, who, I was told, were commissaries of the Committee of the Bonnet Rouge.* They took down my name, and commanded me to go and join the other rascals who were in the same establishment, and to lodge myself in it as I could.

With a drooping heart I ascended a staircase, without well knowing whither I was going. I confess that I formed a very unfavourable opinion of the individuals confined in this place, from the account the commissaries had given me of them; but I was agreeably undeceived, for, upon my companions in misfortune coming forward and offering me the hands of friendship, I recognised several amongst them who had long formed the

---

* "Vernay, coachman of *Monsieur*, the eldest brother of Louis XVI., and Baillère, the coachman of a Swiss officer." Such is the note which the manuscript of that period bears, and which we cite on account of its singularity.

delight of my company, by their virtues and the purity of their patriotism; and, in a few days, I became upon terms of the greatest intimacy with the others.

A respectable old man, who occupied a chamber with two other unfortunate beings, came, without having been acquainted with me, and made me an offer of a share of their asylum. I gratefully accepted his generous offer; and I owe it to the memory of this worthy man to state, that during three months, that we were together, he constituted the greatest comfort of my life, as much by the mildness of his character, as by his agreeable conversation and profound wisdom. My other chamber companions likewise bestowed the kindest attentions upon me, and we lived like four brothers.

The regulations of my new abode were very severe. Two commissaries of the revolutionary committee of the Bonnet Rouge, who were relieved every four-and-twenty hours, were appointed to superintend us; and sixteen armed men, under their orders, composed our guard.

The Revolutionary Committee of the Bonnet Rouge, who were more greedy for money than anxious for the welfare of the republic, had speculated in arrests. They had formed a prison out of the barracks of the former French guards, situated in the Rue de Sèvres; and, though it was pronounced by members of the faculty to be most unhealthy, yet, notwithstanding that, the committee crammed into it, during the space of four months, from 120 to 140 persons.

The prisoners were put under contribution for the expenses of the guard, in a most arbitrary manner, and almost all of them were obliged to pay from twelve francs, down to twenty sous each; the total daily sum amounted to three hundred francs, and this sum was received every month, on receipts from a treasurer of the committee.

The daily amount received was  .  .  300 fr.

The expenses were:—

For 16 men of the guard at 3 fr.  .  .  48 fr.
Lighting of 3 lamps  .  .  .  .  .  4
Candles .  .  .  .  .  .  .  .  1
Wood for firing, one fourth of a load .  .  9 ——— 62
Daily profit to the committee  .  .  .  238 fr.

The room appropriated for the lodging of the commissaries was the place where their friends assembled, and the most splendid dinners were there served up: ten to twelve livres (ten-pence) each was nothing to them; while the poor fathers of families, whom personal revenge had placed under arrest, could scarcely procure the common necessaries of life. It may easily be conceived how cruel our situation was with such personages.

Our complaints, our supplications, and our cries for justice and humanity, were all stifled; and, if we chanced to give way to tears of grief, a damp dungeon was our reward; and even the women were not exempt from this cruelty, whatever happened to be their condition.

Our wives, our children, and our friends, paid very dear for the pleasure of sometimes seeing us; for these tigers, full of rage and cruelty, subjected them to all kinds of evil treatment.

Our abode was unhealthy, and the rooms, although very small, contained as many as ten persons each; and these monsters, in contempt of the law, which grants furniture of absolute necessity to the prisoners, forced some of them to sleep two together.

I had already been three weeks in prison, when a friend came to pay me a visit, in company with a police-officer, to be present at the removal of the seals at my house, upon which my future liberty was to depend; the order was presented to Verner and Laqueriére, then commissaries on guard, and, although it was perfectly regular, they did not think proper to conform to it, without having first given information to their committee. My friend immediately repaired thither; but the committee refused to obey the order of the police, and, to punish the temerity of him who had dared to solicit in my favour, he was ordered to be followed by Renaud, bailiff of the committee, and arrested the same evening.

Every day was distinguished by some new act of cruelty and tyranny; the prisoners were regularly called over at noon, by one of the commissaries going out, and one of those coming in, and the most brutal and scandalous sarcasms were their ordinary language. At half-past nine at night we were shut up in our chambers, like so many wild beasts; and if a prisoner, of whatever age, sex, or infirmities, happened to be ill at the time,

he or she was obliged to wait till the next day for the assistance which their situation might require.

During our detention, we have often heard these wretches say
to our wives, who came to implore our release: "You ought to
regard your husbands as if they were dead, and to conduct
yourselves accordingly, for it will be long before they will regain
their liberty." And at different periods they have almost all
declared: "If the Convention should give a decision in their
favour, and even the president himself should bring it hither,
we will not obey it, only as far as it may suit our own ideas,
and after we have deliberated upon it in the committee."

The section of the Bonnet Rouge gave a fête to the memory
of Marat, on the 2nd Frimaire. The procession, on its return,
passed under our windows, with two movable forges in the line;
the commissaries of the Revolutionary Committee took care to
have them stopped opposite to us, and caused a pike and some
chains to be made in our presence, insulting likewise our
misfortunes by the most atrocious invectives; and the scene
terminated by a circular dance, at the suggestion of Lebrun and
his companions, who sang the *Carmagnole*, pointing us out in
derision, and exclaiming, *to the guillotine!* We imagined our last
hour had arrived, and undoubtedly such would have been the
case, if the wishes of these monsters had been accomplished;
for they had taken the precaution of having us shut up in our
rooms, under lock and key about three o'clock in the afternoon,
in order to deprive us of all means of defence, in case the people
should second their wishes.

I had already pined three months in imprisonment, when, on
the 30th Nivôse, about ten o'clock a.m., we saw our barracks
besieged by an armed force; fear took possession of our minds,
and each questioned the other as to the cause of this visit,
without being able to divine the meaning of the mystery, when,
at length, about eleven o'clock, a number of my companions in
misfortune were called out and transferred elsewhere. I was
called in my turn, with nine others, and Lebrun, who commanded
the armed force, communicated to us the order to set out for
Picpus. We requested that we might be permitted to collect
such of our clothes as would be necessary for us; but Lebrun,
who has never been surpassed in atrocity, would not even allow

us to go for our shoes, and forced us to set off immediately, some without hats, and others in slippers, although no conveyances were provided for us.

He guarded us with a double file of soldiers, to the number of a hundred, and we were thus led, on foot, through the whole extent of Paris, to Picpus.*  Our march did not produce any thing disagreeable to us, and, had we not met a few blackguards near the Pont Neuf, who addressed abusive language to us, we should have experienced nothing but marks of pity and interest from those who saw us.

On our arrival at Picpus, only five of my companions were received, and the others, of which I was one, were taken back to the barracks.  The indisposition which one of my fellow prisoners experienced, owing to the forced march which we had just made, having excited the compassion of the commander of the guard which accompanied us, he permitted us to take a coach at the Rue St. Antoine.  The guard surrounded it, and during the whole distance we were assailed by the bitterest invectives, the men who composed our escort having told the people that we were counter-revolutionists, agents of Pitt and Cobourg, and conspirators.

We returned to our barracks in the midst of hootings and dangers; but we were abundantly repaid for our alarms, by the kind and friendly greetings of the friends whom we had left there; and the tears of joy which trickled down their cheeks at our return proved most gratifying and consolatory to us.

We learned from the prisoners whom we had left at the

---

* "Many prisoners were removed to Picpus: amongst others, a tall young man, condemned to be imprisoned a year for a crime with which we were not acquainted.  He had wrapped himself in the cloak of one of his friends, and, the moment after his entrance, the chamber which he was to occupy was pointed out to him.  It was a very damp spot, which had just been newly repaired. 'How!' exclaimed the young man, 'is it here that we are to be lodged?  It is impossible to live in it.'  He felt the walls, and added, with the greatest sangfroid, 'I will not remain here, that is certain; this wet plaster is sufficient to cause one's death.'  He laid down the mantle or cloak that he had upon his shoulders, took hold of the door, escaped, and was not afterwards heard of.  He might pass easily without interruption, being taken for one belonging to the house.  After that time, the prisoners were much more closely confined and watched."—*History of the Prisons.*—*Note of the Editors.*

barracks, that the Commissaries of the Bonnet-Rouge had endeavoured to justify our removal by the vilest calumny, having
imputed to us the sanguinary scheme of murdering our friends,
in order to escape the more easily.

We were resting after our fatigues, engaged in relating the
particulars of our journey, when we were called, at eight o'clock,
p.m. to go to St. Lazare. This new journey did not excite
so much attention as the former, as a hackney-coach was
provided for us, under the escort of four men and an officer;
and the shades of night saved us from every kind of unpleasant
interruption. At nine o'clock p.m. we arrived at Saint Lazare,
where ten of our companions of the barracks, who had been
there since the morning, alleviated our troubles by sharing with
us their beds and their supper.

The humanity with which we were treated by Naudet and
his wife, as well as by the turnkeys, the great attention which
was paid by the young men who waited upon us, to procure
every kind of necessary, made us believe that we were passing
from the infernal regions to Elysium; and, had we been permitted
to see our friends and relations, without interruption, our detention
would have been preferable to the liberty which was then
enjoyed in Paris.

The number of the prisoners at St. Lazare was soon augmented
by the numerous transfers that were made thither from the other
prisons; after many prayers and entreaties, we obtained permission to see those who loved and regarded us, by means of
*permits granted by the police*, which cost us very dear.

We were already more than three hundred in this prison,
when Michel, administrator of police, came for the first time
to inspect it. The harsh and menacing tone which he employed
in his examination of the prisoners, and the absolute orders
which he gave to those whom he thought rich, to support such
as were not, caused great distress to many of them. The
inflexible Michel could not endure that any representations should
be made to him on the subject, and, when any one ventured
to point out to him, in the most convincing manner, that he
was anything but rich, Michel uttered curses against him, and
threatened to transfer him to the Bicêtre; fortunately, this
tyrannical wretch only made his appearance two or three times.

Michel abandoned the superintendence of the establishment, and Gagnant succeeded him. Novelty always pleases men; the unfortunate calculate everything to their advantage; and we attributed this change to the ill-treatment which Michel had exercised towards us. We all flattered ourselves that the new superintendent would treat us with more humanity, and would not dispose of our fortunes without having previously known what they were. In this expectation we were indulging, when Gagnant was announced, and each prisoner urgently represented his grievances to him, to which he barely vouchsafed a reply, and that was uttered in a pettish spirit; his dark and hideous countenance afforded a gloomy presage of his disposition.

We soon discovered that we had gained nothing by the change. Gagnant informed us, that he intended to establish a dining-ward in the prison, to which he determined to force all the prisoners to go and eat, and where the rich should bear the expenses of the poor.

He solicited permission to this effect, and the administration of the police made a decree, ordering a refectory to be established, and appointing a mode for sending, backwards and forwards, the linen and clothes of the prisoners, who were to be prohibited every sort of communication.

The order was formally posted up in the prison, and the day for opening the refectory was indicated. Gagnant came to St. Lazare to arrange everything connected with the plan; he ordered the prisoners to go into their rooms, had them fastened with hasps, and then went from one apartment to another, to receive payment of the sums to be furnished daily for the establishment of the refectory. He imposed an arbitrary contribution upon the prisoners, notwithstanding their remonstrances; and, when any of them dared to urge that his detention had ruined him, the tyrant replied by irony and sarcasm, and immediately threatened to remove him to the Bicêtre. The refectory was not, however, established at this time.

In proportion as the administration cramped our communications with our friends, the difficulty of seeing our relations was redoubled. We could enjoy this happiness only by dint of money. The turnkey became more greedy on account of this increased difficulty; and the orders for admission from the police became negotiable like stock upon the Exchange. The poor lost every remaining comfort, and the rich could not obtain enjoyment but at the expense of the wreck of their fortune.

The administration of the police made several transfers at this period;* and more than three hundred individuals from different prisons, particularly from the Bicêtre, arrived at St. Lazare. These last-mentioned, excepting about sixty who were confined upon suspicion, were all condemned to be imprisoned for ten, fifteen, or twenty years. (This happened on the 12th Pluviôse). The administrators, Gagnant and Cailleux, who had the management of these transfers, fulfilled the duties of their odious office with unexampled severity and cruelty. They repaired at night to the prisons by torch-light, selected their victims, had them hand-cuffed, tied two and two, and huddled them together into carts, without regard to their age, infirmities, or causes of their deten-tion; all were alike confounded together.

The night passed in arranging everything for the journey; and, at break of day, the carts so loaded were surrounded by horsemen, who received orders to kill the first prisoner who should dare to complain.

The procession was numerous. It was preceded by Gagnant and Cailleux, who caused it to pause in the public places, par-ticularly upon Place Maubert, and the Place des Innocentes, in order to offer the unhappy prisoners as a spectacle to the people,

* We find in another sketch of the prison of St. Lazare a fact which deserves a place here:—

"In one of the removals, determined upon merely to harass the prisoners, Dumoutier presented himself at four o'clock in the morning, accompanied by a large waggon, in order to take away the females who were confined, and to conduct them to the English prison. One of them, whose time of confinement was approaching, having been aroused without any regard to her situation, felt a sudden convulsion, which predicted to her a speedy accouchment. She requested that she might remain a few days, but was charged with deceit and imposture, and her entreaties were disregarded. Her reiterated supplications, her tears, the solicitations of her companions,—all, in a word, proved unavailing, and she was forced to walk along with the rest. This young unfortunate creature crawled along, by the aid of some men, uttering the most piteous cries of grief and despair. She had scarcely crossed the garden, and reached the gate, before her attack increased. There was barely time to lead her into a neighbouring apartment, where she threw herself upon a bed, and gave birth immediately to a child, in the presence of the barbarian and his satellites.—*Note of the Editors.*

and to draw down invectives on their heads. The kind-hearted beings who were desirous of affording such assistance as humanity demanded, were kept back, in order to give place to the wretches who assailed the prisoners by the most brutal abuse. Everything, in fact, announced that these ferocious monsters had formed the design of provoking a tragic scene, which they might see repeated at the prisons.

The carts destined for St. Lazare arrived. The prisoners were distributed through corridors in the third storey; and more than two hundred were thrown upon straw, in a room on the ground-floor, called the Refectory, a damp and noisome apartment; and such was the want of feeling, that robbers and villains of every description were mixed with those who were only suspected of political offences.

The night of their arrival was very stormy. The prisoners from the Bicêtre, who were condemned to chains, committed the most frantic acts; stole the portfolios belonging to the suspected prisoners; broke the stoves and the wainscotting; set fire to it; and at last a man forced a way through the top of a cellar, and succeeded in escaping.

The keeper, Naudet, made his report to the police, and procured an order that the thieves should be taken to the Bicêtre. The police had it executed, but slowly and without noise, setting out two and two in hackney-coaches; in other words, having no longer suspected individuals with them, they were treated with greater humanity.

The day after the arrival of the men from the Bicêtre, the report was spread in Paris that the prisoners of St. Lazare had mutinied, and fought with their keepers, and that many of them had escaped. The keepers, in order to secure the rumour credit, did not hesitate to give a false colouring to the circumstance.

General Henriot hastened with an armed force, and, after having distributed cartridges to them, he thus harangued his men:—"My friends and companions, I enjoin you to exercise the most rigid watch over the scoundrels who are confined in this prison, for they are only waiting for the death which they have merited." He was here applauded by some of the prisoners, but hooted by the generality of them. He then added, "If, however, there should be found any victims amongst them, you

owe them aid and protection;" and, satisfied with himself, he
returned with his aides-de-camp. The night following, one of
the sentinels placed on guard around the house, towards the
side looking to the country, displeased with a prisoner who had
opened his window to ventilate his chamber, insulted him, and
ordered him to close the window, and, upon a refusal, fired his
piece at him, which luckily did not produce any evil consequences.* It may not be altogether improper to observe, that
it was the section of Bonne Nouvelle who were that day upon
guard.

About this period a rumour was circulated in the prison that
the scene of the 2nd of September was about to be renewed;
that all the places of confinement were to be assailed, and their
inmates assassinated. Alarm took possession of our minds, and
each set of prisoners prepared to defend themselves, by establishing amongst themselves a night guard in each corridor.
This measure was judged so much the more necessary, as it was
reported that they were menaced by an attack from thirty of
their companions, whose dark projects were to be assisted by
parties from without.

Ronsin and Vincent obtained their liberty about this time, and
came to St. Lazare to visit their friends, Pereyra and Desfieux.
On their account, splendid dinners had been prepared on the
occasion, in an apartment where their protégés joined them, and
there a list *was drawn out of thirty persons*, to whom Vincent
and Ronsin swore protection, and promised liberty.

These meetings took place exactly at the period when the
report was current that the prisoners were going to be murdered.
The thirty individuals just alluded to carried their heads high,

---

* It was not always mere caprice that exposed the prisoners to this unworthy
treatment, but it was pursued on a regular system, if we may credit the following
passage, extracted from a memoir relative to the English prison:—

"It was expressly forbidden to look through the bars of the windows that
were situated towards the street; notwithstanding which, we approached them.
The sentinels (particularly before the section mounted guard) then called out to
us to retire, threatening to fire upon us. One day, Bertrand, the gaoler, went
out at the gate just at the moment that a prisoner had thus been summoned.
The sentinel mentioned the circumstance, when he replied, 'Fire upon them:
they are villains, aristocrats, game for the guillotine, and must all suffer by it:
I will give thee some small shot, that will not kill them.'"—*Note of the Editors.*

frequently sought to quarrel with the other prisoners, openly threatened them, spoke of their own patriotism, announced their approaching liberty, through the protection of Vincent and others, and declared that one third of the prisoners in the place (themselves excepted) would be burnt, a third more guillotined, and the remainder sent out of France in a vessel with a leak in her.

It may easily be conceived what was the perplexity of the prisoners at St. Lazare, after hearing such menaces from their companions: they redoubled their vigilance in keeping the night guard; and they mutually promised each other to sell their lives dearly in case of attack.

Ronsin and Vincent were again arrested, but upon this occasion taken to the Conciergerie. Pereyra, Desfieux, and Anacharsis Clootz, were brought to trial, and several prisoners of St. Lazare were called upon as witnesses, amongst whom were Joubert and Belge, although of the number of the thirty I have mentioned before. Some others were called upon to give corroborative testimony, and I amongst the rest. I entered into particular details in my declaration, as I deemed it of importance to make known, from what I had heard said, the ramifications of the plot then formed.

Ronsin, Vincent, Hébert, Pereyra, Desfieux, and Clootz, were condemned to death. Their friends at St. Lazare expected to be disturbed in consequence of it; but the affair did not affect them, and their audacity became still more intolerable a few days afterwards. Joubert and his associates figured again in Robespierre's proscription.

Reflections here become unnecessary, as it will be seen, if this narrative be read with attention, that Robespierre was always the concealed chief of the party; that he had pronounced the death of all the prisoners; and that he had placed his spies and accusers in each prison, in order to fabricate insurrections at pleasure, and to conduct his victims to the scaffold.

The death of Ronsin and others made the prisoners of St. Lazare forget their past dangers; fear was succeeded by tranquillity; confidence was once more established amongst us, and our night guards were discontinued; Joubert and his accomplices were feared and despised; and two months passed in the greatest quiet, although the guard of Bonne Nouvelle occasionally renewed their harsh conduct.

Gagnant, the superintendent,—he who had never appeared at St. Lazare but to commit outrages upon the prisoners,—was at length deprived of the functions of his office, and placed under arrest in this same prison. He was welcomed by songs, jests, and raillery, which continued to be employed towards him for a few days after his arrival; but at length he was despised and avoided by all; and Grimoard, late Count du Roure, formerly a municipal officer, was the only one who found any pleasure in the society of such a man.

Bergot, one of the companions of Robespierre, whom his disgraceful death will make known to posterity, succeeded Gagnant in the administration of the prison. This immoral character, whose private life was one tissue of crimes, at first put on the mask of humanity, visited the prisoners in their apartments, offered them protection and assistance, and, under this hypocritical disguise, laboured to render our fate still more deplorable.

Naudet, the gaoler, was not the man who suited his projects, and he seized the moment when he was summoned before a criminal tribunal, on account of the escape of a prisoner, to replace him by a provisional keeper; and, although Naudet was afterwards acquitted by that tribunal, and acknowledged to be innocent, yet he was deprived of his situation, and succeeded by Semé, inspector of the Robespierrian police.

Bergot and Semé, old bottle companions, entirely devoted to Robespierre, were daily forming schemes, over their wine, for rendering the yoke which the prisoners had to bear more oppressive.

In their cups they one day decided, that the wives, relations, and friends of the prisoners, who for a long time had not had permission to see them, except in the entrance court of the place, at a distance of fifty paces from the buildings, should be dismissed, and the doors closed.

This order was rigorously observed; for these atrocious wretches, always stimulated by the wine they drank, watched and severely punished those of the turnkeys whose humanity was sometimes excited by their sensibility to violate it.

We were then condemned to lose the gratification of seeing

all we loved and regarded; and, when any one had the courage
to pass into the Rue de Paradis to salute us, immediately the
brutes who were posted by the police about the prison, beat
them with clubs, and dragged before the Revolutionary Committee of the Poissonnière section, the wives or children who had
been imprudent enough to show themselves to their husbands
or fathers.

Bergot, who was ever on the alert to persecute the prisoners,
denied them the use of candles; and his friend Semé, anxious
to surpass him in severity, carefully saw that this order was
rigorously put in execution. The prisoners patiently resigned
themselves to this new privation.

The deprivation of their money, and the prohibition to send
for more, forced the prisoners to make representations to the
administration on the poverty to which they were reduced, and
on the tax which was imposed upon them, for the support of
their more indigent fellow-prisoners. It may not be amiss to
state, that the prisoners had voluntarily fixed upon a daily sum,
in proportion to their means, and that this imposition was carefully
acquitted twice every ten days, to a treasurer selected from
amongst the prisoners, and was distributed by him each day to
our poorer companions.

Bergot received this representation, and promised to take it
into consideration; but a month passed and no measure of relief
was taken, although we were obliged to pay the contribution.

The prohibition for the receipt of money at St. Lazare was
rigorously observed; the infamous Semé, who was always tyrannical
in his conduct, retained every fraction that was remitted for the
prisoners, whatever their necessities, or however small the sum.

He was one day consulted by the citizen Pierre, a respectable
individual, to know if he would permit him to write to his
family in one of the departments, for three hundred livres, as
well for the purpose of paying two hundred livres that he owed
to various prisoners who had lent him money in his necessities, as to avoid being entirely penniless. Semé granted the
desired permission, and gave him his word of honour, that the
money which he might write for should be delivered to him.
Pierre wrote upon the faith of this promise, and his family sent
him three hundred livres; the latter was received by Semé, who

kept back two hundred and fifty livres, and gave fifty to Pierre, and all the entreaties of the latter, for the delivery of the residue, proved unavailing.

In this interval, the popular commission appeared at different times, and nearly one hundred prisoners were successively examined; but the confidence which had been entertained did not long continue, when it was known whom the individuals were that composed it. The indecency which characterized the questions addressed to the prisoners, the irony with which they were accompanied, and the insulting laughter of the commissioners, served only to inspire us with contempt.

The illusion that had been created on their account soon ceased; the commission was considered a mere mockery, and the political life of the base and abandoned characters who composed it afforded a presage of striking events, which was justified by the result.

The treasurer, established for collecting the contributions for the indigent, could no longer fulfil the functions of his office, as the expense was continually augmenting, and the receipts daily diminishing.

Bergot was again petitioned to supply the wants of the poor, which he promised to do, and at length, a few days afterwards, there was posted up, in the corridors of the prison, an order of the police, of the 27th Floréal, in which the administration took care to announce that, for want of a strict superintendence, a system of immoderate luxury had been introduced into the prisons; that the tables were there served up with indecent profusion; that the sums which the prisoners had obtained might become dangerous; that the police had deemed it wise to make a general search in the prisons, from which there had resulted a seizure of 864,000 livres, independently of valuables; and that they hoped the sums already seized and to be seized, would amount at least to 1,200,000 livres.

That these different sums would be deposited in a private chest, to be delivered to the prisoners who should obtain their liberty, deduction being previously made of three livres a day for the expense of their guard and sustenance.

That, in order to establish an equality amongst the prisoners, and put an end to all distinction, a refectory should be established, to which all indifferently should be obliged to go and eat; that, till then, there should be paid to each of them three livres per day, subject to the deduction of ten sous for the expenses of the guard; and that these sums should be taken from those deposited in the private chest.

That, finally, to deprive them of all mode of communication, there should be established in the prison a box, in which letters, parcels, and linen should be placed, and afterwards carried to their address by messengers.

This decree gave rise to great disputation; it was found false in its statements, and impolitic in its consequences. We all coincided in opinion, that it contained a secret design of provoking us to mutiny.

It was, in the first place, false in regard to the luxury which was imputed to the prisoners, and in the extravagance of the tables, for it was not possible to see more simplicity in dress, or more frugality in living; some receiving their food from the generosity of their relations and friends; others taking their dinners from the *traiteur** of the prison, at thirty and forty sous a head; the greater part, in fine, dining in their rooms, for the sake of greater economy, and often eating their pittance with tears streaming from their eyes.

The distribution of the promised fifty sous a day took place on the 20th Prairial, commencing from the first day of the said month. Most of us thought it burdensome to the republic; for, of 700 prisoners, 200 were in the greatest poverty, and 500 could provide for their expenses as hitherto; notwithstanding that, we were obliged to receive the allowance, and he who was disposed to decline it, even with the design of benefiting his country, was noted down as aristocratic.

As to the refectory, it was considered impracticable, from the difficulty which the relations of the prisoners experienced in procuring them subsistence, and it was concluded that Bergot would not prove more fortunate in his project than Gagnant.

In the meanwhile, Bergot increased his exertions for the success of his plan; the most peremptory orders were given to the contractors, and locksmiths, masons, carpenters, and joiners, were all set to work, with Semé to superintend them.

* One who keeps an eating-house.

The preparations for the refectory went on for some time, yet the prisoners had no idea it would be established. Their reasoning upon the subject was plain enough, as they reflected, that there were seven hundred in the prison, and that their three thousand relations had found it difficult to provide for their daily subsistence; it seemed, therefore, improbable, that one person alone could succeed in furnishing the necessary supply. They feared, with some justice, that the traiteur, being obliged to make large purchases, would be treated as a forestaller, and pursued by the mob into the prison, and that the prisoners, who had been studiously held up to the execration of the people, might be ill-treated and assassinated, as wretches who were burdensome to society.

About this period, the story was fabricated of a project of escape on the part of some of the prisoners, for the purpose of assassinating Robespierre, for he it was who was generally mentioned as the object of vengeance.* The spies of the prison made all the necessary preparations for a grave accusation, and a messenger, Herman, was sent to give information of it. Joubert, whom we have already seen play a part in the affair of Ronsin and others; Manini, an Italian; and Coquery, a locksmith, appeared in the quality of denunciators of the pretended scheme for an escape. Allain, Selles, and Gauthier were called in their turn, as the three ringleaders of the plot; and the first of the questions proposed to each of these three individuals, taken separately, was this:—"What dost thou think of Robespierre?" and, when the examinations had been taken down, Herman retired.

The Luxembourg had already been charged with a similar project, and the death of nearly two hundred individuals upon the scaffold seemed to attest its truth. It appeared, then, natural enough that the germ of such a plot should be carefully spread,

---

* This pretended conspiracy, organized at the same time in most of the prisons, was carried on at St. Lazare with particular perseverance. As this example of the most infamous baseness deserves to be thoroughly made known, we refer for further explanations to another narrative of the same facts, by Dusaulchoy. Our readers will there find new details, and sometimes the same details presented under different points of view. The piece which we quote forms nearly half of the work.—See Note H. in the Appendix.—*Note of the Editors.*

in order to render it probable; and, with a view of succeeding
in this object, all the prisons were inoculated at the same time,
by the transfer into each of a prisoner from the Luxembourg.
Citizen Selles arrived at St. Lazare, and it must be remarked, that
it was a few days after his arrival that the project of escape, in
which he played one of the principal parts, was said to have
been formed amongst the prisoners.

The subject of this imaginary project was discussed in the
prison, but no one believed in it.  The colleagues of Joubert,*
Manini, and Coquery, employed all their eloquence to gain it
credit, swore by their patriotism it was true, and were prepared
to attest it before the revolutionary tribunal, before which, they
said, the affair was to be carried, when at length the report ceased.

The idea of the refectory was still entertained, and the intimacy which existed between Semé and Bergot enabled us to
discover, in this establishment, two plots, which, in the sequel,
were verified.

The first was a speculation formed at the expense of our
stomachs; and the second a secret design to excite us to mutiny
at any price.

On the 23rd Messidor, a vague rumour was in circulation
throughout the prison, that the refectory would be opened the
following day.  The keeper, Semé, declared the contrary, upon
his honour, to those who questioned him, and assured them that
they might order their dinners as usual.

On the following day, however, it was notified to the prisoners,
that they would dine together that same day, and all the provisions which they had sent for were seized at the door for the
benefit of the gaoler and his creatures.

This extraordinary intelligence at first greatly surprised the
prisoners and stupified them; but they took courage, and, fancy-
ing they perceived a latent design to provoke them to mutiny,
they recommended each other to exercise the greatest prudence
which was the only means of frustrating it.

The hour of dinner having arrived, a bell announced it in

* Joubert, or Jobert, has published a relation, in which he confidently disavows
what many other prisoners have asserted respecting him in their memoirs.  We
owe it to our impartiality to quote a part of his recital.—See the explanations,
Note I. in the Appendix.—*Note of the Editors.*

the corridors, and each gloomily went down with his napkin, his knife and fork, his plate, and the bread and wine which had already been distributed to him, and placed himself at a table for fifteen to thirty persons; for it was thus that they were at first divided.

The prelude of the service was long, and an hour passed in expectation of the dinner to be provided by Périnal, the *traiteur*. He at length appeared; and the table of thirty persons, at which I was placed, was served with two dishes of vegetable soup, miserably thin, with three pounds of boiled beef, two pounds of calf's liver, thirty eggs, with a small quantity of sorrel, a dish of French beans, containing about a quart, and sixty apricots, which, we were told, were a present from the *traiteur*.

This light and miserable dinner was the only food which the prisoners were allowed to have for twenty-four hours, as there was no supper permitted. The admission of wines, brandy, coffee, liqueurs, syrups, milk, fruits, and vegetables, was absolutely interdicted, as well as of medicines, whatever necessity any one had for them; so that the sick as well as the healthy in the prison were condemned to the same regimen,—namely, bread and water, and Périnal's dinner.

It may easily be conceived how painful was the situation of these unfortunate victims of the cupidity of Bergot and of the villainy of Robespierre; yet they had the prudence to support with courage and resignation their fresh mortifications.

Bergot wished to be a witness of his triumph, and was present at the dinner. He visited all the tables with a sardonic smile, carried off the knives which he perceived, and refused to listen to the complaints which were addressed to him respecting the disgusting style of the dinner, the small quantity of food, and the wretched quality of the wine; and the request which was made in the name of the sick for permission to procure things indispensable for their condition, was referred to the medical officer.

Bergot was not indifferent to the prudence of the prisoners, and he was evidently discontented with the order which reigned in the refectory. The mortification which he evinced on going away persuaded us that we had conceived a just idea as to an intended scheme for exciting insurrection amongst us.

The prohibition to the admission of eatables into the prison established among the turnkeys a very lucrative sort of trade. Smuggling was carried on, and the entry-duties were dearer than under the old regime; for the chopine (half-pint) of brandy, according to their tariff, was at six livres, a fowl twelve livres, eggs twelve sous (sixpence) each, the evening paper twenty-five livres, and at equal rates we paid for everything.

Our first dinner gave rise to loud remonstrances, but the second did not on that account improve ; for the table of thirty, at which I was placed, was served with a very bad thin pea-soup, thirty herrings, thirty artichokes, and thick dirty sauce, and two small ham patées, the meat of which had been too long kept; and the chopine of wine allowed to each prisoner was of a still more wretched quality than had been supplied the day before.

The administrator, Grepin, who replaced Bergot that day, visited the refectory, heard the complaints of the prisoners, tasted the wine, which he found execrable, and, after laughing at our situation, disappeared: notwithstanding, we were not better served.

Complaints against the *traiteur*, Périnal, increased. We proved to him conclusively that he made at least twenty sous per day by each prisoner out of the fifty which he received from the administration for their support. He was too ingenuous to deny it, and he and his cooks added sarcasm to robbery, telling us that he had orders to treat us in a revolutionary style.

Neither justice nor humanity, then, could we obtain! Our remonstrances were stifled; and they all, not even omitting the petty Périnal, insulted our misfortunes.

While we were indignant at the miserable dinners that were furnished us, the agents of Robespierre, who in appearance were prisoners, praised to Périnal the excellence of his wine and his meats, and, after leaving him, came to excite us against the man ; but, as we knew them, we took care to keep upon our guard.

Our lives were besieged on all hands. Périnal was poisoning us, and the guillotine was already eagerly waiting for us. We were necessitated to make up our minds to every hardship, and to hope for nothing but from divine justice.

In vain we implored the police to do us justice against Périnal, which was always promised, but as often neglected. The *traiteur* became more insolent in consequence of it, his wine and his dinners more detestable, and his wife and waiters more arrogant.

We were at length reduced to deplore our fate in silence, when the prisoners of Robespierre announced in the prison, on the 26th Messidor, that the following decade was to purify St. Lazare by the agency of the revolutionary tribunal; that the aristocrats, the priests, and the authors and accomplices of the pretended scheme of escape, would be summoned before it.

The dried cod-fish and the rotten herrings, which were frequently served to the prisoners during the dog-days, had already injured their health. Many were confined to their beds; and the agonized cries of these unfortunate beings seemed to affect the wife of Semé. Soupé, a medical attendant, came, in company with Wilcheritz, another superintendent, to visit the sick, and ordered medicines for them; but Semé opposed the admission of these remedies, on the ground that the administration had not given orders, and consequently the sick remained without assistance.

Wilcheritz heard complaints against Périnal, tasted the foul wine which had that day been distributed, and pronounced it execrable and unwholesome; however, we were forced to receive, and were called upon to bless the hand which administered this slow poison to us.

The report as to the purifying of the prison circulated abroad. Coquery and Manini, authors and denunciators of the project of escape, were transferred into another prison; and on the 30th Messidor some gendarmes came to fetch certain of the prisoners, who were condemned to death the following day.

On the 1st Thermidor, twelve others left St. Lazare, all members of the Revolutionary Committee of the city of Troyes, men of bad reputation, who had indulged, in the prison, in the most sanguinary style of discourse; and we learnt, on the 2nd, that they had been all acquitted and liberated.

On the same day, 2nd Thermidor, the wine which was served out having been found of a still worse quality than before, the prisoners, not suspecting that the administration of police were in connivance with Périnal, although it had not done justice to their complaints, took the resolution of sending a bottle to the Committee of General Security, and one to the administration of police. The latter ordered it to be tasted; and there resulted from the procès verbal which was sent in reply, that the wine was of bad quality and unwholesome. The following day, however, it proved no better, nor was Périnal more honest. What did all this prove, but that there was a design of irritating us so far as to induce us to mutiny?

On the 3rd, Semé, the gaoler, of whom we had so much reason to complain, and whose surveillance was every moment marked by oppressive acts, was discharged, as being too mild and humane, and succeeded by Verner, head turnkey of the Luxembourg.

This man, of a ferocious aspect, who had afforded proofs of his villainy in the removal of the prisoners from the Luxembourg to the Conciergerie, was then established, in appearance, at St. Lazare; but Semé, although formally dismissed, nevertheless filled the office of gaoler afterwards.

Verner distinguished his entrance into the prison by informing the prisoners, in a hand-bill, that, after the lapse of a fortnight, they would not be allowed to send or receive their clothes and other things, except between the hours of nine a.m. and noon, and that, every decade (ten days), nothing would be permitted to enter into and go out of the prison. He stated further, that the police, wishing to intercept every kind of communication with the persons out of the prison, were about to undertake to wash for the prisoners, and that, in consequence, two shirts only would be left for their use.

He likewise notified, that he would receive representations only in writing. He forbade them an entrance into his apartment, and ordered the wickets of communication in the doors to be closed; and my Lord Verner did not even give himself the trouble to answer, either in writing or verbally, the humble and respectful petitions which were addressed to him on different subjects, and particularly respecting the thefts which they daily experienced in the transmission of their linen.

The prisoners thus saw the rigour of their situation continually increasing; their letters to their families, deposited in the box of the prison, with money to frank them, did not arrive at their different addresses. The messengers and the turnkeys, initiated into the mystery of what was plotting against the prisoners, became unfaithful. Some of them had kept for themselves the linen which had been confided to them to carry to the families of the prisoners. All was thus given up to plunder, when, on the morning of the 5th, the Robespierrists announced that, in the afternoon of the same day, several of those who were charged with a share in the pretended plot for escape would leave St. Lazare to go before the revolutionary tribunal, and, from the nature of their assertions, we gave credit to the fact.

About four o'clock p.m. we saw two waggons, under the escort of fourteen gendarmes, enter the court of the prison. The apparition terrified the minds of all, and alarm rapidly spread through the place. Each feared for himself, until the moment when the turnkeys, stationed in the different corridors, had made known the prisoners who had been fixed upon, by leading them to the Office of Records, where a bailiff of the revolutionary tribunal was waiting for them.

These unfortunate victims were placed in the waggons, after they had been so completely stripped of everything which belonged to them, that on their arrival at the Conciergerie they had nothing in their possession. They were counted over by Verner and Semé, with an insulting laugh, and, thus huddled together, they parted from us, and carried with them our esteem and regrets.

# APPENDIX

## NOTE A. Page 7.

HER head and her breasts were immediately cut off; her body was opened, her heart torn out, and her head placed on the end of a pike, and paraded through Paris; her body was dragged, at some distance, after it.

"The tigers, who had just torn her to pieces, indulged themselves in the barbarous pleasure of going to the Temple, and exhibiting her head and heart to Louis XVI. and his family. Indeed, all the horrors and cruelties which the most cold-blooded ferocity could conceive, were exercised towards Madame de Lamballe. *

* When the Princesse de Lamballe was brought forth she was asked to swear eternal hatred to the King, the Queen and to Royalty. "The oath," said she, "is foreign to the sentiments of my heart and I will never take it." She was instantly given over to the ministers of death. These ruffians pretended to caress her, stroking her cheeks with their hands yet dripping with human blood, and thus they led her along the line. Amidst all these insults her courage never deserted her. On reaching the heap of dead bodies, they bade her kneel and ask pardon of the nation, "I have never injured the nation," she replied, "nor will I ask its pardon." "Down!" cried they, "down and ask pardon, if you wish to live." "No," said she, "I scorn to ask pardon from assassins that call themselves the nation; I will never bend my knee or accept a favour at such hands." Her soul was superior to fear. "Kneel and ask pardon," was shouted at her by a thousand voices, but in vain. Two of the assassins now seized her arms, and pulling her from side to side, nearly dislocated her shoulders. "Go on, scoundrels," said the heroic Princess, "I will ask no pardon." In a rage to see themselves thus overcome by the constancy of a woman, they dashed her down and fell upon her with their knives and poniards. Her head was soon hoisted upon a pike and her heart, after being bitten by one of the ruffians, was put into a basin. Both were carried in triumph through the streets of Paris. The body was stripped naked and with bowels hanging out was exposed to view.—*The Bloody Buoy.*

"A fact occurred, which modesty will scarcely furnish us with language to relate; but we ought to reveal all the truth, and leave nothing untold. When Madame de Lamballe was mutilated, in a hundred different ways, and the assassins had shared amongst them the bleeding remnants of her body, one of the monsters cut off the virginal part, and made himself a pair of mustachios of it, in the presence of the spectators, who were horrified by the sight." *

## NOTE B. p. 17.

A pamphlet, entitled *The Whole Truth on the Real Authors of the Events of the 2nd of September*, has furnished details which too often excite the horror and pity of the reader.

Some important circumstances which are contained in this pamphlet are worthy of being extracted, as further illustrative of this history.

"Arrived here on Sunday, the 2nd of September, p.m. This day, usually dedicated to repose, only renewed in the minds of the idle populace the hope of gratifying their revenge.

"In the morning, a proclamation was published in Paris, urging the patriots to fly to the assistance of their brethren.

"It was therein declared, that there was not a moment to be lost; that no pretext for delay should be alleged, not even the want of arms; that Verdun was taken; and that the enemy was rapidly marching towards the capital.

"About midday the cannon of alarm was fired. Shortly afterwards the tocsin resounded on all sides, and the general was beaten. Terror took possession of the minds of all the inhabitants; they hastened to arm themselves, and the general cry, *Let us march against the enemy* was heard throughout the city. *But . . . . our most cruel enemies are not at Verdun: they are here in the prisons.* Many individuals spread abroad this rumour, and others repeated it, and gave it credence. 'Our wives, our children, will be left to the mercy of these wretches, and will be immolated,' exclaimed some; while others rejoined, 'Let us strike before we depart—let us run to the prisons.'

* Vide also Note C., Massacre at the *Hôtel de la Force*.

" This dreadful cry, a fact which all impartial men will cor-roborate, was re-echoed at the same moment spontaneously and unanimously through all the streets and public squares and places, where the inhabitants were assembled together and associated, even in the National Assembly itself.

" This fear might naturally arise from the state of things. After having destroyed the throne which oppressed them, the French people might have expected these implacable reprisals would be made by all other thrones; after having broken the principal keystone which supported the royal arch of Europe, they ought to have dreaded being crushed themselves. But we regret to say, that certain men took advantage of this natural state of feeling, and made these sentiments of terror answer the purposes of their intended crimes; and at this period the *ingenious invention* of the prison conspiracies was made, and by those very individuals who since, possessing greater power, have managed so well to complete and bring it to perfection.

" I was going to my post about half-past two o'clock: in passing through the Rue Dauphine, I suddenly heard loud hootings. I looked around, and perceived six hackney-coaches, in a line with each other, escorted by national guards of the departments (federated soldiers of Marseilles and Brittany).

" These coaches each contained four individuals, who had been arrested in the preceding domiciliary visits. They had just been at the Mayoralty Office, before Billaud de Varennes, Deputy Attorney of the Commune, and they were now sending them to the Abbaye, to be temporarily imprisoned there. The mob became tumultuous, and the shouts redoubled. One of the prisoners, doubtlessly heated and carried away by these murmurs, put his arm out of the coach-door, and struck one of the federates, who accompanied them, upon the head with his cane. The man immediately drew his sword in a fury, jumped upon the step of the coach, and plunged his sword three different times into the heart of his aggressor. I saw the blood issue from the bosom of the victim in a copious stream. ' *We must kill them all ; they are rascally aristocrats,*' exclaimed those who were present. The murderer's companions instantly unsheathed their sabres, and massacred the three unfortunate associates of him who had just been sacrificed. At this moment I perceived a young man,.

in a white morning-gown, get out of the same coach. His interesting, but pale and dejected countenance, announced that he had been very ill. He had summoned his tottering strength, and, after having already received a wound, cried out once more,—'*Mercy, mercy, pardon,*' but all in vain; a mortal blow united him with his companions.

"This coach, which was now conducting only lifeless bodies, was the last of the cavalcade. It had not stopped during the carnage, which had not lasted two minutes. The crowd increased; their shouts grew louder; the conveyances arrived at the Abbaye, into the court of which the dead bodies of the victims were thrown: the surviving prisoners alighted, for the purpose of being introduced to the Civil Committee; two of them were massacred the moment they got out, and the others succeeded in gaining admission to the committee. The members had not had time to enter into the least examination, when a multitude, armed with pikes, swords, sabres, and bayonets, hurried into the room, tore away the prisoners, and murdered them. One of the number, already wounded mortally, clung to the coat of a member of the committee, struggling against death, which was fast chilling his vital powers.

"It was five o'clock in the evening. Billaud de Varennes, deputy of the attorney of the Commune, arrived, wearing his scarf, his small puce coat, and the black wig, which were known to distinguish him. He walked over the dead bodies, made a short speech to the crowd, and thus finished:—'*People, you immolate your enemies; you do your duty.*' This brutal harangue served to animate them; the assassins increased in ferocity, and tumultuously demanded fresh victims. How was this increasing and inextinguishable thirst for blood to be quenched? A voice was heard from the place where Billaud stood; it was that of Maillard, who was afterwards known by the name of Tappe-dur (strike-hard).—'*There is nothing more to be done here; let us go to the Carmes.*' They hurried thither, and, five minutes afterwards, I saw them drag the dead bodies by the feet into the channels. An assassin (I cannot say a man), dressed in a very rude manner, and who apparently had a special commission to expedite the Abbé l'Enfant, feared that he had missed his prey. He took up some water, threw it upon the bodies, which were all covered with blood and mire, rubbed their ensanguined faces, turned them over, and thus endeavoured to assure himself that the Abbé l'Enfant was of the number of the victims.

" The expedition to the Carmes was terminated; a band of murderers returned, covered with blood and dust: the monsters were *fatigued* with carnage, but *not satisfied with blood;* they were out of breath, and demanded *some wine, wine or death!* What was the reply to their irresistible will? The Civil Committee of the section gave them orders for twenty-four pints, on a neighbouring wine-dealer. They had very soon drunk to satiety, and contemplated, with gratification, the dead bodies which were strewed in the court of the Abbaye.

" ' *What are we doing here?'* exclaimed the same voice (Maillard returned from the Carmes), ' *let us go to the Abbaye; there is game there.'* The assassins repeated in chorus—' *Let us go to the Abbaye';* and they hastened thither, armed with their pikes and their bloody sabres. Scarcely two minutes elapsed before they dragged out the slaughtered victims; several had already been added to the heap in the court of the Abbaye, when there was formed, *as it were by inspiration*, a commission called Popular, of which the newspapers gave an account the next day, and which they called an *equitable tribunal.*

" Twelve of the myrmidons of Maillard, no doubt, directed by him, were, *as if by chance*, amidst the people; and there, being well known to each other, they united themselves together *in the name of the sovereign people*. Either stimulated by their own private assurance, or under the secret influence of some superior authority, they took possession of the registers of the commitments, turned them over, and examined them; the turnkeys trembled; the wife of the gaoler, and the gaoler himself swooned from terror; the prison was surrounded by furious men, who cried out in a terrific manner; the clamour augmented, the door was assailed, and was about to be forced open, when one of the commissaries presented himself at the outside grating, and called upon them to listen to him. His gesture obtained him silence; the doors were opened, and he advanced with the book of the commitments in his hand; after ordering a stool to be brought, on which he mounted, that he might the better be heard, he thus addressed them; 'Comrades, friends, you are good patriots;

your resentment is just, and your complaints are well founded. Open war with the enemies of the public welfare; no truce nor tenderness ought to be held with them. I feel, as well as you, that it is necessary they should perish; but, if you are good citizens, you must love justice. There is not one of you who does not shudder at the dreadful idea of steeping your hands in innocent blood.' 'True, true,' exclaimed the people. 'Well, then, I ask you, when you, without hearing or examining anything, rush, like furious tigers, upon men who are your brethren, whether you do not expose yourselves to the bitter and despairing regret of having struck the innocent instead of the guilty.'

"Here the orator was interrupted by one of those present, who, armed with a sword, his eyes sparkling with rage, rushed through the crowd, and thus refuted him: 'Tell me, then, Mr. Citizen, speak, do you also wish to lull us into deceitful security? If the cursed beggarly Prussians and Austrians were at Paris, would they seek for the guilty? Would they not strike at random, like the Swiss of the 10th of August? Well! I am no orator, I do not lull any one into security, and I tell you that I am a father of a family, that I have a wife and five children, whom I wish to leave here under the protection of my section, in order that I may go and fight the enemy; but I do not intend that, during that time, the rascals who are in this prison, to whom other rascals will come and open the doors, shall go and murder my wife and children. I have three boys, who will one day, I hope, be more useful to the country than the scoundrels whom you wish to preserve; as for the rest, you need only let them come out,—we will give them arms, and will fight them with equal numbers; whether I die here or die at the frontiers, I shall be killed all the same, and I will sell them my life dearly; and no matter if it be by me or by others,—the prison will be purged of those rascally beggars.'

"'*He is in the right, you must enter;*' they pushed forward and advanced. 'A moment, citizens, and you shall be satisfied,' said the first speaker: 'here is the book of the commitments; it will serve to give you information, and you will thus be able to punish the guilty, without being unjust; the president will read the commitment in the presence of each prisoner; he will afterwards collect the opinions, and will pronounce his decisions.'

At each observation, the mob cried aloud on all sides; '*Yes, yes, very well; he is right; bravo! bravo!*' At the end of the speech, several men stationed on purpose exclaimed: 'M. Maillard, Citizen Maillard, president; he is a worthy man; Citizen Maillard, president!' He was himself on the watch for the nomination, and, being anxious for such a ministry, immediately entered into his functions, and said, that *he was going to labour as a good citizen*. The commission was organized, his myrmidons surrounded him, and they soon agreed upon a brief formula of examination, which was merely to consist in the identity of names and surnames; they determined that, to avoid all violent scenes in the interior of the prison, they would not pronounce sentence of death in the presence of the condemned, but should only say, *à la Force*.

"They were finishing the regulation of these formalities, when a voice was heard through the window of the hall of deliberation, which announced itself as being charged with the wishes of the people. 'There are,' he exclaimed, 'many Swiss in the prison; lose no time in examining them; they are all guilty, and not one of them ought to escape.' The crowd immediately cried out,—'It is just, it is just; let us begin with them.' The tribunal immediately pronounced unanimously *à la Force!* Maillard, the president, went to announce their fate to them. He entered their presence, and said to them, 'You assassinated the people on the 10th of August, and they now demand vengeance; you must go to *La Force*.'

"The unfortunate men fell upon their knees and cried out, '*Mercy, mercy!*' 'We are now,' phlegmatically replied Maillard, 'about to remove you to *La Force;* where you may, perhaps, afterwards obtain mercy.' But they had only too well heard the cries of the multitude, who swore to exterminate them, and they therefore answered him with one voice,—'Ah, sir, why do you deceive us? We too surely know that we shall only go out from here to our death.' At the same time two assassins appeared from without, the one a journeyman baker, the other a Marseillese, who said to them, in the most inflexible tone,— 'Come, come, decide at once,—walk.' Immediately the most horrible lamentations and groans were heard. In the midst of this dreadful scene, which would have shocked any but such monsters as Maillard, the voice of one of the commissaries who surrounded these unhappy men, was heard exclaiming, 'Well, let us see who will be the first to go out?' All the Swiss shrunk into the prison, mutually embraced each other, pressed eagerly together, and uttered the most piteous and grievous cries at the appearance of inevitable death. The impress of despair rendered still more interesting the faces of some old veterans; their white hairs inspired respect, and their looks, like those of Coligny, appeared to restrain the assassins who were nearest to them; but the fury of those who were behind, and who could see nothing, still increased. Redoubled shouts called for victims. Suddenly one of the unfortunate beings presented himself with intrepidity. He wore a blue frock-coat, and was about thirty years of age; he was about the middle size, his countenance was noble, and his air martial; he possessed the apparent calm of concentrated despair, 'I pass the first,' said he, in the firmest tone. 'I am going to give the example: we soldiers are not guilty, our commanders alone are so; yet they are saved, and we perish; but, since it must be so, farewell.' Thus, forcibly pressing his hat on the back part of his head, he exclaimed to those who were before him,—'Which way must I go? show me.' One of the two doors was immediately opened for him: he was announced to the multitude by those who had come to seek him and his comrades, and he haughtily advanced. All the operators drew back, and abruptly separated into two parties. There was formed around the victim a circle of the most bloodthirsty characters, with sabres, bayonets, axes, and pikes in their hands: the unfortunate object of these terrible preparations stepped two paces backwards, calmly cast his eyes around him, crossed his arms, and remained a moment motionless; then, as soon as he perceived that all was ready, he rushed upon the pikes and bayonets, and fell, pierced by a thousand wounds.

"The last sighs of the unhappy victim were heard by his ill-fated comrades, who answered them by dreadful cries; several had already endeavoured to conceal themselves in the heaps of straw which were in one of the rooms of their prison, when twelve of the most brutal assassins from without came and dragged them out, one after another, and barbarously murdered them, as they had done the first. One alone had the good fortune to escape: already seized by the coat, and struck the first blow, he was on the point of suffering the same fate as the others, when a Marseillese darted forward and made himself a passage through the arch of steel which was about to close upon him: 'What are we going to do?' he exclaimed in his dialect; 'comrades, I know this worthy youth: he is not a soldier of the 10th of August,—he is only the son of a Swiss, and has surrendered himself to prison, because he has been assured that every Swiss by birth would be massacred.'

"During this moment of suspension in the slaughter, the young man hastily drew some certificates from his pocket, and raised them to the full extent of his arms in the air: his youth, an ingenuous countenance, the tears which flowed abundantly from his eyes, his air of frankness and simplicity, and the papers which he earnestly exhibited, holding himself still in the most visible attitude; all appeared to move and arrest the bloody actors. 'You see,' exclaimed the Marseillese, taking advantage of the favourable moment, 'you see that he is innocent.' 'Set him at liberty,' replied the multitude. Immediately the Marseillese took him by one arm; an assassin took him by the other; the murderers lowered their arms, and several embraced and congratulated him. He left, as it were triumphant, the embraces of death which encircled him, and was carried away in the midst of cries of *Vive la Nation!* with the most lively and boisterous demonstrations of joy.

"This moment of clemency was but of short duration: the list of other prisoners was read; Grandmaison, Champclos, Maron, Vidaut, and others, accused of the forgery of assignats, were the first called: they were forced to descend, and were then examined in the brief mode agreed upon; they wished to answer all at once, but, by a unanimous judgment of the tribunal, they were immediately sent to *La Force*.

"After the death of Montmorin, a second reading of the list of the prisoners was demanded; the name of Thierry, and still more the title of *valet de chambre* of the king, fixed the attention of the commission. A member commenced the examination, and reproached Thierry, who had just been introduced, with some actions of royalism; he accused him particularly with having shown himself on the 10th of August, at the castle of the Tuileries, armed with a poniard. Thierry denied it, and boldly asserted that he had always been an honest man; that, far from conspiring against his country, he had been the first to defend it against its enemies; that, if he happened to be near the king on the 10th of August, it was his service that took him thither, and that he had done his duty.

"Maillard summoned him to declare in what part of the palace he was during the action. He replied that he did not recollect precisely the place; that he was attending to his business; that, as for the rest, he ought to be cited before a tribunal legally constituted, and that there he would answer. 'You will never persuade us, sir,' said a member to him, 'that you are not an aristocrat; you approached too near to the *Veto*: you pretend to tell us that you were obliged to do what was ordered you: for my part, I will answer you,—"Like master, like man:" in consequence, I call upon the president to order you to be removed to *La Force*.' Maillard pronounced *à la Force*, and Thierry was no more.

"Bocquillon and Buos, justices of the peace, afterwards arrived. 'You are accused by the people,' said Maillard to them, 'of having joined with colleagues as infamous as yourselves, and formed a secret committee at the palace of the Tuileries, intended to avenge the court for the events of the 20th of June, and to punish the authors of them.' 'It is true,' replied Bocquillon, with a calm and serene countenance, 'that I was present at that committee; but I defy any one to prove that I participated in any arbitrary act.' '*à la Force! à la Force!*' exclaimed the members. The president pronounced the words, and Bocquillon and Buos were no more.

"Probably, from the characters of the personages whom we have just seen pass to *La Force*, it may be imagined that guilt alone perished. Doubtlessly, many guilty individuals paid for real crimes with their lives; but the greatest offence which these horrible massacres have done to public morals, is, that acts of such cruel illegality, far from turning to the profit of example, the real end of punishment, always honour the victims of the guilty, and leave their adherents the right of calling upon their memory, as upon that of martyred innocence.

"I have forgotten to relate another enormity committed by
the *soi-disant* agents of the sovereign people. With whatever
rapidity the operations went on, these gentlemen had still time
and precaution, instead of adorning their victims, to strip them
completely. They began by taking away their pocket-books,
watches, rings, diamonds, and assignats, and then put all these
spoils as well in their pockets as in baskets and band-boxes;
and I have the two following proofs that they appropriated all
to themselves.

" 1st.—Two commissaries were sent by the section of the
Quatre Nations, to claim, upon the petition of his relations, a
prisoner who had no mark of a royalist about him: they
succeeded, after much difficulty, in procuring his liberation; but
having perceived that there was no procès-verbal of the valuable
effects taken from the condemned, they took the liberty of
remarking upon it to the spoliating judges. The latter, being
much embarrassed in being discovered by these quick-sighted
denunciators, wished at first to shuffle and elude the subject;
they soon raised their tone in such a cunning and obscure
style, that the people, deceived with respect to the object of the
discussion, and taking the commissaries of the section for prisoners,
were going to massacre them, when the latter, lowering their
voices and softening down the reproaches of an ill-timed probity,
retreated promptly and returned like fugitives.

" 2nd.—The civil committee of the section, charged to get
accounts rendered, could discover nothing respecting all these
valuable spoils, although the prisoners of the Abbaye, particularly,
were most of them people of quality and very opulent.

"The commission divided itself, about two o'clock in the
morning, for the purpose of going to the other prisons of
Paris.

"There yet remained, however, some prisoners at the Abbaye;
but the operators were forced, by fatigue, to abandon their post
for some hours, while they went to rest themselves at the committee, which they had chosen as the scene of their orgies,
where they ordered a plentiful supply of wine. Thus they passed
the night, and returned in the morning to the prison of the
Abbaye, and killed the few that remained.

"I have stated how Billaud de Varennes had come, the evening before, to the court of the Abbaye: Manuel, on his part, had come to the prison about eight o'clock in the evening, by torch-light. He had harangued the Popular Commission, but his eyes expressed more the character of constraint than of the sanguinary joy which animated those of Billaud.

"Billaud de Varennes returned the next morning, the 3rd of September, near noon, to the committee of the section. He was speaking, standing upon the steps of the staircase, when a man named Rulhière, a prisoner of the Abbaye, already pierced by many pike-wounds, ran naked into the court, falling and rising again alternately. I saw him advance again several tottering steps forward, and struggle for more than ten minutes against death, which at last vanquished him. The following are the abridged, but *bonâ fide*, words of Billaud de Varennes to the assassins:—'Respectable citizens, you have just destroyed a set of scoundrels; you have saved the country; all France owes you eternal gratitude; the municipality knows not how to make a return to you. Undoubtedly, the booty and the spoils of these scoundrels (pointing to the dead bodies), belong to those who have delivered us from them; but not deeming this a sufficient reward, I am deputed to offer each of you twenty-four livres (a pound sterling), which are to be paid to you immediately (loud applauses from the assassins). Respectable citizens, continue your work, and the country will be grateful.'

"After the speech which I have just reported, Billaud de Varennes entered into the committee, and directed it to give the twenty-four livres which he had just promised to the operators. The committee, possessing no funds, demanded from him the means of satisfying the engagements he had imposed upon them. He laconically desired them to make a list, and went away without giving any other solution, leaving the committee trembling and terrified at this terrible responsibility to the operators.

"In fact, scarcely had he quitted the room before the wretches entered in a body, and loudly demanded the sum which had just been allotted to them by Billaud de Varennes. Never was there a more horrible spectacle.

"One held a sabre, another a blood-stained bayonet, another a broken pike, covered with human brains; another had torn out a palpitating heart, which he carried at the end of a mutilated halberd; another had cut off the virile parts, which served him to exercise disgusting jokes towards the women. These were the trophies, the abominable justifications, on which they founded their threatening claims: '*Do you think that I have only gained twenty-four livres,*' boldly exclaimed a journeyman baker, armed with a club; '*I have killed more than forty of them for my share.*' Two women were met in the morning, carrying some soup and meat in a porringer. '*Whither are you going?*' said their neighbour to them. '*We are carrying breakfast* (replied they) *to our men, who are working at the Abbaye.*' '*Is there still work?*' asked an assassin who had just slept himself sober in the court. '*If there is no more,*' answered the two women, '*it will be very necessary to make it.*'

"Anxious to satisfy the furious claimants, the committee occupied itself in instantly drawing up a list of the whole of them, told them the money was at the municipality, and requested them to go and receive it themselves: they consented, and set out provided with the list, but there was no money at the Committee of Inspection of the commune. They waited there in vain till eleven o'clock in the evening: at midnight they returned, swearing, cursing, foaming with rage, and threatening the committee collectively that they would cut their throats, if they were not instantly paid. No reply would be heard to this imperative decision; a member of the committee wished to remonstrate, but the sabre was raised over his head, and he remained mute; in a word, '*money or life*' was what they were determined to have. At this irresistible argument a member of the committee, a woollen-draper, requested permission to run to his house for some money, and it was granted to him: he returned immediately, and advanced on his own responsibility one half the allowance of the assassins.

"The committee were thus rid of these monsters for the night; but, after having slept off the immoderate drink of eight and-forty hours, they returned at an early hour the next morning for the other half. Two commissaries civilly conducted them to the commune. I have learnt that they were ultimately paid by the minister Roland, and I affirm that they were not seen again.

"On the 3rd of September, in the morning, Billaud de Varennes entered the council-general of the commune, amicably holding by the hand an assassin covered over with blood, and presented him *as a brave man, who had laboured well,* according to his expression.

## NOTE C. p. 39. *

*Account of the Massacres in each Prison.*

We borrow from the History of the Revolution of the 10th of August, circumstantial details of the various massacres which took place at Paris. We shall commence by that of the priests at the Abbaye, at the Carmes, and at Saint Firmin:—

"By the shutting of the Barriers, several of the conveyances, which were leaving Paris, had been detained. These contained some unfortunate priests, who, in order to obey the terms of the decree, were departing in companies, four, six, and eight together, for the purpose of sharing the expenses of the journey, and of lessening, by the association of their virtues, the burden of their miseries. The coaches which conveyed them were taken to the Hôtel-de-Ville, and from there sent to the Abbaye and to the Carmes, the sacred depositories of these new martyrs. The crowd of people who followed them from the Hôtel-de-Ville to the Faubourg St. Germain, increased every moment. The Marseillese repeated over and over again, with horrid imprecations, that they were going to make them dance the *carmagnole:* three carriages were thus conducted to the door of the Abbaye. The priests from the two first were allowed to alight and to enter the cloister of the Abbaye; but, when the first priest alighted from the third coach, the director of the massacres spread the report amongst the people, that they had a secret understanding with the other prisoners; that they had made signs to them, to which the latter had replied; and the massacre began by this third coach. The assassins shortly afterwards entered into the cloisters and passages of the convent of the Abbaye St. Germain, and nearly twenty ecclesiastics lost their lives there.

"When the massacre of the few priests who were at the Abbaye was finished, a messenger went to give orders to the

* This note refers to the note of the Editor, p. 39.

committee, which had been assembled since morning in the
building adjoining the church of the Carmes. The priests who
were there soon saw that their last hour was approaching.

"For two days, all the ecclesiastics, warned by numerous
indications that they had only a very short time to live, had
passed their last moments in mutually exhorting and blessing
each other. Through the gratings and the windows which looked
into the garden, they saw the sabres and the pikes glittering,
and they could hear the threats which were directed against
them.

"About half-past three o'clock, they were all made to quit
the church indiscriminately, although it had been usual to allow
the sick, the aged, and all those who wished to engage in
prayer, to remain there. It was remarked that this was the
third time that day that the names had been called over.

"Half an hour after the church had been emptied, the assassins entered it with their arms, in the midst of cries, oaths, and
menaces. The door of the church, from which one descended
by a staircase into the garden, was guarded by gendarmes, and
was opened without any resistance; but the principal door of
the church, which opened into the Rue Vaugirard, remained
closed during the whole of the execution. The people did not
take the least share in it.

"At the time of the irruption into the garden, the unfortunate
priests, to the number of one hundred and eighty-five, divided
themselves into two groups. The former, composed of thirty persons amongst which were the three bishops, directed their steps
towards a chapel or oratory, which was at the extremity of the
garden. They there knelt down, and implored the pardon of
God for their offences, and blessed and embraced each other for
the last time.

"Ten assassins advanced towards the chapel. One of the
priests went to meet them: he was about to address them, when
a musket-ball deprived him of life. This was the first blood
that was shed that evening.

"On their arrival at the chapel, the assassins tumultuously
demanded, ' *Where is the Archbishop of Arles ? Where is the Archbishop of Arles ?*' He to whom they addressed the question was
the Abbé de la Pannonie. The archbishop was close to the

abbé; the latter, thinking that by his death he would perhaps save the life of his worthy bishop, contented himself by casting down his eyes without reply, imitating by this religious devotedness that which Madame Elizabeth evinced on the 20th June, when she determined, at the risk of her life, not to contradict the report which was spreading among the assassins, that she was the queen. Admirable testimony of heroic sentiments, the fruits of true religion!

"By his age, however, and by his venerable countenance, so exactly answering the description they had received of him,— one of the murderers recognised the prelate, and, addressing him, said, '*It is thou, then, who art the Archbishop of Arles?*'— '*Yes, gentlemen, I am.*' '*Ah, unfortunate man! it is thou who hast shed the blood of the patriots of Arles?*'—'*Gentlemen, I never shed the blood of a human being, nor did I ever do ill to any one in my life.*' '*Well! I am going to make thee shed blood now!*' And instantly, on finishing this dialogue, he struck him a blow with his sabre upon the forehead. The archbishop received it without shrinking. A second was aimed at his face; after this second blow, the contraction which pain occasioned, and the blood which flowed from the wound, disfigured the prelate so, that even his colleagues could not recognise him. A third blow made him fall, and he supported his sinking body with his left hand, without uttering a complaint or a murmur. As he was thus lying, one of the wretches thrust a pike into his bosom with such violence, that the head of it remained in the wound. He then leaped upon the throbbing body, trampled upon it, plucked the watch from the pocket, and presented it to his comrades, as a trophy of victory.

"Thus perished this venerable archbishop, at the entrance of the chapel, at the foot of the altar and the cross of our Saviour.— By the standard under which he had fought, he died.

"The two other bishops were in the chapel with the rest of the priests, all kneeling at the foot of the altar; a railing separated them from the assassins, who made several discharges among them, with the muzzles of their muskets almost touching the victims, and in this manner killed the major part of them; but the Bishops of Beauvais and Saintes survived this first massacre, the latter having had his leg fractured with a ball. The band of assassins dispersed themselves in the garden, and joined those who were murdering the priests that were scattered about that vast enclosure. An atrocious spectacle was here presented,—men hunted down by their fellow men like so many wild beasts. The victims were pursued in every direction. More than forty were thus slaughtered: some might have saved themselves by scaling the walls, and by throwing themselves into the Rue Cassette, and into the courts of the adjoining houses; but, thinking that their absence might cause the massacre of their companions, they entered again, with the exception of a very few. When the assassins saw that some escaped in this manner, they sent two of their comrades into that street, and there, with a sword in one hand, and a pistol in the other, they pursued those who attempted to escape that way.

"The firing in the garden had continued about a quarter of an hour, when a man, who was the chief director of this massacre, ran towards the murderers, and made them cease firing, by exclaiming—'*Gentlemen, it is not thus that you must act; you go awkwardly about it; do what I shall tell you.*' Upon these words he ordered that all the priests should be made to go into the church. They then drove back, with the flat parts of their sabres, all those who still breathed. The two bishops were of the number. The Bishop of Saintes, already wounded, was taken with a degree of attention, in the arms of the assassins, and placed temporarily upon a bed.

"There were still at this time about a hundred priests. The manager of this new manœuvre then gave orders to take them two by two, and to lead them back a second time into the garden, whence they came. The assassins had been stationed at the foot of the staircase which descended into the garden, and there they massacred them, one after another.

"When the turn of the Bishop of Beauvais was arrived, they went to fetch him from the foot of the altar in the church, which he held clasped with his arms. He serenely arose and went to meet his fate. The Bishop of Saintes was one of the last who was asked for. The gendarmes on guard surrounded his bed, which at first gave some trouble in finding him. These men, who were equal in number to the assassins, suffered him to be carried away. He could not walk, and replied to his executioners, who ordered him to follow them; '*Gentlemen, I do not refuse to go to death like the others, but you see the state in which I am; I have one of my legs broken; I pray you to assist me, and I will willingly go to my execution.*' Two assassins supported him under their arms to the staircase, where he received the blow of martyrdom.

"The massacre ended at eight o'clock in the evening; all were killed, as we have seen, in the garden, with the exception of one single priest, who had concealed himself under a mattress. He was discovered there, while the assassins were terminating their crime by a debauch, and were drinking with the gendarmes, dancing at the same time the *Carmagnole*. This unfortunate priest was destroyed the last; he was the only one who perished in the church. When the massacre was almost consummated, an order was given to open the doors of the church, that the people might enter, and give this horrible catastrophe a sort of popular legislation.

"The fate of these unhappy priests had been so definitively settled for several days, that the gravedigger of the parish, St. Sulpice, had received in advance an assignat of a hundred crowns, in order to prepare, at Montrouge, the grave which was to receive their bodies. They were deposited there the next morning. Ten waggons carried them to the place."

### Massacre at the Cloister of the Bernardines.

"I speak of this prison before the Conciergerie and the Hôtel de La Force, in order to follow their topography in Paris. There were, in all, nine theatres of carnage, two on this side, and seven on the other side of the river; the former to the north, the others to the south.

"The Carmes, St. Firmin, and the Abbaye, were in the southern part of Paris. The victims who were slaughtered there were principally the martyrs of religion.

"The four other prisons, which were likewise situated on the south, were the cloister of the Bernardines, the Salpêtrière, Bicêtre, and the Conciergerie of the Palace of Justice, which is in the Isle Notre-Dame.

"The cloister of the Bernardines was the depôt whither had

been transferred the prisoners destined for the galleys, from the lower St. Bernard, before its destruction. Seventy-three prisoners, there waiting to be sent to their destination, were all murdered."

### Massacre at the Hospital of the Salpêtrière.

"In this prison were confined the women of abandoned lives, and other prisoners, who had been condemned to a punishment more or less severe by the Correctional Police. Forty-five of these unfortunate creatures were massacred on the morning of the 3rd. Amongst the number was the widow of the famous Desrues. The following observations respecting this woman are contained in a work recently published at Paris:—'This unfortunate woman thought she was on the eve of gaining her liberty. There had, in fact, been a commission named under the ministry of M. Duport-Dutertre, to restore to liberty those of the prisoners of the *ancien régime* for whom the nature of their crimes, the length of their captivity, and their good conduct, claimed indulgence. The commissioners, who went to the Salpêtrière, received from the heads of that establishment such satisfactory testimonials in behalf of the widow of Desrues, that, ascertaining she was claimed by one of her uncles, they promised her liberty. Unfortunately the functions of these commissioners ceased when M. Duport-Dutertre quitted the ministry. This woman had seen, during the *ancien régime*, her husband perish upon a scaffold, and her children enclosed in hospitals, and had been herself branded by the executioner, and condemned to perpetual punishment. Under the new *régime* she received a melancholy death, at the very moment when, she thought, the doors of her prison were going to be opened."

### Massacre at the Hospital Bicêtre.

"It was here that the carnage lasted the longest, and was the most bloody and horrible. This prison was the den of every vice, the hospital in which the most afflicting diseases were treated; it was the sink of Paris. All it contained were killed. It would be impossible to fix the number of the victims; I have often heard it estimated at six thousand. The work of death did not cease for a moment during eight consecutive days and nights. Pikes, sabres, and muskets not sufficing for the ferocity of the assassins, they were obliged to employ cannon. Two sections suffered them to take those which were confided to them for the protection of their fellow-creatures. For the first time, prisoners were there seen defending their dungeons and their chains. The resistance was long and sanguinary; at length, the assassins, by the following means, became superior. They enclosed in a court a certain number of malefactors, and secured the gates; men who were posted there were driven away by the butt of the musket, and those of the unfortunate wretches who attempted to make an attack upon them, in order to escape, were shot. They then procured a cannon, and, while they appeared to point it to the angle of the court where the greatest number of prisoners were assembled, the latter fled to another side to avoid the fire, when the direction of the piece was suddenly changed, and the flying group were fired on with grape-shot. The more rapidly the victims fell, the greater the joy and the laughter of the assassins became; and, when at last there remained but a small number of prisoners, which they would have been long in destroying with the cannon, they had recourse to small arms. In fact, the reptiles had devised a new source of amusement, that of firing on their fellow men running.

"At the close of the massacres, Pétion, who had not repaired either to the Carmes or to the Abbaye, went to the Bicêtre. There his compassion was for the first time excited at the sight of the slaughtered victims. The cannonading had ceased. The prisoners who remained to be put to death had taken refuge in the cellars, the cells, and the vaults, where the cannon, and even the light of day, could not reach them; the assassins were occupied in drowning them with pumps in these subterranean retreats. Pétion spoke to them of humanity and *philosophy*.

"The murderers, who found it quite as philosophical to finish these unhappy beings as those of the Abbaye, for whom they had not seen Pétion make intercession, harshly repulsed the Mayor of Paris. The mayor, in quitting them, addressed to them the following words:—' *Well, my good fellows, finish.*' However dreadful the expression may be, it is only the parallel to that which he addressed to the furies of the 20th June, when

he said to them, under the eyes of the king:—'Citizens, you
have conducted yourselves with wisdom and dignity.'"

*Massacre at the Conciergerie.*

"To this prison the Swiss officers who were at the Abbaye,
had been transferred.   Their trials had commenced at the
Revolutionary Criminal Tribunal, by that of the brave Bachmann,
their major.   He was then upon his trial, and these judges were
holding their sitting, when the carnage of the prisoners commenced
in their presence, at the door of the tribunal,—at the very foot
of the great staircase which led to it—and they did not attempt
to prevent it.   They showed some respect to the Swiss major,
who was then under process of trial; but only because they well
knew that his punishment was certain.   He was preserved only
that his punishment might be increased by the sight of the
slaughter of his eight comrades, and they were in the hope that
they might be able to draw from him some confessions against
the queen.   But the man who had seen approach, without alarm,
and even with pleasure, the 10th of August, naturally contemplated, without emotion, the 2nd of September.   Bachmann,
silent and cold, answered nothing, and did not condescend
to discuss his innocence, of which he would have felt ashamed:
he demanded death, and received it like a hero.   Enveloped in
his red cloak, with nothing under it but his shirt, he mounted
the scaffold with a firm air, gazed with disdain upon the mob
which surrounded it, uttered, shuddering, these prophetic words,
—'*My death will be revenged,*' and his head fell!

"Besides the Swiss officers and the Marquis of Montmorin,
no other persons were assassinated who had been imprisoned
merely for having expressed opinions contrary to those of the day.
The malefactors killed in the court of the palace of justice were
to the number of seventy-five; which, united to the ten soldiers
above-mentioned, form a total of eighty-five dead.

"A single individual, a female, forming one of the seventy-
five, merits particular remark: she was a shopkeeper of the
Palais Royal, who had been accused of having mutilated her
lover, a grenadier of the French guards.   She had already been
condemned, but had been fortunate enough to obtain a respite

from the execution of her sentence. She was tied to a post,
her feet were nailed to the ground, and her breasts cut off
with sabres; the monsters employed to finish her sufferings
applied the steel and the fire in a way which modesty and
humanity forbid us to mention, From this revengeful appearance
of cruelty, we should be led to imagine there were many French
guards amongst the assassins."

### Massacre of the Grand Châtelet.

"There was none confined in this prison for political causes.
They consisted principally of persons suspected of forgery, or
of uttering forged assignats, and those who, having taken them
by accident, had endeavoured to put them again into circulation.
Of this number was a brother-in-law of M. d'Eprémenil, who
miraculously escaped by the intervention of a national guard of
Bordeaux. Accident having thrown me into his company, a
few days after the 2nd September, he confessed to me that, in
going out of the Châtelet, under the disguise and with the arms
of an assassin, he sank up to the knees in blood, and that he
passed more than two hours at the fountain Maubuée, to remove
the marks of it, in order that he might not wound the sensibility
of the individuals at whose house he was going to seek for an
asylum.

"The slaughtered bodies were heaped up on the lateral parts
of the Pont-au-Change. Thither were also carried the dead
from the Conciergerie. Waggons taken from the stables of the
hotels in the Faubourg St. Germain, yoked with horses hired
the day before, driven by men all dripping with blood, successively
bore off these mutilated bodies, and carried them to the depôt
pointed out by the Commune, the stone quarries of the plain
of Montrouge, at a league distant from Paris. Upon these
waggons were even seen women and children seated, holding
in their hands, and showing to the passers-by, the mangled
limbs of the murdered bodies."

### Massacre at the Hôtel de La Force.

"This prison, which was divided into several buildings, had
been chosen as an assistant to the prisons of the Abbaye and

Châtelet: the former could receive no more prisoners, and even the infected dungeons of the latter, although sufficient under the old police, had been insufficient for the disorders, robberies, villainies, and assassinations, which the revolution had engendered. The part destined for the debtors had been recently burnt, and they had been transferred to the convent of St. Pélagie, where they were set at liberty to the number of fifty-three.

" An individual named Truchon, commissary of the commune, came to the Committee of Twenty-one, who were still assembled, to make his report, that the massacres having begun at the prison of La Force, he had thought it his duty to permit the women to go out, and that he had set at liberty twenty-four of them; that among these were Mademoiselle de Tourzel and Madame de St. Brice, whom, however, from prudent motives, he had conducted to the section of the *Droits de l'Homme*, to await their sentence there. The extraordinary commission troubled themselves no further with the fate of these two persons, than with that of the Princesse de Lamballe, and of the other ladies whom Truchon had thought proper to leave at La Force.

" Tallien, another commissary of the commune, said, that he had used all his efforts to prevent the effects of the people's fury; but that he had not been able to prevent their *just* vengeance. A third commissary, named Guirauld, came to give a detail of the judgments which were pronounced in the turnkey's ' rooms. He extolled the justice of the people. ' Twelve jurors,' said he, 'are questioned upon their consciences as to what they think of the prisoner. They place their hand upon his head, and upon the question being asked, whether they are of opinion that the prisoner should be liberated, if they answer YES, he is instantly murdered with pikes; if they say NO, he is set at liberty, amid cries of *Vive la Nation !* '

" The massacre of La Force began by the unfortunate Rulhière, ci-devant commandant of the watch of Paris, and then of the horse gendarmes. He was brother of the celebrated academician of that name, author of the poem of the *Disputes*, and other esteemed works.

" M. de la Chesnaye, one of the six commandants of the National Guards, and an Abbé Bardi, strongly suspected of having assassinated and robbed his own brother, likewise perished in the evening of the 2nd. But I must, above all, fix the attention on the deplorable fate of the Princesse de Lamballe.

"This unfortunate princess, having been spared on the evening of the 2nd, had thrown herself upon her bed, overwhelmed with anxiety and horror. She only closed her eyes to open them again almost immediately, alarmed by the most frightful dreams. About eight o'clock in the evening, two national guards entered her apartment, and intimated to her that she was going to be transferred to the Abbaye. She answered them that she liked as well to remain in the prison where she was, as to go to another. In consequence, she absolutely refused to go down, and earnestly entreated them to leave her in quiet. One of the national guards then approached her, told her that she must obey, and that her life depended upon it. She answered that she would do what they desired, and prayed those who were in her room to retire. She put on her robe, recalled the national guard, who gave her his arm, and went down into the formidable turnkey's room, where she found the two municipal officers, wearing their scarfs, · sitting in judgment on several of the prisoners. Pétion, who saw them again the next evening, has not thought proper to name them; but it was soon known that they were Hébert and L'Huillier. On her arrival at this frightful tribunal, the sight of the ensanguined arms, and of the assassins, whose hands, clothes, and faces were stained with blood, caused her such horror that she swooned several times. When she was in a condition to undergo her examination, they commenced it. The following is the examination, as has been collected by the family of the princess, from the mouth of an ocular witness :—

Q. Who are you?

A. Maria Louisa, Princess of Savoy.

Q. Your employment?

A. Superintendent of the household of the queen.

Q. Had you any knowledge of the plots of the court on the 10th August?

A. I know not whether there were any plots on the 10th August; but I know that I had no knowledge of them.

Q. Swear liberty, equality, hatred of the king, of the queen, and of royalty.

A. I will readily swear the two former; I cannot swear the latter; it is not in my heart; (here one present said to her in a whisper; '*Swear; if you do not swear, you are dead.*') The princess did not reply, raised her hands as high as her eyes, and made a step towards the door.

"The judge then said: '*Let Madame be set at liberty.*' It is well known that this phrase was the signal of death. The report had been spread that it was not the intention of the judge to send her to execution; but those who have, by these means, wished to attenuate the horror of her death, have forgotten to state what precautions had been taken to save her. Some say, that when the door was opened, she had been recommended to cry out, *Vive la Nation!* but that, terrified by the sight of the blood, and of the dead bodies which she perceived, she could only utter these words: '*Fie! horror!*' and that the assassins, applying this very natural exclamation, to the cry which they demanded, of '*Vive la Nation,*' had instantly struck her. Others pretend that she only uttered, at the door of the room, these words: '*I am lost!*'—Whatever she said, her death was so firmly resolved, that, scarcely had she passed the threshold of the door, when she received a blow on the back of the head from a sabre, which made the blood spring forth. Two men held her tightly under the arms, and made her walk over the dead bodies. She fainted every moment, while passing through the narrow passage which leads from the Rue St. Antoine to the prison, and which is called the *Cul de Sac des Prêtres;* when, at last, she was so weak, that it was no longer possible for her to raise herself up, they finished her by stabs with their pikes, upon a heap of dead bodies. She was soon stripped of her clothes, and her corpse was then exposed to the gaze and insults of the populace. It remained more than two hours in this position. By degrees, as the blood which flowed from her wounds, or from those of the bodies near her, sullied the limbs of this unfortunate victim, men placed there purposely were occupied in washing it, in order to make the spectators remark its beauty, even in death.

"I have not firmness enough to describe all the excesses of barbarity and licentiousness with which they dishonoured it, but shall content myself with stating, that they loaded a cannon with one of the legs. About noon, they resolved to cut off her head, and to carry it through the streets of Paris. The other members of her body, scattered about, were likewise delivered up to a troop of cannibals, who dragged them through the streets· Her head was carried first to the Abbaye St. Antoine, where she had passed some time, and was shown to Madame de Beauvau, ci-devant abbess of that abbey, and the particular friend of Madame de Lamballe. Thence it was carried to the Temple, as I shall shortly state, then to the Palais Royal, then to the Hôtel de Toulouse, the residence of the Duke of Penthièvre, her father-in-law, where she had long resided: some of her sad remains were afterwards collected and interred.

"Shortly after, a parley was held with the commissaries for the admission of the head of Madame de Lamballe into the Temple. They protested that they did not wish to offer any violence to the hostages, but that they desired a deputation should enter to accompany this head *to the foot of the throne*, and make those who were the cause of it see the result of their conspiracies and their plots. The two commissaries of the temple, alarmed at the sight, acceded to the wishes of the assassins, and went to inform the king and the royal family of the demand of the people, and of the necessity they were in of going to contemplate the sad spectacle. The inspector of the Temple, the mason Palloy, and the officer commanding the National Guard, remained near the King. The commissaries sent for the procession, which entered, with the horrible trophy, into the principal court of the Temple, and traversed the passage of the Bailli, and came into the garden, under the windows of the lateral building, called the *Petite Tour*, which the royal family then inhabited. When the head of the Princesse de Lamballe had arrived there, the commandant of the National Guard intimated to the King to present himself at the window; this prince, who imagined that his last hour was come, prepared himself to die. Concealing his grief beneath his dignity, he replied firmly to the gaoler, who had made a speech to him on the subject, in a revolutionary style, '*You are right, Sir.*' He afterwards presented himself at the window, and retired almost immediately. The Queen and Madame Elizabeth had fainted, and did not behold the frightful sight.

" The order which reigned at La Force, thanks to the members of the commune, who gave their judgments there, has enabled us to ascertain the number of victims: they amounted to a hundred and sixty-four persons, not including malefactors, suspected individuals, vagabonds, etc."—*Extract from the History of the* 10*th of August, by Peltier.*

## NOTE D. p. 42.

" On the 8th of September, 1792, at nine o'clock in the morning, I was attacked in the Rue Baillif, by two men, one of whom gave me a blow with a stick upon the head, which knocked me down; his companion was going to plunge his sword into my body, when they were pursued by two men, who, not having been able to overtake them, told me, in conducting me home, that they had seen me pass under the wooden galleries of the Palais Royal, and that they had heard two men say, in speaking of me: 'It is he—we shall not miss him this time;' and that they had followed me to assist me in case of need.

" On the 5th of October following, at eight o'clock in the evening, I was passing over the bridge Notre Dame, returning from the Conciergerie, whither I had been to carry a copy of 'My Agony' to M. Poupart de Beaubourg, who had written to Desenne, requesting him to send one to the prison to him. On my return, I crossed the Pont Notre Dame, and was then attacked by three men, one of whom rushed upon me, and attempted to stab me with his sabre; I parried the blow with mine, and disarmed him; I seized him by the collar, and fortunately a woman cried out *assassin*, which made the other two take flight. I dragged him to the guard-house, placed at the foot of the bridge, and I afterwards learnt that he had been shut up at La Force, where he had remained six days.

" If I could believe that M. Manuel was a traitor and a scoundrel, I should suspect him of having ordered these assassinations, as one of those who attacked me in the Rue Baillif was recognised as one of his trusty adherents, who tenaciously followed me everywhere before the 2nd of September; and, as he whom I arrested on the Pont Notre Dame, and who was imprisoned at La

Force, got out immediately, on his liberation being demanded by Manuel, at the General Committee of the Commune."—*Note of M. de St. Meard.*

---

In a notice preceding the declaration of Citizen Jourdan, reference is made to certain accounts of the disbursement of sums of money paid by the treasurer of the Commune of Paris, in behalf of the council-general, for expenses occasioned by the revolution of the 10th of August, and by the events of the 2nd and 3rd of September, and following days. They are too tedious to be translated. It may be sufficient to observe, that they abundantly prove the share which the Commune of Paris had in the massacres, and show that the assassins acted by the authority of, and were paid by, the wretches who laid regular schemes for the atrocities that were committed.

The procès-verbal of the commune are given in the volume we have been translating. They are not of sufficient interest for an English reader. The whole of them clearly testify that it was by the chief instrumentality of the members of that body, that the massacres of the 10th of August, and of the 2nd and 3rd of September, took place.—*Note of the Translator.*

## NOTE E. p. 172.

"Several remarkable circumstances occurred in this number (13). We even went so far as to turn the tribunal itself into mockery. Eighteen beds, touching each other, were separated by high boards, between which each individual lay as if buried. Upon each of these beds sat a judge. The accused was mounted upon a table in front of the beds, and the floor was occupied by the registrar and the public accuser. Our sittings usually commenced at midnight, when, confined within our strong doors and gloomy vaults, we were almost certain of not being disturbed. The accused was always found guilty: could he be otherwise when tried by the Revolutionary Tribunal? The moment he was sentenced, the dreadful apparatus was displayed; his hands were tied, and the sufferer advanced to the rail of a bed to receive the stroke which was ready to fall upon

his neck. By one of those events which so frequently occur in
revolutions, the public accuser became in his turn the accused,
and was consequently condemned. He underwent his sentence;
but suddenly returned covered with a white sheet, and terrified
us by a picture of the tortures which he suffered in hell; enu-
merated to us all his crimes, and predicted to the judges the fate
that awaited them: that they would be carried about in carts
filled with blood; that they would be shut up in iron cages;
and that the world would be dismayed at the horror of their
punishments, as it had been terrified by their unheard-of cruelties.
We had in our room a man named Lapagne, the Pantin of
number 13; he had been mayor of Ingouville, a suburb of Havre,
to which place he had been sent by the Jacobins; and at that
time he was worthy of serving under them, having been a chief
of robbers, and condemned to be broken on the wheel for murder
under the *ancien régime*. Our ghost seized this man by the
collar, and, reproaching him for all his crimes, with the most
dreadful imprecations, he dragged him away to hell. 'Lapagne!
Lapagne! Lapagne!" cried he in a hollow voice. Lapagne,
terrified and confused, followed his guide; and his terror gave
additional solemnity to this scene, which was lighted by a single
lamp, that left two-thirds of the dungeon in absolute darkness.
This ghost was myself.... It was thus that we amused ourselves in the midst of death, and that in our prophetic imitations
we spoke the truth in the midst of spies and executions."—
*Note by Riouffe.*

## NOTE F. p. 172.

J. P. Brissot to Barrière, deputy of the Convention, at the Ab-
    baye, the 7th of September, the year 2 of the one and indi-
    visible republic.

"The people cried out to you for bread; you have promised
them my blood. Thus you decree my death, even before I am
tried by a tribunal. Thus you insult the people, to whom you
ascribe a love of blood, and the tribunals, whom you suppose
to be the instruments of your passions. Ah, if my blood could
produce abundance, and extinguish all divisions, I would myself
shed it this moment.

"In order to excuse this sanguinary language, you allege that I am conspiring in my prison; you allege that I have said: '*Before my head shall fall, others shall fall in the very heart of the convention.*'

"This is a fresh calumny, invented with a view to irritate the public mind against me. I defy you to cite a single witness, a single proof, of this conspiracy or of this language. I abhor the shedding of blood; I would not even wish for that of my persecutors, who would delight in drinking mine. Philosophy, justice, order, and humanity,—behold the true foundations of republics; and it is well known that my only crime is, that I could not approve of any others. Behold my conspiracy, that which I follow up in my prison. Yes, I conspire with my triple grates, with my triple bolts; I conspire alone or together with all the philosophers of antiquity, who teach me to endure my sufferings for the sake of liberty, of which I shall always be the apostle. Behold the plot which must be added to the list of those which are imputed to me, and the proofs of which are sought in vain, since they are imaginary. But victims are wanted .... Strike, then, and may I be the last republican immolated to party spirit!"

## NOTE G. p. 175.

"I met in this prison a man of a very singular and original character. He was so disgusted with his existence, that he never spoke of anything but dying, though his desire for death did not deprive him of a stock of gaiety, which was proof against every shock.

"This prisoner's name was Gornay. He was about twenty-seven years of age. He had formerly been a grenadier in the ci-devant regiment of Artois, and had since served in the hussars of Berchigny. He was confined in the Conciergerie as accused of emigration. It was Ronsin who had him arrested at Châlons-sur-Saône, and sent forward to Paris.

"His gay and affable manners had gained him the good graces of a pretty young woman, who came regularly to the Conciergerie to attend to her asthmatic father. After having fulfilled this pious duty, she went to pass three or four hours with her dear prisoner. It was an inexpressible pleasure to her to provide for his wants, and even for what she called his *menus plaisirs*, amusements.

"Gornay was fully sensible of her generous conduct. He had promised to marry her upon his being released from prison; but the unhappy man always nourished in his heart the desire of dying.

"When his act of indictment was brought him, he took it coolly in his hands, rolled it up, set fire to it at the lamp, and lighted his pipe with it. His companions observed to him that it was madness thus to run in the face of death, when he had such positive means of defence. Gornay appeared to be moved by their solicitations, but his mind was bent on dying.

"Before he departed for the tribunal, he drank some white wine, ate some oysters with his companions, and smoked his pipe, discoursing with them with perfect ease upon the destruction of our being. 'That is not all,' said he; 'now that we have breakfasted well, we must think of supper; so give me the address of *a restaurateur* (tavern-keeper) in the other world, in order that I may have a good repast prepared for this evening.'

"When his indictment was read before the tribunal, he admitted that every article of it was perfectly true; and his advocate having observed that he was not in his right mind, he replied, 'Never have I been more in possession of my senses than at this moment when I am on the point of losing them. Officious advocate! I forbid you to defend me: let them drag me to the guillotine!'

"Upon being sentenced to death, he crossed through the court-yard, and saluted his companions with his usual gaiety, and without the smallest alteration being visible in his countenance.

"After his arrival at the hall of the condemned, he ate and drank with a good appetite, and was just the same as usual.

"On ascending the fatal cart, he addressed one of the turn-keys with whom he was a little familiar.—'Friend Rivière,' said he to him, 'we must drink a glass of Kirschwasser together, or otherwise I would not forgive you to the day of my death.' Rivière brought the liqueur, and Gornay appeared to drink it with much pleasure. While crossing the court-yard of the Palais, some persons hooted at him. 'Cowards that you are,' replied he, coolly, 'you insult me! Would you go forth to death with as much courage as I do?'

"Upon his arrival at the foot of the scaffold, he exclaimed, —'I have at length reached the point I wished!' and tranquilly gave himself up to the executioner."


## NOTE H. p. 203.

"Let us follow the steps of Hébert and his *acolytes*, in their endeavours to raise the mob against the *maisons d'arrêt* (Houses of Detention).

"In the course of the month of Nivôse it occurred to them to order the removal, with great ceremony and in open day, of two hundred persons at once, into the *maisons d'arrêt*, and from the *maisons d'arrêt* to the prisons. Drawn slowly along from street to street, in long carts, manacled, and tied two and two, the unhappy objects of their choice were exposed to the hootings and insults of the mob, to whom they were represented as *brigands of La Vendée*. The carts were purposely stopped, for entire hours, in the market-places; and the gendarmes had orders to put to death the first who should utter a complaint, or make an attempt to disengage himself. Among these victims were old men, women, and children. Several of them, overwhelmed with weakness and fatigue, and sunk under the weight of humiliation and shame, fell down in fits. The wives of the sans-culottes, affected at this cruel scene, immediately ran to fetch them a few drops of wine or brandy. They offered them this trifling assistance, with the frank expressions of nature and of feeling. On a sudden, the municipal Cerberus, offended at their relieving the sufferings of misfortune, rushed among them in a fury, loaded them with abuse, tore the glass from their hands, dashed it on the ground, and drove back, with violence, those who had dared to offer it—those whose only offence was that of being humane and compassionate. Such was his barbarity, that some of these good females have even been punished for their benevolent pity.

"Two hundred brigands, who were sentenced to imprisonment in irons, were transferred from Bicêtre to St. Lazare, in order to persuade the people that St. Lazare contained none but brigands. In this prison, sufficiently secure for men who wished to owe their liberty to the law alone, but very unsafe for beings inured to every crime, it was hoped that these wretches would revolt, and would employ every possible means to effect their escape. In order to excite them to proceed to the greatest excesses, they were treated in a manner to drive them to despair. They were thrown pell-mell into the refectory, without beds, without seats, without straw, without fire to warm themselves, and even without food. They roared and bellowed, and filled the air with cries and imprecations. The refectory hall was covered with a handsome wood-work, which was soon torn down and burnt. Uneasiness and alarm were spread through the prison and the surrounding houses. The neighbours were in terror, dreading at every moment an irruption of counter-revolutionists and assassins. In this state of things, Henriot, mounted on horseback, collected the mob around him, and advanced, at the head of an armed force, into the court of the prison. 'Citizens (cried he, addressing himself to the guard, and pointing to the windows of the prisoners' room), the men who are in that building are wretches whom death awaits: they dream of nothing but crimes and counter-revolutions. If a single one should dare raise his voice, or attempt to escape, fire upon him; we give them all up to you.' ..... At these sanguinary words a cry of indignation issued from the windows where the prisoners were crowded. Henriot appeared disconcerted; he, however, soon recovered himself, and resumed: "It is possible that among these conspirators there may be one or two patriots; if so, you will grant them favour and protection." He then reined up his horse, and, inwardly congratulating himself upon the unfavourable impression which he had left against the prisoners, he rode out of the court.

"The unhappy prisoners, having witnessed this revolting conduct, looked forward to nothing but the most frightful death. They no longer doubted but their enemies wished to renew the horrible butchery of the 2nd of September; and resolved, if an attempt should be made to massacre them, to employ, in their defence, every means in their power. In consequence of this determination, they kept themselves on their guard. Four out of their number were charged with passing the night in each corridor, to stand sentinels, and to arouse their companions in misfortune, in case of any event. One circumstance alone served to inspire them with a little confidence:—the Citizen Naudet, at that time gaoler, was a humane and tender-hearted man, who treated his prisoners with all the kindness due to misfortune; and who allowed them all the alleviations consistent with his duty.

"While these unhappy victims were thus a prey to insupportable alarms, Henriot excited the public opinion more and more against the *maisons d'arrêt*, by the hypocritical orders which he had inserted in all the newspapers. His spies and agents, together with those of the police, spread themselves through all the public places, and circulated the basest and most perfidious calumnies. But the first arrest of Ronsin and his gang having taken place at that time, the massacre was adjourned. The robbers of Bicêtre were conducted there, and the poor inmates of St. Lazare were permitted a short respite.

"The measures taken against us were not, however, less rigorous: the sentinels who guarded us were not less convinced that we were brigands and conspirators; they even frequently fired at the prisoners who placed themselves at the windows; and it was remarked, that those who allowed themselves to act thus barbarously against peaceable men were members of Hébert's section.*

* "The watch-word given to the sentinels was of the most frightful nature; they were forbidden, under pain of death, to speak to us, toreply to our questions, to make us the smallest sign: and these instructions made such a terrible impression on the greater part of the sentinels, that when they saw us at the windows they grew pale with fear, lest it should be supposed they were keeping up a communication with us. Several of them, whose brains were disordered by the dread of the guillotine, made no scruple of levelling their pieces at us, to make us retire; and upon three or four occasions fired at us, but happily without effect. These incidents threw the whole prison into confusion: we shuddered with indignation at finding ourselves treated in this manner, and it required all the prudence of the gaoler, Naudet, to maintain tranquillity. These poor sentinels were excusable for their terror: a gendarme had been guillotined for having taken charge of a letter which a woman wrote to her husband, a prisoner at St. Pélagie. I have, however, met some of them who had the boldness and humanity to address me some words of consolation, while marching up and down, without once looking at me. I shall never forget a stout man, whose countenance was marked with kindness and good nature; he had the courage to write upon the wall, with his pike: 'Unhappy prisoners, have patience; the day of justice is at hand.' . . . . Good citizen! If I ever meet you again, with what pleasure will I press your consoling hand!"

In these frightful times, three citizens, whose affairs were thrown into disorder by their confinement, and who found themselves deprived of all means of corresponding with those who were charged with the management of their interests, lost their senses, and threw themselves, one after the other, out of the window. These three unhappy men had faithfully served under the banners of the revolution : one was Etienne, who had formerly been a notary; the other a friend of Marat's, whose name I have forgotten; and the third a patriot from Belgium.

" It was not sufficient, in the opinion of our persecutors, to deny us the pleasure of embracing occasionally our wives or our friends; it was also necessary to deprive us of the consolation of seeing them from a distance, and of sending them the expressions of our love. As they could no longer obtain permission to enter the prison, these dear objects, and the only ones which attached us to existence, came regularly into the first court, where we had an opportunity of seeing them from our windows: we saw them near enough to read upon their features the expression of tenderness, uneasiness, and grief. They could hear us say, 'Our hearts know no other enjoyment than that of being entirely yours; the ties which unite us alone give us strength to support the burden of our woes.' We could let fall a few tears upon our children, whom their mothers lifted towards us in their arms : the paternal benediction could descend upon the heads of these innocent creatures. But it frequently occurred that the savages who tortured our souls, upon witnessing these affecting scenes, only beheld them with envy and rage; and orders were shortly after issued, to forbid the entrance to the court. The gate was closed, and this spot, in which our looks had wandered over all that was most dear to us, now offered only a dark and gloomy solitude. Those who love to delight in the pure expression of feeling, and of nature, can form an idea of the state of languor and dejection into which we were plunged by this cruel privation.

" On the other hand, nothing seemed to give hopes of an end to our captivity; each day brought us new companions, and none departed. We heard nothing spoken of but the terror which was spread through Paris and the departments. We learned that no one could any longer dare to interest himself in our favour, or to solicit our release. We looked upon ourselves as deserted by all the world; we saw society load us with its contempt and hatred, and we went so far as to forbid even our very wives to demand justice for their persecuted husbands.

"As we provided food at our own expense, both for ourselves and our indigent companions, we could not be deprived of the liberty of writing, to send for what we wanted. Ticket-porters, under the authority and inspection of the gaoler, entered the ward-rooms, and we were there allowed to communicate with them. But this liberty might afford a means of publishing abroad the vexations which we experienced, and give us an opportunity of being informed of the daily calumnies that were circulated respecting us; our oppressors, therefore, considered it imprudent, and resolved to deprive us of this our last comfort. The most efficacious mode of effecting this object seemed to them to be to confine us in so strict a manner, that they might act as it pleased them, and proceed to every extremity, without any danger of our representations or complaints ever reaching the people, or the National Convention. They accordingly persuaded the committees of public safety, and of general security, to pass a decree, ordering that we should be provided with food in common, and that the nation should pay the expense; the police officers also signified to us, that our clothes should be washed for us, and that all sort of correspondence was entirely interdicted.

"The humane character of Naudet, our gaoler, not being suited to such measures, he became an object of suspicion to this same administration (the police), and it seized the opportunity of some trifling difference, to remove him, and replace him by another gaoler, the Citizen Semé, a rough and punctual executor of the oppressive orders which were given him, but, at the same time, an honest man, and incapable of adding to our sufferings of his own accord. Even this man did not appear to them sufficiently determined to torture his prisoners, and to invent false accusations against them; he experienced the same fate as his predecessor, and they substituted in his place a being entirely to the taste of the administration, a ferocious brute, who seemed to live upon our sufferings alone. With such a Cerberus, they were very sure of being warmly seconded, when the moment should arrive for attempting our destruction.

"Another precaution still remained to be taken by our tyrants: we had knives, razors, and scissors, which we might use in our defence, should they attempt to massacre us. Several of us, according to our fortune, had reserved some assignats for our current expenses, our future wants, and the assistance which we distributed among our poorer companions in misfortune; we might, said they, with these assignats, corrupt our keepers, and transmit the recital of our sufferings outside the walls. They therefore considered it expedient to deprive us of all these objects, and to become our heirs before our death, and so put it out of our power to make the smallest resistance.

"In consequence of this resolution, we one morning received orders to remain within our chambers, and not to go out of them under any pretext whatsoever; the corridors were closed; we were no longer allowed to communicate with each other; we asked ourselves the probable motive of their prohibition, and, while delivered up to our apprehensions, the commissaries of police entered, followed by an armed force. As we easily believe what we desire, we for some moments gave way to the idea that it was the Popular Committee,—that committee in which all our hopes were centred, and which was only a bait, a means of murdering us more securely, concerted by Robespierre and his accomplices. They come to deliver us, cried we! How great was our error! Alas, we were soon undeceived!

"The visit proceeded, the corridors were filled with guards, who were forbidden to speak to us, or to answer us a single word; a police officer, accompanied by a peace officer, and followed by the gaoler and two turnkeys, came into each chamber, according to their numbers, and did not leave it until he had made the most diligent and most indecent search, and read all our papers, ransacked our pockets, examined our mattresses, and our portfolios, and stripped us to our very shirts. Knives, scissors, pen-knives, razors, assignats, and jewels, were all seized; the very watches, which were generally looked upon as mere useful pieces of furniture, were held to be fair game; they however consented, as a great favour, to leave with those from whom they had taken money a sum not exceeding fifty livres.

"This inquisitorial visit continued, without intermission, during three days and three nights.* One may judge of the uneasiness of those whose chambers were last in the corridors, and what frightful conjectures we drew from this circumstance, upon our again meeting one another!

" This event was shortly after followed by orders prohibiting the introduction of all sorts of provisions into the prison, and establishing a common refectory. They carefully avoided giving us notice of this day, lest we should make any previous preparations; it was on a sudden, on the 24th Messidor, that the ticket-porters ceased making their appearance, that we were forbid to enter the ward-room, and that we received notice, that, unless we meant to die of hunger, we should each of us use our utmost exertions to secure a place in the refectory.

" I shall not dwell upon the two long hours we were obliged to pass at the door of this refectory, elbowing, pressing, and stifling each other; I shall only remark, that, as food for old men, for weak and delicate females, and for sick invalids, they gave each of us, for the twenty-four hours, two rotten herrings, some stinking cod-fish, and a half pint of a mixture of litharge, beet-root, indigo, etc., to which they gave the name of wine.† One of the first days of this new regulation, Bergot visited the tables, not in order to see that we had good and plentiful food, but to take away their knives from those among us who had

* "It would be difficult to paint the gross brutality of Bergot, the officer of police, upon the occasion of this visit; I have seen him carry the refinement of barbarity to such a point, as to tear from a prisoner a snuff-box, on the lid of which was painted the portrait of his wife.—'These gentlemen,' said he, 'console themselves with these portraits, for the absence of the originals, and forget that they are in prison.' . . . The monster!—but he has met the just punishment of his crimes, being outlawed, together with the rebel commune, which has suffered the same fate!"

† On the 9th Thermidor, the honest Périnal was completely entrapped. He was getting in two barrels as his provision of wine: but unfortunately the car was overturned in the very middle of the court; the barrels rolled down upon the ground, burst, and exposed to the view of the prisoners, who were observing what was passing from the windows, two distinct currents; one of a muddy red, in the midst of which were distinguished, in their perfect state, both the indigo-wood and the other drugs of which it was composed, and the other of perfectly pure water. Unfortunately, one of the new commissaries of police was there at the moment, and the complaints which we had before made to him, on this very subject, were fresh in his recollection. He sent M. Périnal to prison: but in a few days afterwards he was reinstated in his office.

the address to conceal them previously from his ferocious vigilance. If we complained of the detestable food which was given
us, he replied, in a furious tone, ' 'Tis but too good for rascals
that are going to be guillotined.' He then turned round to the
cook; 'Let me not see you pay any attention to those rascals ;
if they don't like what you give them, let them leave it.'

" Périnal was the name of this second Mignot, to whom these
verses of Boileau's may be so justly applied:—

> "'Périnal c'est tout dire, et, dans le monde entier,
> Jamais empoisonneur ne sut mieux son métier.'

" The honest fellow! he seconded to perfection the wishes of
his principal, and made no other reply to our complaints than,
'If I followed the instructions of the police, you would be still
worse off.'

" I should, however, mention, in his justification, that he was
in some degree forced, by the sacrifices which he had made, to
treat us in this manner. We did not at that time know the
secret, but have since learned it. Upon making his bargain,
the police officers had exacted from him, as a consideration for
his being allowed the exclusive right of poisoning us, a sum of
eighty thousand livres as a *pour-boire*, for these officers were not
at all averse to drinking, if we might judge by Bergot, who
never appeared without his face being entirely illumined by the
juice of Bacchus, and without getting intoxicated among the
turnkeys, and even with the common porters. One day that he
could only walk in the figure of an S, and that his voice was
interrupted by hiccups, he wanted to enter the prison in this
condition: the guard refused to recognise his authority, and he
was put under arrest. It required all the eloquence of the gaoler
to prevail upon the officer who commanded the post to set this
beast at liberty, and particularly to promise not to make a report
upon the subject.

" It will, I think, be allowed, that two rotten herrings and a
little poisonous cod-fish, in the space of twenty-four hours, were
not well calculated to give strength to the stomach; and this,
also, at that season (for it was then in the dog-days) at which
that sort of salted food has even been proscribed by the regulations of police: but the indignation of all must arise against

those wretches who treated in this manner men and citizens, the greater part of whom were superior to themselves in every respect.

"We had several infirm old men among us, who required some good wine to support their strength: we had also some women, both sick and pregnant; several of whom had children at their breasts, who required the same assistance. It was refused them without mercy. The citizen Giambone, a banker, was in a dying state; his wife was devoured by a cancer in her breast: the first requested as a particular favour to be allowed to send for some syrups and other little matters which were ordered him; the second prayed for a few drops of milk. 'No, and be d....' was the answer of our Cerberus. They still entreated, and still received the same answer.

"Though we were not allowed to receive the public newspapers, we were not, however, entirely ignorant of what was passing.* We interrogated the new-comers; the number of persons guillotined was always the grand object of our questions. We shuddered at the recital of the number of victims who lost their heads every day: we heard of the conspiracy of the Luxembourg and of some other prisons, and found it difficult to conceive how a handful of prisoners, without exterior relations, without arms or without resource, could have formed such plots. We judged of the other prisons by our own, in which the greatest order and submission was observed, and in which we were all retained more by our respect for the law than by the bolts which secured us.

"It gave us pleasure to think that we had no men among us capable of forming plans of escape, or bold or abandoned enough to think of conspiring in their prison against the national representation. Alas! we knew not that the storm was impending over

---

* "This prohibition respecting the journals, by keeping us in ignorance of what was going on outside our prison, gave opportunity to certain persons, whose imagination could not remain at rest, to circulate among us each day the most extraordinary news, sometimes of the most alarming nature, and sometimes very favourable. Thus we were incessantly driven from terror to hope and from hope to terror. The richer individuals were not, however, in such a situation, being able to procure the newspapers by dint of bribery. I have seen 25, 50, and 100 livres paid for a single number of the *Journal du Soir* or the *Courrier Républicain*, and the turnkey who procured it justly considered the favour the greater that he risked his head in the attempt."

our devoted heads; that, at that very moment, our enemies were busy in imagining a pretended conspiracy, which was to be imputed to us; that at the very same table with us sat a number of monsters charged with that very object, and with the trust of marking out the unfortunate beings destined to undergo the punishment of a crime which had no other existence than in the infernal imagination of their vile denunciators.

"An Italian, named Manini, a man known since the revolution as an informer and spy, and who continued to follow up these professions in the different prisons in which he had been confined, was the inventor of this pretended plot: he united himself with a locksmith named Coquery, a stupid fellow whom he had bent to his purposes, both by promises and threats. This Manini, according to his plan, denounced several individuals confined in the prison of St. Lazare, as having offered sixteen thousand livres to the locksmith if he would engage to saw through a bar of the only window of the first-floor which was secured with bars; and this in order that they might escape, and then proceed, in pursuance of their project, to massacre the members of the committees of public safety and of general security, particularly Robespierre, from whom it was intended, as they said, that Atain (a young man, the son of a fruitwoman, who was always alone and never spoke to anybody) was to tear his heart, and devour it.

"This window opened upon a sort of terrace, from which it was separated by a space of twenty-five feet broad. The bar being got rid of, they were, according to Manini, to pass through the window a plank, which was to serve as a bridge from the window to the terrace. It was to this narrow and unsteady bridge that the pretended conspirators were to confide their fate; and doubtlessly they would have contrived to set the sentinel who was placed immediately under the window to sleep, as well as those who were stationed in the neighbourhood: they would otherwise see and hear everything, and it was not to be supposed they would remain tranquil observers.

"Such was the chef-d'œuvre of Manini's imagination, as supported by Coquery. This denunciation being received, as may be supposed, by Robespierre and his friend Fouquier-Tinville, they despatched Herman, the minister of justice, to St. Lazare, to order two other agents of theirs, who were in the prison, to implicate all they possibly could in this conspiracy. In order to afford these two wretches, Joubert and Robinet, a greater facility in drawing up the lists which they were asked for, Herman ordered them the full liberty of inspecting the registers of the prison, and he himself frequently came to pass the morning along with them in arranging their proceedings.

"I sometimes went into the apartment of this Robinet, where I occasionally seized a glimpse of my wife through the window which looked upon the grand entrance-gate. One day that I called upon him, 'You are an honest patriot,' said he to me; 'I will tell you a secret, on condition of your not mentioning it to any one: if you reveal a single word, you are ruined.' He then continued: 'Joubert and I are charged by the committees of public safety and of general security with drawing up a list of all the aristocrats and the counter-revolutionists in this prison : as soon as we shall have prepared this list, all the patriots will be released.' I shuddered at these words. Observing my air of alarm and surprise, 'All those who have not shown themselves staunch revolutionists, must pass through it,' said he, making a sign with his hand as of cutting off the head. He then showed me a list of eighty-two individuals; among whom were several whom I knew to be excellent citizens, and respecting whom both Joubert and he had made vague and false remarks. I could not refrain from observing to him how very delicate a point it was to make accusations upon such slight grounds, and what fatal consequences might result from it. 'We have nothing to fear,' replied he: 'it is determined that all those heads must fall: we are well supported. Remark, besides, those words at the bottom of the list. We state we do not donounce, that we only give our opinion respecting the above-mentioned individuals, as has been required of us. If we should get into any scrape, which there is little chance of, those words will save us.'

"I cannot express all the horror with which I was seized at this barbarous language, which this infamous wretch spoke in a gay tone, and mingled with the chorus of *Vive la République!* I related what I had seen to my unfortunate companions, and we waited the event, with mingled fear, alarm, and hope, that these wretches would not be believed.

"Three days passed in this painful suspense, during which Joubert and Robinet conducted themselves like men sure of their affair: they openly declared that they were making lists. They inspired so much terror, that the prisoners were constantly at their feet: if any one differed from them in opinion, they threatened to send him to the guillotine. Joubert obtained favours from several women by terrifying them with the idea of being inscribed in the list if they refused. One of these unfortunate females was not the less sent to the guillotine through the medium of this execrable monster. They both taxed the wealthy, and, notwithstanding what they obtained from them, enrolled their names with aggravating notes: they did not even spare those whom they called their friends. 'A revolutionist,' said Joubert, 'has no friends.' Being solicited by the citizen Jolly, a gunner, to erase the name of his mistress, and of Giombone and his wife, who, said this young man, had never ceased to give proofs of their attachment to the revolution,—'Be silent,' answered he, 'or I will put you down yourself.' A prisoner having complained of the conduct of his fellow-prisoner,—'Do you wish me to rid you of him?' said Robinet, 'I will put him on my list, and his affair will be soon done.' It was thus that these monsters,—these subaltern Neros,—conducted themselves in the midst of those whose destruction they were plotting; and I have only sketched an outline of the picture of their villainies.

"The day at length arrived on which we were to witness the results of the labours of these devourers of human flesh. It was the 5th Thermidor; that day, and those which followed it, will never be effaced from my recollection. About four o'clock in the evening, two long covered carts were brought into the first court. Our hearts beat, our blood froze, on seeing them from our windows. Who do they come to seek? Is it a removal to another prison? Is it to carry us before the revolutionary tribunal? The report was spread that they were come to seek several prisoners to remove them to Chantilly; but the joy which we could read in the countenances of Joubert and Robinet told us but too well that the two carts were destined to transport victims, to glut the sanguinary thirst of the cannibals of Robespierre's tribunal. About twenty turnkeys entered the corridor with a dark and gloomy air; and divided three by three to seek those whose names were called. We were drawn up in a line, and stood trembling in silence: our unfortunate companions, whom we then beheld for the last time, passed before us; the paleness of death was on the forehead of some, the calm of fortitude on that of others; they pressed us in their arms, bid us farewell, and exhorted us to courage. 'You have more need of it than we,' said they 'for you remain.' A moment after, we saw them ascend the fatal carts, whence they once more saluted us, and exclaimed, 'We are going to die innocent.' They departed, and we saw their eyes fixed upon us, with the expression of suffering and regret. What a dreadful night we passed after having witnessed such a sight! How terrible was the following day! We knew they were before those judges with whom innocence met the same punishment as crime! And when we learnt that every one of them had lost their heads, what hope remained for us? especially when we heard Joubert and Robinet declare that only thirty prisoners would be spared out of all those confined in Saint Lazare.

"On the 6th and 7th, we suffered the same anguish, the same agony; we saw our brothers, our friends, torn from our embraces, and led forth to the scaffold; but on these last two days, through a refinement of barbarity, they had the carts brought into the court four hours before the time, in order to make us all slowly undergo the dreadful torture of suspense, not knowing whether we were or not in the number of the proscribed whom the executioner was waiting for.

"André Chénier, a man of the most valuable talents and acquirements, and whose only crime was his having taken advantage of the liberty of the press, by inserting in the *Journal de Paris* some letters against the Jacobins, together with the poet Roucher, were in the number of the victims of the second day. At the moment when they came to seek Roucher, one of his friends was finishing his portrait. 'Wait a moment,' said he to the turnkeys, and dictated these four verses, addressed to his family and friends, which he desired to have written at the bottom of his portrait:

> 'Ne vous étonnez pas, objets touchans et doux
> Si l'air de la tristesse obscurcit mon visage:
> Lorsqu'un crayon savant dessinait cette image,
> On dressait l'échafaud, et je songeais à vous.'

An eminent man of letters was accompanied by his son, a charming child of seven or eight years old, whose education was all the thoughts and consolation of his father. Robinet conceived for this child a brutal passion, which can only dwell in the hearts of beings, in every sense out of the order of nature. He took him one day into his chamber, shut himself up, and treated this innocent creature in a manner which the pen cannot describe: the child spoke, notwithstanding all the threats and prohibitions of this odious satyr. The father was informed of what had happened, and redoubled his care of his child. It is supposed that it was to revenge himself, and in order to get rid of a being in whose presence he would always have been forced to blush, that Robinet inscribed his name upon his list.

"On the 8th, we were in expectation of a fresh removal, but were informed that we were allowed three days' respite, as the prison *Des Carmes* (of the Carmelites) would furnish provision for those three days; and that they would not return to Saint Lazare until the 11th. This delay added to the tortures of the suspense which tormented us; death was in our hearts; almost certain of being sacrificed, we made our arrangements, wrote to our relations and to our friends; in fine we prepared ourselves for the passage from life to death.

"During the three days that our unhappy companions continued to appear before the tribunal, who were the witnesses that deposed against them? Manini and Coquery,—always Manini and Coquery! Joubert and Robinet had only to draw out the lists. As for the first two, they boldly asserted, in presence of the accused, that they were themselves present when they were conspiring to effect their escape from Saint Lazare, and to massacre the representatives of the people. One of the accused defied Manini to point out each of them by his name upon looking at him; he put on his spectacles, and could not point out a single one, but Coffinhal did not the less declare them guilty.*

* One of the greatest crimes in the eyes of such men as Dumas, Coffinhal, or Fouquier, or rather the common pretext under which they condemned the rich, the nobles, and the clergy, was their not having kept up any intercourse with the patriots confined in the same prison. It would appear from this that

"It would require an entire volume to describe all the atrocities committed by this tribunal of vampires. I shall confine myself to a few facts which are connected with the prison of Saint Lazare.

"There were two women confined in this prison, whose names resembled each other very closely; one was called Maillé, and the other Maillet. The officers made a mistake, and carried away the former in place of the latter. They perceived their error upon their arrival at the tribunal. 'It is all the same,' said Coffinhal, 'let us proceed to the next.' Thus was Madame Maillet guillotined for a crime imputed to Madame Maillé. 'We have killed two birds with one stone,' said Coffinhal to Fouquier; 'we have by this means, despatched the trial of Madame Maillé also.' They sent for her in the middle of the night, though she was lying in bed under a nervous attack, and we learned on the following day that she had been guillotined without appearing at all before the tribunal!

"On the evening before, her son, who was not yet sixteen years old, and had been in prison since the age of fifteen, was condemned to lose his head, as an accomplice of Manini's conspiracy, because he had thrown a stinking herring, which was too bad to eat, in the cook's face.

"The ci-devant Abbess of Montmartre, aged eighty years, and no longer able to speak or stand, and Madame Meorsin, an old paralytic woman, who was obliged to be carried about in arms, were condemned, as guilty of having attempted to make their escape, by passing out of a window, on a plank six inches wide, and forty feet from the ground, in order to reach the garden, the walls of which they must then have scaled.

"I shall mention one more fact which is still more atrocious:— One of my unfortunate companions had been in daily hope, since his imprisonment, that, by the exertions of his friends, he would soon be released; one of his friends at last arrived with the pleasing intelligence, that his acquittal had been granted, and that the order for his release would arrive on the following

they admitted that patriots were imprisoned. By no means: the word patriot, according to their vocabulary, signified a maker of lists, a creature of the committees of general terror and of public calamity.

day; but, alas! he never saw that day, for that very evening
the fatal cart arrived, and his name was called over as one of
its intended victims; he immediately represented to the persons
that he had been acquitted, and that the order for his release
would arrive on the following day, but all in vain; he was
peremptorily required to ascend it: he screamed and wept, and
swore every oath that he had been acquitted, and that he was
to be released from prison on the following day, but all without
effect: his complaints were unattended to: they were deaf to his
cries, and he was forced to ascend the fatal cart, and, though
acquitted, was guillotined.

"I shall here conclude, though the subject is inexhaustible;
but I have said enough to show into what hands we had fallen.
None escaped; the fate of all was alike; crime and virtue shared
the same scaffold, and the most abandoned and infamous,
and the most sublimely virtuous, were alike victims of these
execrable villains."

### NOTE I. p. 204.

"A message was sent me to go to the apartment of the gaoler
Semé; I there found two citizens whose features were unknown
to me, one of whom addressed me:—

"'I know you to be a sincere patriot, I am fully convinced
of your good principles, and I expect you will justify the opinion
I have evenly conceived of you.

"'Here is an order from the Committee of Public Safety, to
make a search through all the prisons for the enemies of the
Revolution.'

"I took the order and read it through.

"He then asked me if I had any knowledge of a plan of
escape having been concerted in St. Lazare. I replied that I
had none, and that if such a plot had really existed, it would
have been very difficult for it to have escaped the notice of the
patriots who were in that prison.

"He then asked me if I was acquainted with the person of
Manini, to which I replied, 'that I was not; that his features
were entirely unknown to me.'

"'He is easily recognised,' replied he; 'he is the only prisoner who wears spectacles. Endeavour to inform yourself of everything respecting him; he has declared that he has discovered a project of escape at St. Lazare; I have no great confidence in him, he is a great talker. Here is the list of the accomplices which he has given me;' and he began to read the names to me.

"I saw, with horror, the names of several of my friends marked upon this list, and of several citizens, both men and women, who were utterly incapable of conspiring against their country. I made strong representations upon the subject of this denunciation, even at the risk of compromising my own safety. I took up the defence of those with whom I was acquainted with so much warmth that I succeeded in having their names erased from the list.

"I was not so fortunate in my application for the young Maillé; I in vain represented that he was but a giddy boy of sixteen years old, whose only thought was the pleasure of a joke. 'Let us leave him as he is,' said they, 'he may, perhaps, get out of it.'

"'And Duclos, in whom I have never remarked any thing but the greatest attachment to his country?' 'Oh! as for him, he is a chevalier of St. Louis,' replied they.

"They asked me to affix my signature to my observations, which I did without hesitation.

"He who interrogated me then said, looking over the list which he had in his hand, 'There are about a hundred of them; there ought to be many more than that here.' I replied, 'I do not think there are many conspirators here:' 'We have found three hundred of them at the Luxembourg,' replied the officer, 'we will easily find as many at St. Lazare.'.... I requested Madame Glatigny to apprise Duclos of the fate that awaited him. After much trouble, she succeeded in inducing him to think of preparing his defence; and, by degrees, we communicated our fears as to the result, in order that he might be prepared for his fate. He beheld it with coolness and courage, and the citizen Duroure assisted us in the preparation of a memoir for him to read on his trial, to prove his patriotism and his innocence. I embraced him before his departure, and conjured him to defend himself with courage and confidence.*   He followed my advice, was acquitted, and returned to the prison of St. Lazare, to the great joy of us all."

* The moment Duclos was brought before the Tribunal, Joubert sent an express to the public accuser, with a declaration of the prisoner's patriotism, signed by three well-known patriots; had it not been for this circumstance, neither his innocence nor his eloquence would have been of any avail.

END OF VOL. I

www.ingramcontent.com/pod-product-compliance
Lightning Source LLC
Chambersburg PA
CBHW030353270326
41926CB00009B/1082